Praise for *Cloistered*

"This is a memoir of emotions felt viscerally. But there are also remarkable spiritual insights, intellectual reflections on life and death, and, of course, plenty about the intense relationships that developed between Catherine and the other sisters. Engrossing and moving."

—Belinda Jack, author of *George Sand:*
A Woman's Life Writ Large and *The Woman Reader*

"A profoundly moving memoir which gripped me . . . It's about spirituality and asceticism and silence and sisterhood, but also about how flawed human beings can abuse power and how hermetically sealed communities, which should care for and protect their members, can be dangerously vulnerable to threats from inside their walls."

—Mark Haddon, author of *The Curious Incident*
of the Dog in the Night-Time, The Porpoise, and others

"In an era of relentless superficiality, Catherine Coldstream's memoir of her years living as a nun draws us back into the cloistered world of the inner life. It shows us what it is we may have abandoned in our lives of emotional and material dependency: a commitment to hope and faith; the transforming structures of a spiritual imagination. Here are beautifully crafted lessons in spiritual survival; the meditative practice of deep loneliness; of days wrapped in prayer and contemplation."   —Sally Bayley, author of
The Green Lady, Girl with Dove,
No Boys Play Here, and *The Private Life of the Diary*

"A mesmerizing memoir of great clarity and nuance, *Cloistered* is an account of religious life that is as authentically vulnerable

as it is poignantly honest. It will transform the perceptions of its readers regarding the unique traditions of convent life, including its struggle and pain as well as its beauty and glory."
—Revd Dr. Ayla Lepine, associate rector,
St James's Church, London

"This fascinating, disturbing memoir takes its place in a rich tradition of writing about convent life by ex-nuns and is distinguished by its passionate, lyrical writing, which perfectly expresses the author's ardent search for meaning, freedom, and love."　　　—Michèle Roberts, author of
Cut Out, Paper Houses, and *Negative Capability*

"When she was twenty-four years old, Catherine Coldstream lost her father, who had been everything to her. From the depths of her grief, she set out on a journey of poverty, chastity, and obedience in a Carmelite monastery in an area of outstanding natural beauty. During the following twelve years, Sister Catherine plowed, planted, and harvested vast fields of solitude and faith. There she experienced the power of prayer, the sometimes damaging politics and surveillance of monastic life, the numinous heights of music, and her own sharp intelligence. This incredibly beautiful and moving book is for all of us."
—Dr. Carmen Bugan, Orwell Prize Fellow and author of
Burying the Typewriter: Childhood Under the Eye of the Secret Police,
Time Being, and *Poetry and the Language of Oppression*

Cloistered

My Years as a Nun

CATHERINE COLDSTREAM

ST. MARTIN'S PRESS
NEW YORK

First published in the United States by St. Martin's Press, an imprint of St. Martin's Publishing Group

CLOISTERED. Copyright © 2024 by Catherine Coldstream. All rights reserved. Printed in the United States of America. For information, address St. Martin's Publishing Group, 120 Broadway, New York, NY 10271.

www.stmartins.com

The Library of Congress Cataloging-in-Publication Data is available upon request.

ISBN 978-1-250-32351-4 (hardcover)
ISBN 978-1-250-32352-1 (ebook)

Our books may be purchased in bulk for promotional, educational, or business use. Please contact your local bookseller or the Macmillan Corporate and Premium Sales Department at 1-800-221-7945, extension 5442, or by email at MacmillanSpecialMarkets@macmillan.com.

Originally published in Great Britain by Chatto & Windus

First U.S. Edition: 2024

10 9 8 7 6 5 4 3 2 1

For Margaret and for Adrian,
without whom – for very different reasons –
things would not have happened as they did

Contents

CONTENTS

PART III

The Truth

Come, my Way, my Truth, my Life:
Such a Way, as gives us breath:
Such a Truth, as ends all strife:
Such a Life, as killeth death.

The Call, George Herbert (1593–1633)

Everything was the same – the smell of beeswax, the red lights of the sanctuary, the words the children were whispering beyond the altar screen. But Nanda knew that whatever might happen in the future, nothing for her would ever be the same again.

Frost in May, Antonia White (1899–1980)

Prologue

In my mind I am still running. Running towards the road. Running. Running. Running. The darkness is fresh around me, the air slicing across my face in wild, clean shafts. The rush of oxygen is fizzing, moonlit, completely unexpected. I'd forgotten what night tasted like, the great dome of it, just as I'd forgotten what it was – after ten years cloistered – to run cold and wild and wet, beyond enclosure. I'd forgotten what it was to stand under the sky and feel the far stretching of infinity. I'd forgotten what it was to stand and look up and turn and twizzle my head this way and that, amazed, engulfed in stars. I'd forgotten what it was to move and breathe and spread wide my arms and feel . . . no walls!

Now I am running fast and newly free, my feet sunk in wet greenery on the grass verge. My socks are damp. My ankles brushed by foliage. The first shock, after the careful terror of the locks and keys, the infinitesimal turning of the handle, had been the floodlighting that rose up before me, sweeping the gravel forecourt like a great white whale as I stepped out. For a moment I had thought that was it – the game was up. There would be an alarm. There would be footsteps rushing, voices, torches. My mind spooled. I just stood very still and looked, took in the frightening, glorious wide space in front of me, the beam of the lights over gravel, and decided there was nothing for it but to go on. Beyond the lights were dark trees. Beyond that there were fields, black carpets of freedom only bumpily illuminated in places by the moon.

Halfway down the long drive I stop and look back for a moment, expecting to see lights popping on in the windows, faces looking out, but there is nothing. No change, no movement about the sleeping house. The monastery slumbers. The low moon hangs vigilant over the hushed, teeming landscape. Cells are shuttered, slices of corridor seen from a distance static, deadly quiet. And then, only then – at a hundred yards – do I begin to breathe. To stop and note the startling feelings that are welling up inside me. I am astonished at the freshness of the night. Amazed to find myself feeling safe. Surprised at the sense of boundless space. Surprised, especially, to hear my voice saying out loud, quite clearly and confidently to God or whatever guardian spirit may be listening: Thank you. Thank you. Thank you.

And then I am moving on again, breathless under the stars. I've taken virtually nothing with me, just my viola and a plastic bag containing a few necessities. When I next look back at the vast, towering house that rises like a fortress against the sky, I see it for what I now think it is, a place of danger and of dishonest murmurings. I look at it with relief and incredulity. Incredulity that this place held me for so long. Incredulity that I am safe. Incredulity at the beauty of the surrounding natural world. It is so good! Safe, safe, safe – I am *safe*, I keep repeating to myself, as though I cannot quite grasp or get used to the idea. My voice peters out. I halt again near the Lodge, close to where the gravel drive meets the country road, and look back one last time at the now toy-sized gothic spectacle. How small and powerless the house looks at two hundred yards. How foolish and flimsy, like a cut-out against the beauty of the infinite moonlit sky. Relief surges through me, and I breathe and turn finally – finally – towards the road.

*

I had come to Akenside Priory a decade earlier, in 1989, young for my twenty-seven years, a sheltered Londoner, eldest daughter of my father's late-life second marriage. We three children were his 'second eleven', the strawberry blonde batch born to an unconventional woman younger than his first daughter. I was more strawberry than blonde, a faded redhead, and easily emotionally exhausted. Life was febrile in our bohemian family home in Islington, as my parents were ill-matched, not only by virtue of the age gap.

My mother was beautiful, not just to our (indulgent and familiar) eyes but to everyone's. My sister Frankie and my brother Rob were striking in youth, too, all of us echoing at least some aspect of our Nordic mother's sculpted looks. My father, bespectacled and grey-haired, was professor of Fine Art at UCL, and had painted her 'at the height of his powers' but after that nothing went right, and neither of them made the other happy. It was a stormy marriage. We children grew up in the firing line, ducking and dodging, taking the odd bullet, anxious to keep both our very different parents happy. We were programmed to be polite. Tiptoeing around my mother we lived in an atmosphere of simmering emotion, an environment in which eruptions could occur at any time.

Mum took out much of her frustration on my introverted sister in more subtle ways than flying bullets, unwittingly unkind words that caused Frankie to become what grown-ups called 'withdrawn'. Mum had had childhood traumas of her own, including parental abandonment, and no model of family life on which to base her own maternity. Sadly, she did not know her own unruly power, nor own up to and resolve her manifest unhappiness. She was fire to my father's more gentle ice. My brother Rob became strategically cool, and just a touch aloof – childhood illness, stoically endured, gave him resilience. Unlike my younger siblings who knew how to separate themselves emotionally, I did not so much become as remain 'excitable', and – my father's word – 'impressionable'. I was, and would continue to be, painfully anxious to please for far too long.

As the eldest I was spokesperson and go-between, tormented messenger between the separate bedrooms. It was a role I grew into naturally, my elastic empathy stretched in all directions. Dad was on the top floor, with views towards the New River Walk, while Mum sequestered herself off the first-floor landing, in a room that overlooked the Shrubbery. This tree-enclosed park was where children, who were allowed to shout and fight, kicked balls around. But after Frankie and I were beaten up there, our legs slashed with a broken bottle by an older girl, my father told us to keep to the main road. The furthest we were allowed to walk was Upper Street, and even then our father would be hanging out of the window looking anxiously for our return.

Our father. He cared for us until it wore him thin, and most of his hair dropped out, and his grey flannel suits became loose, a doting grandfather of a dad, intent on compensating for what my impractical mother lacked, and for what he'd dropped us in – the consequences of a classic mid-life crisis. For all his antiquity, and even after his body had begun to tremble with old-age illnesses, he was the rationally controlled, the steady one to whom we looked for wisdom and advice. Mum was a fully signed-up actress and an opera singer, a subscriber to *The Stage*, and the possessor of a voice and an Equity Card that took her On Tour far from home for whole seasons at a time when we were small. In those troubled days it was my aunt Winnie who came to live with us, Dad's older – *even* older – sister, a white-haired angel in sensible shoes and cornflower blue cardigans (fixed with brooches) who was kind and conscientious, and 'married to God' as she used to describe her single, childless state. She taught us to be thankful and to say grace before meals.

Life was relatively straightforward when we had a mother, a father and an aunt, a trinity of very different persons. Febrile it might have been, volatile too at times, and the firing line – Mum's unwitting speciality – was a pervasive worry. But worries that you've always known, like all routine difficulties, are much easier to cope with than the shock of sudden change. When Winnie died of cancer while I was in my teens, and we lost our ethereal aunt and fairy godmother (and Dad his second mother), our father began his slide into morbidity. The trembling began, then took over, overshadowed with depression, and neither he nor Mum knew what to do. For better or for worse, and amid recriminations, they went their separate ways, although it was really Dad who went, in near despair, to live in makeshift style near the studio where he could paint in peace, which is what mattered and what he was born to do. He was a begetter of art, a maker of pictures and people, a gentle man ill-equipped for marital battles and – in his seventies – exhausting journeys back and forth on the local overground, the North London Line.

At home he was forever on his guard, strangely invisible around the house, timing his schedules to avoid my mother, sometimes a late-night diner and always an early riser. He used to get up early to catch the light, intent on keeping his morning vigils at the easel. Out of the house he'd creep before any of us were up, the green tartan holdall of paintbrushes in his hand, a whiff of turpentine about his person. Paint rags were strewn around his spacious, rarely tidied room, as were tufts of cotton wool dotted with dingy colours,

the ochres and siennas – burnt or otherwise – that consti-
tuted his favoured palette. He saw the world in shades of
light, and skin, and hair, and earthenware. Nothing was ever
completely black or white, or bright or bold, but always quivering with a delicate sensibility. He was endlessly deep and
kind, and everything and everyone was perceived with fellow
feeling. He forgave our temperamental mother her many
derelictions, because he knew she couldn't help it, and he
forgave us our eventual failures and rebellions. He forgave
everyone everything, which is not what all fathers are like, I
learned – but ours was, full of bounty.

When his health broke down and our rickety old house
was sold, and my mother vanished to a flat (and a world) of
her own, the first eleven took over. They, my much older
relatives and their advisors, would manage Dad's affairs from
now on. It felt as though the world was falling about around
me. Everything was now out of our hands; we were no longer
a family unit. With no home left, once Dad had been scooped
up and taken under an older relative's wing (and shunted
between hospital ward, hotel and nursing home) we children
were left without anywhere to go. After an eccentric, over-
protected childhood, with no idea how life worked in the
world beyond our art-filled, over-sensitised bubble, we were
suddenly adrift. It was a challenge none of us would rise to
without difficulties.

In a London turned inhospitable, we had to be resourceful, or at least have a go at going off the rails. In my case,
Europe beckoned. The possibility of studying electroacous-
tic composition in France while working part-time for a
contemporary music publisher proved irresistible. So did
creative and amorous adventures in Paris, Darmstadt and
Cologne. I threw myself into it all with my usual excitability.

Soon I was playing with synthesisers and discussing Sartre and Stockhausen in French. I was falling in love with unsuitable propositions in dark polo necks. I was moving through existentialism and hitting nihilism. The clouds were gathering. I was still scribbling scores in Paris when, one snowy day two years later, my father's life ground to a halt. The phone call came late at night and I stood and watched the flakes of snow drift past my window.

A world without Dad in it was inconceivable, just as the vacancy of his body – when I saw it in the hospital two days later, the snow still falling – was a moment not only of shock but of clarity and heightened awareness. If a universe without my father was inconceivable, and he was no longer in his mortal body, it followed (less the product of deductive reasoning than what seemed a lightning-flash of numinously tinged intuition) that he must be somewhere else, as disembodied spirit. If I could no longer catch the exact tone of his voice, or hear his laugh, or see the grey-green of his eyes light up, I could feel his presence. I could even speak to him. Dad's intellect and personality had always transcended his feeble physicality, and now it seemed to me his spirit was all around me. Overnight, with only the imprint of a first-hand impression, and a predisposition to look for comforting connections, I had become a believer in the afterlife.

Meanwhile, I was still me and I was twenty-four. A lot had been lost since our house was sold and the family had been scattered and everything had gone into storage. My mother was by now a city hermit whose primary relationship was with a typewriter, living life on her own terms and rarely in touch. Rob was away travelling and would be doing so indefinitely. Frankie was soon to be moving up north to start life afresh near Newcastle, where she was joining potter friends who, like her, wanted a more affordable place to live than London. With little left to tie me to earth, my search for ultimate meaning intensified. I began reading Dostoevsky, Kierkegaard and CS Lewis, I began asking questions. I was looking for an afterlife, had been doing so unconsciously for years, and when I found it, through stained glass and lit by candles, it seemed quite obvious, staring me in the face. The afterlife had been there all along. The afterlife was a suitable proposition.

I was a regular choral singer in those days, part of the choir at the Anglo-Catholic church in Paris, and loved the singing. It had never occurred to me until then to pay much attention to the liturgical words. Soon those words were jumping off the page, every syllable alive, demanding my full attention. Having previously dismissed the formal Christian teachings as outmoded, suddenly they were lit from within. It was not that everything automatically made sense (it didn't) but that I recognised I was in the presence of a vital and important mystery, and in a context where I could at least begin to tease this out. I could ask questions. I could let the spirit that moved there take me where it wanted.

What did it want? It seemed the first thing was to take me on a long journey south, to visit a family friend in Provence, one who was kind, and wise, and gentle, and let me listen to Bach for hours on end in her sitting room, and cry on her shoulder, and talk long into the night. Appropriately, her name was Angelica. I stayed until the brink of summer. After that it put me on a train back to Paris, all ginger freckles and sunburn, my viola slung over my back, where I searched for a seat and found one next to a quiet woman dressed in grey. Was the only spare seat on the Avignon to Paris TGV that day next to a woman intent on her book, one studying

Hebrew, a woman who would turn her head and smile, and finally introduce herself as a Dominican nun? Was the pale radiance emanating from her calling out to me? Of course it was. If Angelica had been a guardian, Sister Else was a timely messenger. We talked until we arrived in Paris, and she sent me on my way with a blessing and a phone number. She had a specific message for me, a message I only obscurely understood. Only later would I connect it with the beginnings of vocation.

Sister Else had not preached, or done anything but listen and supply some gentle insights, but she had given me the number of what she called a 'retreat centre' somewhere in the Paris suburbs, a place she urged me to go and stay. This sounded bland and alien, but I thought it worth a try. I needed a dedicated space. I would benefit from some spiritual guidance. She had spoken in unhurried undertones, in a voice that seemed to come from a place of higher knowledge. I hardly remember a thing she said, but I do remember the soft impression that she left, and the way her words – like all the words in church in those lost, expectant days – pointed to something overwhelming, something expressive of mercy, goodness, and eternity. When the train pulled in at the Gare de Lyon and we stood together for a moment on the asphalt, promising to keep in touch, I pushed the scrap of paper she had given me down deep into my pocket. Later I would find it, and see the words Communauté de l'Épiphanie, in her perfect handwriting, an echo of the afterlife.

The afterlife is a thing of fascination: it has eyes and it has a soul. The afterlife is vital (of necessity) and is both buoyant and serene. It has an overarching mind and a kind heart. And, because it is not just an 'after' but a 'life', the afterlife is everywhere and always. It is alongside, all-encompassing and indivisible, which is why we nuns called it quite simply 'The Life'. The religious house I chose, or that chose me, was only a few miles from my sister Frankie's new base. While she was in Victorian Jesmond, I was drawn out to the wild expanses of the countryside. In those days Northumberland promised new beginnings to us both. Visiting a range of monasteries of contemplatives in the north, and the odd modern convent of more active outgoing sisters in London, it was finally the radical and ancient Carmelite order that proved compelling, alluring, irresistible.

The Life claimed me then, and I was happy of it. Scribbling scores and singing in choirs and playing my viola, even in Paris, were all very well but I was thirsty for the ultimate, for the source of all those lovely things. My father and my aunt were both by now in heaven, I supposed, and so I decided I would seek them, and all other original forms of goodness there. The day the afterlife came to meet me on the road, like a stranger destined to become a friend, I could not have welcomed it with more open arms. I could not have shed more earnest tears nor have been more relieved.

The Life of Carmel was everything I thought I wanted. It gave me answers and it gave me a new kind of home. It gave me skies and trees and lofty ceilings, and a cell with a view. The Life gave me community – an unfamiliar one at first and something I had to put my own self aside to learn – and a resilient purpose. It came with a Mother, universally regarded as being Reverend (and Superior), one voted in every three years by the mature majority, and a bevy of sisters known collectively as The Brethren. Over and above all of this, it gave me a central and defining relationship, one with an invisible being we thought of as our spouse. An immanent embodiment of the afterlife, the unseen spouse was the reason for everything we did, and for why we were there, cloistered religious sisters hidden within the four walls of our cells, and of a closed community.

For the first few years, the monastic life nourished and reorientated me. It alone, thanks to the unseen Presence, had power to lift the mourning veil of my early twenties, and to instil a new set of values and embed a new source of hope. But the helplessness of grief, like clouds, and other fluctuations, does not last unchangingly forever. Faith, too, matures and presents us with more solid challenges as we go on. An active faith sometimes entails an active questioning. It was inevitable that, one day, I would have to face not only the light but the dark that my new vocation housed. It was perhaps also inevitable that complexity and decay, and even human cruelty lurked not far off, this world being what it tends to be when you are impressionable. The Life was not, and never could be, perfect in reality.

Our father, nevertheless, remained in heaven, and I made it my business to seek him there. This book is about how I succeeded and how I failed. It is about how difficult lessons were learned. And it is about how God is bigger than all of that. Bigger even than the best of his earthly representatives and divine messengers. After the early snow of my father's departure, and after the frosty funeral, a long passage awaited me across an unfamiliar landscape. In the cloister of Akenside Priory I would find a transcendent source of love that would outlast pain and loss, and stay with me, even after my own departure.

PART ONE
The Life

'What the mind does after losing one's father isn't just to pick new fathers from the world, but pick new selves to love them with.'

Helen Macdonald, *H is for Hawk*

1. Matraque

I woke my first morning to the sound of violent shaking, like the emptying of an oversized coal scuttle down the back stairs. It intruded with a brutality for which I was completely unprepared. I sat up, puzzled. Why coal, I thought, and why such a lot of it, and why this dramatic delivery in the middle of the night? I opened my eyes just a tiny crack. I was sure it was not yet dawn. The sound rose and grew, until it morphed into a deafening Doppler effect outside my door, then receded in strange waves, sympathetic tingles extending down my arms into my fingertips. I lay down again. Something rattled and dislodged itself on a corner shelf. Even the floor was shaking.

In the first flicker of awareness, I turned over, confused. Was I back at my aunt's red-brick mansion-block flat in London? Were there lorries? No, Winnie had been dead ten years. Then I felt the thinness of the sheets and remembered where I was.

I found a blanket pressed up against my chin, my neck chafing at its abrasive touch. The half-empty pillow, bumpily compressed beneath my head, breathed trailing feathers, two of which drifted languidly across my neck, long-legged dancers in slow motion. I tried to brush them away, wincing, and was relieved to find that they simply hovered, did not scuttle. I'd sensed a fleeting spidery presence in the night – a horrid pattering across my face – but had held my breath, willing myself into oblivion by urgent prayer. The curious sensation had passed, the room was still; my first small battle had been won.

I opened my eyes and breathed more deeply, and, as I did so, sensed something faded and astringent, perhaps old rubber mixed with dust. Hot-water bottles, disinfectant and Vosene shampoo, and the bar of green carbolic they had left out for me the night before. But none of this was surprising; I had not come looking for comfort.

Sister Ellen had told me to lie in. Someone would come for me after six, but until then I was to wait, to ignore the noises of the night, and to rest or try to sleep. Had I been able to hear above the din I might have detected the clicking of half a dozen switches, the ignition of a stream of lights along the adjacent corridor, the padding of feet in nearby cells, the emptying of cisterns. But I was disorientated. When eventually the knock came it was a single one, brisk and strangely loud. A hovering silence ensued, as when someone unseen awaits a delayed response, and then, at my murmured greeting, the hush of soft, departing footsteps. Sandal upon stone, the brush of a habit hem along a skirting board.

On this, my first dark dawn at Akenside Priory, I turned on the hard mattress and fell into shallow sleep again, and it was almost eight o'clock when I found Sister Ellen leaning over me, shaking the rough brown bedcover, and urging me to get up quickly. 'The *appeau* has gone, Catherine, you'll be late for the procession if you don't hurry! We can't have that on your first morning, can we? Just throw your things on, comb your hair and come down without washing. You can catch up later on.'

The instructions were clear. I was to follow her down to the antechoir, my feet noiseless in brown corduroy slippers, a regulation pair I'd been given on arrival, and then fall into line behind the three white-veiled novices, together with Jennifer, another aspirant, and wait for 'the knock'. This, a sharp tap of knuckle on wood, was the prioress's signal to move, impossible to miss in the surrounding quiet. From then on it would be a case of following, watching and imitating the others. Self-explanatory, Sister Ellen said – I just 'needed my wits about me'. In a silent order there was a lot to be learned just by looking.

She waited for me outside the cell door, then kindly but firmly steered me around endless passageways it seemed I'd never remember, and guided me down the dark panelled stairs that led to the central and enormous hall. Beyond, in the light-filled antechoir, I found the nuns lined up, starched and ready, hands hidden under thick cream cloaks, two dead-straight, veiled arrows poised and prepared for the solemn procession into choir.

Finding my place was easy. Sister Felicity stood out from the surrounding sea of habits, being taller than the rest, angular and awkward in every way. 'Head for the front,' Ellen had said, 'and wait behind the tallest sister in the room. It's usually the youngest in community who lead the way when we process in "order of religion", so it'll be your turn next. I'll explain it later,' she had whispered as we rounded the final corner.

Although she did not turn or look towards me, I knew that Sister Felicity had sensed my arrival from the tiny forward shuffle of her long, pale, sandalled feet and the unease that expressed itself only in a nervous cough, a fragile twitching around her neck. I longed to catch more than a glimpse of her face, half hidden as it was by her voluminous headdress, but the knock had already been given and we were moving as a body towards the open door. Following the pace set by the leaders, I tucked my hands into the pockets of my newcomer's essential baggy cardigan, hiding as much of me as was possible, and found myself merged – like a drop of water becoming one with the ebb and flow of a great ocean tide, I was carried forward. It was not long before I was seated in a wooden stall, breathing in plainchant only delicately tinged with incense.

'*Deo gratias . . .*' The chant rose clean and clear, brushing the air with its sweeping movements, caressing with its lulls and pauses. *Deo gratias* – thanks be to God. The whole rhythm was one of perpetual ascent, and seemed to carry my voice weightlessly, as though transported by transcendent light. The ancient psalm tones were intuitively accessible, profoundly expressive and easy to mould to human gratitude. I had much for which to be thankful, I already felt, not least this mercy of monasticism. Thanks be to God, I sang. I joined not only my voice, but my mind and heart and soul to the common intention. How glad I was, at last, to be behind the high, enclosing wooden bars known to us as 'the grille'. How glad I was to be seated in a stall that felt like the most secret and special place on earth. How glad I was to be claimed, repurposed, already hidden deep in Carmel's choir.

On the chant flowed, a serene undulation, words sung with inwardness and restraint by a body of twenty women, whose voices joined to form a single monophonic stream. Many of the words were comforting and familiar. *Gloria Patri*, the doxology circled like a refrain. The sisters, both old and young, both black- and white-veiled, bowed low at the words, as was customary at the suffix that followed every canticle or psalm or prayer. At the words *Sicut erat in principio* the doxology invoked not only the song of the angels one night, two thousand years ago, but also the first beginnings according to the ancient Hebrew scribes and seers, who knew about creation *ex nihilo* and the One True God. As psalm gave way to psalm, and to the allocated scripture reading, I tasted that gathering-inwards of the bodily senses, that harnessing of every human faculty of thought, imagination and attention that went with prayer. There was a name for it: recollection. The result was a cool yet balmy peace, an enfolding into one great wave of unbelievably perfect love.

Mother Julianna, at the top of the monastic choir, led the prayers, and I noticed the special quality of quiet that surrounded her every syllable, a halo of communal attentiveness. She had long been the community's Mother Superior (known in Carmel as the prioress), and was as rugged as she was revered. A huge and venerable woman, she seemed to me primordial, pre-existent, connected invisibly to some heritage that defied biology. Her Carmelite roots went deep. And afterwards, as she stumbled towards the door, bent practically double on her sturdy stick, each step she took produced a rumbling. Once, she would have been a woman of striking breadth and stature. Now she was gnarled and disfigured, her back an asymmetric hump, her long black veil bobbing like the tarpaulin of a great ship's sail as she moved, lumbering, leading the way back from the solemnity of worship to the working day.

In the hall, a swarm of habits and veils dissipated into corridors and alcoves, down passageways and into further secret spaces behind closed doors. Each moving body was purposeful and mute but for the flap of sandal straps, the pad of slippers on the tiles.

Later, Sister Ellen caught up with me in a 'talking place', one of those alcoves built into the original structure of the great old house where the soft exchange of a few essential words was permitted. The monastery (so-called since it was a strictly 'enclosed' or secluded house of prayer rather than an active convent, from which nuns typically might go out to teach) was a silent world, one where every footstep could be heard, and where those rare things, words, were weighed like gold or precious stones. Sotto voce, Ellen told me to meet her later that morning back in my cell. She had a notebook, a pencil and 'a little list'. We laughed coyly at the comical phrase. A little list. But there really was a great deal of information to transmit and she, as my newcomer's guide or 'angel', was the one to transmit it, if only in the most hushed and reserved of terms.

It was a cloudy October day, devoid of autumn charm. I made my way back to the top floor, somehow managed not to get lost, and waited for her as instructed. Soon she was knocking, then settling herself on the creaking wooden window seat beyond my bed, indicating a choice of floor or chair with broad, freckled hands. Her soft round face was gentle, her eyes a greenish blue. The window, that only partially framed her homely bulk, rattled from time to time, quivering slightly in the autumn wind. Her eyes were wide open and pleasantly enquiring. I looked around me and then chose the floor, having seen young sisters half kneeling on their thick brown habits, the bulky skirts of which were generous enough to roll into a hard, squat cushion, an improvised stool. Not yet having a habit, and being dressed in a simple skirt and top, the floor was cold, and I pulled up my feet behind me and sat on my calves. When Ellen did not react, I knew that what I'd done was seen as normal. She began to talk.

Hers was the face of a plaster Nordic saint, her skin a sandy colour brushed with cream. A few strands of fine, curly hair peeped out from where the rest was flattened beneath the close-fitting cap, which in turn showed itself under the white

wimple and crisp black veil, the latter the sign of a fully professed Carmelite nun. Questioning me gently, she spoke of
antiphons and doxologies, touched the gilt-edged corners of
her breviary (fine, petal-like sheets of compressed spirituality) with reverential care, glanced smilingly heavenward at the
mention of the holy name of Jesus, and arranged her soft lips
into a perfect circle when she formed the words 'Our Lord',
always prefaced by a slight hiatus, a glottal stop that acted as a
kind of vocal genuflection.

Eventually she asked me how I'd slept.

'Ah yes, the morning *matraque* is a custom that came over
from France,' she said, 'after Catholic Emancipation,' and we
both laughed again. 'It's our traditional morning alarm, and
different from the *appeau*, the bell for the Office. I must show
you how it works some time, Catherine. It's similar to a basic
football rattle, but a lot heavier. It's just a brass handle
mounted on a thick slab of oak. But yes—' and here she was
detained by a mini fit of giggling, a dimple appearing on her
right cheek '—it does make a terrifying sound if you're not
used to it. I should have warned you, but there was so little
time last night. And last time you were here, of course . . .'

Last time. Yes, I remembered how they'd put me in a cell
in another part of the building, far from the top corridor,
during my trial run, a euphoric two-week summer stay. The
garden was all roses and summer fruit, and I'd been in what
they called the Old Infirmary. Certainly I had not heard anything from that distance, but had slept, curled and foetal, my
body glad to close in on itself and shut out everything that
could possibly intrude. That first room had been big and
bright, and smelled of disinfectant and sticky rhododendron
flowers. Now I was a postulant (from the Latin *postulare*),
someone requesting entry, knocking on the old oak door of

the order for admittance, and the mornings were dark and black as coal indeed. And this time I'd come intending to stay for ever. My cell was at the end of the long top corridor lined with cells that once had been servants' quarters.

The great manor house bore all the hallmarks of the ancient family who had built it, spacious rooms arranged around the black-and-white-tiled central hall, which was overlooked by a panelled gallery on the one side, and by a sweeping carved staircase on the other. Majestic stained-glass windows rose alongside the deep, gloomy wooden stairs, and the light that danced there was multicoloured. Once upon a time there must have been stags' heads, shields and ancestral portraits on the wall, but now – ever since it had grown derelict following the war and was then as good as given to the nuns – it was bare and stark, the only decorations on its surfaces being crucifixes and the odd holy picture. Over each of its doors the word *JESUS* was drawn in gothic, calligraphic print. Other than that, there was a kind of emptiness; the main thing you noticed was the echo.

The place was indeed cavernous and lofty, with corridors that connected up unexpectedly with other corridors, confused here and there by several sets of stairs – front, back and spiral – not to mention the annexes and outbuildings that sprawled in all directions. But the beauty of it was its bareness, the views over the lake, the grounds that encompassed orchards, lawns and meadows, leading to untamed woodland regions and finally to a high-walled kitchen garden. Beyond that was the Mere, a broad reservoir of water that formed an effective boundary to our thirty acres of Eden. Who knew what lay beyond it, what landscapes might be found there apart from the bending trees? None of us, I suppose, because once you had immersed yourself in the Life, everything Outside – including its most innocent landscapes – merged into one simple, rather distant blur. Inside was where it was at. Inside was where we believed we could experience life to the full.

'You probably noticed how quietly I knocked before I entered, Catherine?' Ellen said. Her wide eyes were soft with gentleness and concern. I nodded.

'That is because the cell is very much your own private space. Yours and the Lord's. It is the fundamental unit of the eremitical – that is the 'hermit' – life. It's sacred, and no one but you, and in exceptional circumstances the prioress, can ever enter it.' She noted my puzzled look, and added, 'Yes, and of course me, as your angel in the early stages. I'll meet you here weekly while you find your feet.'

I thanked her. The intensity of the cloister held huge attraction for me. It was the presence I had sensed so powerfully my first visit, and that again now was calling to me, urging, pulling, pushing me to a response. But still, I needed someone to show me the ropes, and help me get to grips with the timetable. From rising at the *matraque* before dawn (and washing in a bucket of icy cold water with a frayed flannel), to the snuffing out of the last candle after night prayer, or Compline, to the extinguishing of every light for sleep, the day held its own complexities. Finding your way from A to B was only part of it.

'It'll take you some time to get used to everything, Catherine, and no one can run before they can walk. We know you are keen, and that you have a genuine attraction for prayer. You feel God is close beside you. That is good. But you have only been a Catholic for a year and, well – you are still quite inexperienced. Many of our ways of thinking will be strange to you, as a convert. Our separated brethren, the Anglicans, mean well . . . in their own way, of course. But this is different. Here, you have been guided to the very fountainhead of truth. You will be taught each afternoon with the others in the novitiate, and those instructions will continue daily, except for Sundays and feast days, until you are deemed ready to take your final vows.'

The mention of final vows sounded exciting to me, and she noticed my smile and added firmly 'But let us not run ahead. You are here in good faith, and the Lord has his own special plans for you. It'll be another six months before you are admitted formally to the novitiate, by the ceremony of "Clothing", at which point you will be required to cut your hair in preparation for the habit. That is, if you are approved by the chapter.'

I nodded. It was important to demonstrate my acquiescence. Important to avoid presumption, and to make myself ready and available for whatever trials and reversals might lie ahead. However strong the pull towards the cloister, however powerfully I felt the call, it was important to remember that God's inscrutable will was everything.

'Once the chapter – the body of finally professed nuns – have voted (and, please God, you'll be accepted) it'll be another year before you are ready for first vows.'

Her look was kind but just a little distant for a moment. She seemed to be checking something, counting, or making a mental note.

'Then, as you know, it will be at least another three years before you are eligible to take vows for life, and then only, of course, *Deo volente* – if God so wills.'

It seemed a distant prospect as I sat there on my calves, my ankles tingling, but even then I knew that the taking of vows was only the beginning. On the farthest horizon was the beatific vision, the delightful union of the soul with God, and the happy basking in his presence for all eternity that awaited those who were faithful to their calling to bear witness to his love and glory in this world, and to draw others after them. To know my soul safe, I thought – safe, and to have saved others, that was what it was all about.

'God's will is all that matters, Catherine. That's why you have the chapter of the monastery, and the rest of the community, and especially Reverend Mother, to guide you. When they meet to pray and confer, and discern the way ahead on your behalf, you can be sure that they will be guided by divine wisdom. For your part, by obeying what the Holy Spirit says through them, you can be sure you are responding in the most perfect way possible, and thereby honouring the highest principles. But all that is a long way off.' She smiled. 'You have the six months of your postulancy to get through first!'

By now my legs and ankles had gone to sleep, and my feet were prickling. I squirmed and rearranged myself on a different patch of floor, my calves stretched out in their ridged woollen socks before me. Ellen smiled.

'We must get you a proper prayer stool, Catherine. They make sitting for long periods so much more manageable on our cold floors. I'll ask Sister Barbara for one, and check that there's one for Jennifer, as well.'

I thanked her. Jennifer would also be glad of a prayer stool, I was sure. I'd seen very little of her, as I'd arrived earlier than her the previous afternoon. I'd expected to go through into the cloister straight away, as arranged, but they'd kept me back, waiting in the extern quarters for Jen. Eventually she'd arrived, and we passed through a low, rounded wooden door like two mice creeping through a mousehole, and found ourselves on the other side, in a world of silence and resounding space. Since then, the Life had swept us both up and carried us forward, Jennifer being ministered to by her angel, Barbara – a slightly more senior and authoritative character than gentle Ellen – and settling into one of the larger cells on the remote first floor. Meanwhile, I was thrilled to be in the top dormitory corridor, where most of the other young sisters lived.

'Is everything else all right for you, Catherine? Have I forgotten anything, and do you feel you have all you need?'

'Yes, sister, I'm very happy to be here, and really ... I couldn't be more delighted with my cell. It's perfect. It feels so secluded and high up and yet so peaceful, and it's so wonderful being able to look out and see the trees and the lake.'

'And we are all so happy to have you. Both you and Jennifer. It's a rare thing to have two postulants arrive at the same time! God has blessed us . . .'

For a while Sister Ellen mused on, reflecting on the order's recent history, telling me about the changes since the Church's controversial reforms of the 1960s. These, a product of the Second Vatican Council – known informally as Vatican II, or simply the Council – were to my mind a far-off event, having been convoked the year I was born, but were clearly still regarded as 'new' to these sisters living so self-contained and remote – and thanking God aloud for all he'd done to build up the community. I would learn more about Vatican II later on, when the conflict between the new and the old ways made itself felt and sent me running to the library to delve into whatever texts and dusty documents I could find. (The selection of books there was limited, as one would expect in a community living under obedience, all volumes being vetted by the prioress.)

'We keep very much to ourselves, as I'm sure you can see,

Catherine. But do remember, the cell is not only a sanctuary from the world, it is also a dedicated space for something better. As a bride of Christ, it is both a crucible and a bridal chamber, the hidden place apart where you meet most lovingly with your spouse, but also where you will, one day, be called upon to do battle with your demons. It won't be easy. It never is. But trust me, the love of God will not forsake you. Like the early hermits on Mount Carmel who lived in caves, we contemplatives all need our sacred solitude. Cultivate silence, Catherine, do not run from it. And let God's love in solitude be the only comfort that you seek. On the mystical mountain of Carmel, which is the charism, or divinely given character of our holy order, we are all hermits.'

Charism, crucible, mystical mountain, times of trial. I drank in the new vocabulary. Sister Ellen closed her eyes. The two of us sat there for a moment, intent on solitude though physically together. For a moment we dipped into that space where only the wind rustled and the lake lapped beyond the window. Otherwise, all was still. And then she rose and walked with indefinable beauty and composure towards the door.

2. The Charism

With its roots in the ancient Greek word *charis*, meaning gift or grace, the Christian concept of a spiritually gifted or 'charismatic' life goes back at least to St Paul, whose words to the community at Corinth spelled it out. 'There is a variety of gifts, but one Spirit,' he wrote, only two decades after the original Pentecost experience, that of the rushing wind and the dancing tongues of fire. 'It is the same Spirit who is working through all these gifts in different people and in different ways.' He went on to exhort his followers to seek not the spectacular (such dramatic gifts as tongues or healing) but the highest and yet the most modest of the gifts, that of *agape*, or selfless love. 'Love is always patient and kind,' he reminded them. Unlike the graces, or *charites*, of Greek mythology – attendants to the beautiful and sensual love goddess, Aphrodite – the grace-filled Christian was to be dedicated to a path of self-denial, to greater or lesser extents according to their vocation.

As I was to learn during my initiation, we in Carmel were called to live according to a particular way of life called the Teresian Charism. It would be an over-simplification to say that it all went back to St Teresa, as what Teresa de Jésus was doing in Ávila in the sixteenth century was not entirely new. She was building on an existing charism, a way of life and set of values first established on Mount Carmel in northern Israel over 300 years earlier. It was always meant to be a 'desert charism', an ascetic way of life characterised by solitude, silence and intense prayer, but – the medieval plagues and other scourges having done their worst – life had got a little lax by the time Teresa, a fiery young noblewoman, came along and spotted what needed changing or reforming among her peers.

Reforms were already violently afoot in other parts of Europe, and the inspired (and astonishingly astute) nun of Ávila knew what to do. Although she framed her founding of a new branch of the Carmelite order as a counterforce to 'those wicked Lutherans' – she was a daughter of the Catholic Church, after all, and understandably keen not to rub the Inquisitors up the wrong way – her own critique of the great, sprawling convent she had joined implied criticisms of the powers-that-be that were not unlike those the protesters were levelling at Rome. Clear-sighted people everywhere could see that things needed shaking up. What Teresa's new take on an ancient way of life amounted to was a return to the sources, a reinvigoration through intensification of intent, which, in the case of Carmel, meant a return to radical austerity and simplicity.

Just as the other main religious 'families' (or orders) within the Church had their own rules, often written by inspired and inspirational founders – St Benedict's being the prototype – we Carmelites lived by a rule associated with those first beginnings on Mount Carmel. No, there was not a holy sister called Carmel sitting in a cave, writing away, since all those early hermits in the craggy wilderness were men. Although mention is made of a brother called Brocard who might have been the founding prior, unlike Benedict he did not put pen to paper, but went to Albert, Patriarch of Jerusalem, with a request for the document that would confer official status on the ragged colony of hermits. And so it was that the Order of Carmel was born and approved, and the name of Albert Avogadro, that pen-wielding patriarch, forever stamped upon the Rule.

The Rule of St Albert was the sacred script that was meant to define our lives, and one we heard read aloud every Friday in the refectory, our otherwise completely silent dining hall. The reading from a pulpit, just like the serving – in an apron, with the help of a trolley – was done on a weekly rota system, so that most people got a turn at doing a bit of everything. Even the prioress was supposed to roll up her sleeves and do her share of the dirty work, as well as the nicer things like reading and telling other people what to do. The other important text we heard read, eked out at a point a day, was the Rule's companion volume, the Constitutions, based on Teresa's own interpretations of the Rule, written in 1581.

Together, the Rule and the Constitutions formed a fine and detailed mesh, a kind of network of ideas and ideals, on which we Carmelites were to rely. Of course, a high bar was set for everyone, and nothing about the Life was meant to be easy. The charism we had been given was regarded as 'supernatural' which meant it had come down directly from God, albeit through his chosen channel. It called us to live more than naturally, in other words to become our best and highest and most perfect selves, with a bit – or usually rather a lot – of help from on high. Being medieval, all of this holy blueprint stuff was originally expressed in Latin and first intended for the all-male, fraternal communities living in caves on Mount Carmel; the Rule blithely *frater*s away, and so did we. We were called to live 'fraternally', as brethren. It seems 'sororally' never quite cut the mustard.

Being a nun is a kind of voluntary androgyny, although we never really thought of ourselves as anything other than celibate girls, or (if you were especially mature) women. Being celibate meant having renounced intimate or sexual relations, and that was that. For my part, I'd become so focused on the otherworldly, through grieving my father's death, that gender didn't even register, or resonate as an issue. I was me, and not to be biologically confined. What lay beyond the physical was where the action was at, and it loomed much larger than anything as underwhelming as boobs and periods. Why spend your life thinking about your body when you had a soul? Why settle for the finite when the infinite was on offer?

And so we floated around in a more or less safe and sexless haze, even hands and ankles hidden under the thick habit – although you might stop and ask, what was that warming of the heart, that rapturous uplift one sometimes felt when thinking of the unseen spouse? What was the thirst for union with him in prayer, through sacrifice, if not a sublimated form of a more natural passion? These considerations might bear thinking about, certainly if you find illumination in psychology. But sublimated our sensuality was, because everything in the Life tended towards detaching us from the earthly, and freeing us for what was seen as a greater good, the heavenly, the ultimate beatific vision. The teachings were all so extreme, and the prevailing atmosphere of faith so powerful, that the material sacrifices came relatively easily, and seemed almost natural once you put your mind to it.

Beatitude was something we were intensely interested in. You could say that we were obsessed, both with it and with the way that we believed would lead us there. Beatitude, or blessedness, meant a very special kind of lasting happiness, one that could more than make up for our privations in this 'vale of tears', as our finite little lives were termed. We had an infinite, cosmic perspective, and the big picture – from the moment of creation to its final, transfigured end – was always vibrantly before us. It was part of what we contemplated on an ongoing basis. Everything connected up with it. We human beings were made for eternal happiness with God, and we looked forward to the natural end of life as a doorway on to something better, something intensely joyful and enduring.

History showed us the exemplars, those men and women we called saints, who had gone before us into the realms of light. There were different ways of talking about this, from the language of milk and honey – St Bernard's 'Jerusalem the Golden' springs to mind – to elaborations involving cherubs, harps and clouds. All of this was metaphor, and rightly so, because what human mind could conceive of infinite things, while bound by finitude and corruption here on earth? Metaphor was what was needed, as was poetry (and analogy, if you were a philosopher-theologian like Thomas Aquinas) to help point the way, to uplift, hint and encourage in view of the untold glories that were to come.

The Carmelite order was richly endowed with such saints, as well as those more generally inspirational figures the tradition looked to in a broader way. The earliest of these was Elijah, the first great biblical prophet of Israel. Since he long pre-dated Christ, we could not really claim him as our own, but spiritually he was the figurehead for the order, to the extent that our motto, 'With Zeal Have I Been Zealous for the Lord God of Hosts', or *Zelo Zelatus Sum* if you like your sibilants, was taken direct (or so we liked to think) from his prophetic mouth. In spirit we all stood with him on the mountain, whether Horeb, Carmel or Tabor, all peaks mentioned as places of divine encounter in the Bible, and thought of him as a model of prayer and of the way of steadfast witness, which is what we were all about.

Like most reformers, Teresa was not popular with her parent order, who persecuted her and her fellow reformer, Juan de la Cruz – John of the Cross – most disgracefully. As a result her followers, the 'discalced', or barefoot nuns and friars, broke away to live in smaller, more intense communities. While the house Teresa had joined as a young woman had over a hundred nuns, the new, reformed houses were to have no more than thirteen members; twelve, like the disciples, plus the prior or prioress, *in loco Christi*. Fittingly, the friars lived separately, in houses of their own, but were allowed out to preach and administer the ritual sacraments of the Church. The nuns, unsurprisingly for their time and culture, were physically shut away in communities where simplicity of life and silence were paramount, behind walls and grilles that signified (and effected) their radical separation from the world.

If Juan de la Cruz was Teresa's collaborator, recruited specially to help her establish houses for men as well as women, he was much more than a sidekick. He was a kind of holy genius, an original philosopher, a poet, a prisoner of his own short-sighted brethren, and even a runaway when they locked him in a prison cell for his zealous and reforming inclinations. That was when the going got really tough, and he composed his marvellous poem and its commentary, *Dark Night of the Soul*. Eventually both he and Teresa, known as 'La Madre', were vindicated, and passed on their flame to new generations of contemplatives, whom they exhorted to set out 'as though they were always beginning', always open to new insights, always ready to set alight new reforms, to make new departures for the godly wilderness, rather than being content to sit on their laurels. Complacency, they well knew, was one of the more real dangers for established religious houses.

Many other influential Carmelites followed, a series of pale-faced saints and the odd scrivener. Towards the end of the nineteenth century, the young Thérèse Martin, later canonised as St Thérèse de l'Enfant Jésus et de la Sainte Face, joined the order in the chillier climes of Lisieux, in Normandy, and reached millions through her *Story of a Soul*. This spiritual autobiography, written while she was dying of tuberculosis at the age of twenty-four, brought the heartland of the charism – the centrality of simple trust and trusting love – to the fore once again, and even moved the legislators of Vatican II. Some criticised her style, or the cult it propagated, as being too redolent of *fin de siècle* sentimentality; and some, even among my own brethren, dismissed her as a 'sweet pea', someone whose sensitivity outweighed her grit. But her book, and the very modern-looking black and white photos of her, taken by her pioneering photographer sister, Céline, brought her home to me.

In Thérèse of Lisieux I felt I had found a sister. Like me, she was an *enfant* of the somewhat sheltered bourgeoisie, an acutely oversensitive girl by temperament, although a feisty one by faith. Profoundly attached to her doting father, she overcame her natural limitations by giving her heart and soul to God and to a higher purpose. When I came across her story, in the days when the world was strange to me after my own father's death, her voice resonated like an echo of something I obscurely recognised. Looking at the so-called 'little flower', as she once described herself (while thanking God for her resilience), I realised there was someone out there I could relate to, someone whose way of looking at life I could learn from, and whose path through adversity I could make my own.

Certainly, I was too sensitive as a beginner in monasticism. A so-called 'sweet pea' at times, and not necessarily a typical young robust Catholic woman. This whole faith-filled way of life, however, was marvellous and impressive to me as a keen would-be novice. Soon I was to be undergoing an initiation, one in which I was to be remodelled and born again as something dedicated, something different, something new. This process was called the 'novitiate', or, more generally, the state of being 'in formation'. Being malleable enough to be re-formed, to become a 'new creation', meant a whole range of things, from losing touch with the core assumptions of one's native culture (unless you were one of those considered to be from a Good Catholic Family – mine did not qualify), to doing things in exactly the opposite way from what came instinctively or naturally. It was also meant to be about cultivating a life based on the charism, and on the claims of faith, rather than on recognisably rational or evidence-based ways of thinking. Finally, it meant reconceiving your identity, not in personal terms, but as one of a group, a sister with a new identity and a new set of clothes, a new rule of life, and a new and unfamiliar family – a set of brethren.

3. The Choir

There was Sister Magdalena, leaning and stretching with arms, hands and feet at the little wooden organ. Its piped notes kept pedestrian time with us. It was a woody sound, modest and neatly contained. A small strip-light over the music stand made a black-and-white tableau of her head and face, calm with concentration: skin pale as paper, long dark veil, only the face exposed, and the surrounding oval of pure, starched linen. The notes succeeded each other in perfect procession, each one as though hole-punched into the air, while the fluff of our voices meandered across the space, dreamily, in a higher register.

We were in choir, formally arranged in our high-backed wooden stalls. These were divided into individual compartments, all fitted with little ledges for our prayer and music books. Each Carmelite had a dedicated compartment of her own that was, like her cell, special, sacred and humanly particular. Like cells, too, they smelled of wax and wood and linseed oil. Pencils and other effects – the odd personal note or card – found their way into their cubby holes and ledges. A second pair of spectacles, perhaps (National Health, for poverty and modesty's sake), a magnifying glass (if you were old), or a pipe or tuning fork (if you were the sub-prioress, whose duty it was to give out the note, or one of the other musically active sisters). One or two had plastic plectra for the guitars that were occasionally rolled out in the liturgy.

At the bottom, near the adjacent public chapel with its

high sanctuary and altar, was where we, the younger sisters sat, starting with aspirants if ever we had any, and then postulants like me and Jennifer, newcomers who were still in our own clothes. After us were the novices, sisters Philippa, Emily and Felicity, and then the chapter sisters, as the fully vowed members of the community were called. Being a member of the chapter meant, among other things, having the right to vote on certain important questions, including at the triennial elections at which each new prioress was selected and instituted for her term of office. These fully fledged sisters had embraced poverty, chastity and obedience for life, and were arranged strictly by 'order of religion', the length of time they'd been in the community. As a symbol of their death to the world, they each wore a stiff black veil, in contrast to the novices' more flowing white. The stiffest of the stiff black veils belonged to Sister Elizabeth, the novice mistress, as did the straightest back. At the top, far away across the gleaming parquet floor, and thus furthest from the visitors' chapel, was the prioress in her throne-like seat, different from all the others by virtue of its bulk and carvings.

My fellow postulant, Jennifer, was directly opposite me, tall and burly-looking with caramel-coloured, shoulder-length hair in a thick bunch, and at this stage still conspicuously awkward in her stall. Being in our own clothes for the first few months meant that the striking differences between us were all the more noticeable. Being keen to do everything as perfectly as possible (a default acquired during my anxious childhood, or perhaps the result of being a 'convert' – Ellen's theory) I'd made sure to pack only the most muted of flowing garments, to blend with the order's earth-coloured habit which I hoped to embrace as soon as possible. My fellow traveller, by contrast, was in a brightly coloured *Jungle Book* sweatshirt and a thick denim skirt. I'd had little to go on, but she was nothing like what I expected. I was all faded paisley and submissive good will, a pixie by comparison, while Jennifer exuded an atmosphere of excess energy and – was it protest? She certainly was not going to be a sweet pea or a shrinking violet.

For a moment my mind flitted back to our first meeting, when, after a long wait, Jen had blown in like a tornado, all baggage, boisterousness and bluster, and greeted me as her 'partner in crime'. I'd suppressed a little shudder. Crime was not part of my proto-monastic vocabulary. I was keen. I was pious. I'd been steeped in Thomas à Kempis and books about medieval monasticism. Why wasn't she being demure? Wasn't she, like me, only longing to lose herself in God and silent prayer? There was something uncontrolled and almost wild about her from which I instinctively recoiled. Her unusually large white hands were moist with sweat, and her voice, when she got chattering, came out as surprisingly thin and high pitched, like a piccolo emanating from a tuba. 'I thought I'd got away with it,' she was saying. 'Thought I'd got a chance to do a runner, before they finally locked me up.' And then – was it with an eye-roll or a nervous twitch? – 'My sister organised a surprise trip to the dodgems, you see – one last bit of family fun – which was why you beat me to it. As you know, we weren't supposed to arrive on the same day. It was all set up so that . . .'

She rattled on, explaining, gesticulating. My mind was slowly computing.

'Oh yes,' I replied. 'Mother did say you would be entering first.'

'Yup. I was going to come yesterday, first of October. Special feast day. Didn't they tell you much about what was going on? You were supposed to come the next day, to keep us separated. Now, instead of me being your senior novice-in-waiting, it looks like we're going to be the Terrible Twins. Ha!' She rocked and wheezed with laughter.

At that point Sister Paula, who was in charge of the extern quarters, the area outside enclosure where we were still standing, appeared and added, as though it were already a community joke: 'Two for the price of one.'

Jen's boisterous personality was, admittedly, a bit of a surprise. In this quietest of quiet worlds, she was a splash of loud. But then, we were both completely new to all of this, and bound to be disorientated to some extent. I looked down, mindful of the importance of recollection, or 'custody of the eyes', a practice I'd already learned about and was intent on fostering. Sister Elizabeth had had things to say about it during my summer stay, and I'd understood it to be an aid to inwardness and prayer. Both in and out of choir, eyes were to be kept lowered, and, like all the other senses, suitably restrained. We were to mind God's business and our own, never other people's. Prayer was what we'd come here for, and the first step in that direction was humility, the desire, or at least readiness, to make oneself the lowest of the low. Harnessing one's senses was an aid to not judging, not knowing or having an actively expressed opinion about what was going on.

Watching Elizabeth – ironically – was a lesson on how to restrain and harness one's attention. She did not so much walk as glide, and had a quality that was different from the others, perhaps grace, something difficult to put your finger on. A member of the Council, the inner circle of 'advisors' to the prioress (along with sisters Ambrose, Alison and Mary Immaculata), she stood out as being the one who held the greatest influence. She had held it for years, having been made novice mistress while still barely out of the novitiate herself. The old prioress often turned towards her, leaning on her, cupping her great hand to her ear to catch the younger woman's words. Elizabeth carried conviction. She also had a pronounced sense of style that asserted itself in spite of the supposed uniformity of our dress. Her habit, for example, was of a slightly different shade of brown from the rest, a softer and more russet hue. And she had sparkly glasses frames and lace-up shoes instead of sandals.

If looking at Sister Elizabeth was instructive, it was also a source of permitted pleasure. Her natural elegance exerted fascination, and there was undeniable power in those cheekbones. I wanted to look and look again, and decide whether the right word for her oval face was 'chiselled' or 'sculpted' or something smoother. Were her eyes really an impossibly pale shade of blue, or were they sea glass, and was her skin as clear as silver?

I looked back at the open breviary in my hands, the leatherbound tome that contained the words to the psalms and hymns and scripture readings. Here was where our attention was to be focused; here, and on the unseen God who lay behind the sacred words, the being who was both their author and their subject.

However careful you were, however restrained and recollected, you were bound to notice incidental things about each other from time to time. From the way people moved and sat, to whether or not they themselves were being sufficiently recollected. All of us were different, not only in appearance and in voice, mind and gifts, but in how we attempted to live out the Life. Although we were called to conform, there was necessarily a range of motivations, and a subtly diverse range of interpretations of faith, hope and love among us. Some were naturally inward, reserved people, some were scatty, others were surprisingly harsh and loud. Mother called us a cross-section of society, although this was manifestly not the case. But what Mother said went, and did it really matter?

Not everyone was as dignified as Sister Elizabeth or as serene as Sister Ellen. Some were angular and abrupt, others had difficulty reining in their jolliness. Sister Ambrose, I was soon to discover, was a bundle of laughs, and seemed incredibly relaxed for someone living in a state of relentless vigilance. Even in her worried mode there was a mildness about her that was endearing. She gave the impression of absent-mindedness, but always in the nicest possible way. Felicity, or Fliss, and Emily were both novices, Emily smooth-skinned and attractive, while Felicity had a twitchiness about her that drew attention to her pallor. She was not only the tallest but also the thinnest in the community, and desperately sweet-natured. Only years later did I understand she suffered from anorexia.

Opposite me, Sister Philippa sang in a soft, youthful contralto, her face focused and intent. Freckles and a flushed complexion indicated that she was a fellow redhead. Was there a flicker of comradeship between us? Had I sensed a moment of mutual recognition? You knew from the start that you weren't supposed to ask such questions, even of yourself, or give in to preferences or special affections. But I noted the way she stood up and sat down in her role as cantor, moving effortlessly with the rhythms of the verses. Next to her stood a particularly energetic nun called Sister Suzanne, chin up, shoulders squared, head held rigidly ahead, projecting syllables to a far window. Her lips were full, her nose wide and her eyes a burning brown. Little Sister Jane mouthed the words with her eyes closed, her face dwarfed by owl-like glasses. Then Alison, Barbara, Ambrose, Judith and the other middle-ranking sisters. Far away, Sister Mary Immaculata, frail and bird-like, leant on a walking stick as she warbled her contribution to the air around her.

Somewhere between the middle-aged and the truly ancient was the white-haired Sister Paula, a natural chatterbox with a heart of gold. The only Irishwoman among us, she'd come from a teaching order, where she'd held a senior position, and had never quite lost her aura of efficiency or her bustle. When I say white-haired – or red-headed for that matter – it was not that we ever took off our veils, those trusty coverings, but that the odd unruly lock sometimes escaped, especially if you were in and out of the garden, pulling off dirty overalls, something that involved a certain amount of disarray.

In choir we were at our most pleasingly ordered. From the procession in and out of our stalls, to the way we responded to Reverend Mother's knock, to the breathy alternation of antiphons, verses and doxologies, everything was carried out according to minute ritual, words following one another like birds across the taut-stretched skyline of our chant.

The choir was a beautiful place, a sanctuary of music and of soaring space. It was a much broader canvas than the cell, and another kind of window onto God. It was where we practised communal rather than private prayer, and, unlike the lonely but beautiful companionship of the cell, a group effort that demanded the total effacement of the individual. Although we were many, we were one body; many pipes, one sounding organ. This conformity is something that came slowly, through an instinctive binding to the group. While certain personalities asserted themselves in other spheres of life, and indiscretions slipped through the net at times, in choir we sang as one voice, moved only as custom and ritual dictated, and lifted up our hearts and minds to God, in what we very much hoped was perfect harmony. *Levavi oculos meos in montes . . . I lift up my eyes unto the hills.*

In reality, of course, human perfection was harder to achieve than it was to think about, and the beauty of our plainchant was Platonic, in that it existed above all in the mind. *Levavi oculos meos in montes*: if your attention was directed to the highest goal, it seemed everything was possible. If you only Willed One Thing (as my favourite Danish philosopher had once suggested) and kept your mind and senses bridled, you could attain purity of heart. Reading Kierkegaard after my father had died had made a deep impression on me when I was first adrift in London. Sitting in choir, where the light danced and a pure and gentle harmony flooded the mind and senses on every level, it was easy to think you were on the threshold of another world, a place of perfect love and peace where nothing earthly really mattered. Because what could matter more than this transcendence? What in the world was there left to worry about?

4. The Cell

At the heart of our lives was the seclusion of the cell. In the annals of our 'desert' order, it held both a symbolic and a sacred force. It was an aid to purity of heart, and a bastion against all forms of evil. The hermits on Mount Carmel had embraced the cell as a way of turning their backs on the World, the Flesh and the Devil, that triumvirate of deceivers. God, and a godly life, were to be attained to the extent that one purged oneself of their power, and of one's attachment to the satisfactions that they seemed to offer. In this we were not only following the Carmelite way, but also those earlier ascetics of the Alexandrian desert, disciples of St Anthony of Egypt, whose extreme frugality had given rise to the perennially instructive accounts known as the *Sayings of the Desert Fathers*. 'Sit in your cell and your cell will teach you everything,' was one such instruction, attributed to a certain Abba Moses. We were called to be patient as well as pure.

In spite of its rigours, the cell also afforded a feeling of protection. It was a lonely place, yet it was full of presence. It was full of spirit, of watchful intelligence, perhaps full of ghosts. In Carmel, the unseen life was everywhere, and we acknowledged it as part of the everyday. It filled our corridors, and it filled our minds. But the cell was particularly hospitable to it, this inhabiting, being the dedicated space apart where each nun lived 'alone with God'. There, we were hidden with our unseen spouse, and hidden from the world, which was our enemy, and hidden from each other.

My cell was home to a pale, dusky luminescence. There was tremendous beauty in this shifting brightness. The other source, a single bulb that hung, unshaded, from a wire in the centre of the high ceiling, seemed half redundant. The low orange-yellow pulse that it emitted seemed a wintry thing. Sad autumn afternoons and sorrowful evenings were when it came into its own, a proxy and a puppeteer, a contrivance, while the real light slept. Sometimes I did not bother with it. Even the moon gave enough glow to see the surface of the lake by, and prayer, our purpose, did not require many props – only our knees, which grew sore and callused with the years, our dedicated minds and hearts, and our good will.

The low wooden door, with its rope-lift handle and felt-lined latch, was a holy threshold. On entering the whitewashed space, the silence covered you like a cloak, and something in your heart sang, sang into the stillness. Someone, you knew, was listening to you. Someone was there, waiting to give himself to the whole of you, in return for your attention. Going the other way, my cell door gave onto a dim vestibule and then a landing, and from there onto a labyrinth of human complications, unspoken interactions that bred, and shed, and swarmed in the silence of the cold corridors. But the cell was safety. It was repose. Above all, it was ideal companionship.

Yes, the cell was a lonely place but also a lovely one. Lovely in its strength and starkness. Even the loneliness was lovely. You might sometimes have felt shorn of comfort, bereft of human warmth and every shred of fellow feeling, denied the understanding that you craved, and yet you did not feel completely isolated. You felt cleansed. There was a palpable cushion of love around you, one that came from prayer, and – even when your mind was circling, and you felt trapped and tested – there was nowhere in the world you'd rather be. The cell really was a kind of heaven.

As a twenty-something, heaven was often on my mind. Naturally, I'd barely given it a thought before my father died. In those days I was far more interested in books and music, in experimental creativity, relationships and a certain kind of dangerously intelligent and charismatic man. I was interested in experiencing what the wide world had to offer. I wanted to learn and travel, to discover other cultures. I liked learning languages. I was romantically susceptible, and enjoyed the attentions of the opposite sex. Like many young people, I was looking outward at this big, challenging, exciting thing called life, half overwhelmed, wondering what to do with it, a gift I'd been presented with whether I wanted it or not. The otherworldly hardly featured for me in those days. But after my father died, everything changed, and my thoughts turned away from the transient and contingent. I was no longer interested in amassing vibrant experience, however pleasant, I was seeking to understand life as a whole better, looking for something ultimate and absolute.

The unseen spouse had then made his entrance, as had the eternal Father and the irresistible Spirit. This was a trinity that befuddled reason but nourished the heart. In the cell we sat and let its beams encircle and burn down upon us. We exposed every part of us to its searching, ruthless light. Some go to beaches to lay themselves before the sun. We went to our cells and laid our souls completely bare, knowing we would soon be touched by the flame. We knew it would sear and transform us at a deeper level. We were ready to be changed. Something had happened in each of our lives, some jolt, some dislocation, that was powerful enough to override everything else in our experience. We would kneel on low

wooden stools in the cold and – for an hour in the early
morning and an hour in the late afternoon – invite God in, in
total silence. *Veni, Creator Spiritus*, we whispered. We all knew
the words. Come, wind and fire, come, touch us, set our souls
alight . . .

There was a thirst at the heart of this contemplative
approach, a need. The mystics of the order – Teresa, John of
the Cross – and other writers from the desert traditions, such
as the Carthusians, had written about the 'wound of love',
the sense abiding at the heart of every solitary seeker that
there was something more to life, something beyond the
finite and material that alone could make us whole. It had a
personal face, this ultimate being, and because as single
women we dedicated all we had to this relationship, we culti-
vated the feeling that he was our spouse. We, unworthy
though we were, were his brides, Brides of Christ, poor
women earmarked for a glorious nuptial union with Jesus
beyond the grave. We were there because he was everything
to us. We were there because we had 'heard' his call.

The cell was where the designated hours of solitary prayer
usually took place, although you could also take your prayer
time in the choir or the oratory, a smaller and more private
chapel. In summer you could take it in the garden. The important thing was the time spent with the spouse, and the fact that
these two most sacred hours were not meant to be filled with
prescribed actions or words. Unlike the liturgical prayer times
throughout the day, those we carried out as one body in the
choir, reading or singing from a breviary, the solitary prayer
times were spaces in which to let go and commune without
encumbrance. We simply sat there, offered him our availability,
and let him do it. His visits were not always palpable things,
and, as you progressed in the Life, they tended to be less

palpable than at first, back when the 'honeymoon effect' made everything more impressive.

My honeymoon was a protracted one, and the cell was bliss itself to me. All I wanted was to sit there, like Mary of Bethany at the feet of Jesus, and taste his wisdom, listen to his words and feel his presence. To touch and be touched by his reality. In the early days I felt this desire as a pressing need, a portal to connection. I felt I had come home to the one thing that really mattered. Felt I had come home to love. Our Father was in heaven. All earthly things had given way to the heavenly. And now heaven was in the cell.

Beyond our cell doors there were staircases and landings, alcoves and offices (as we called any room where we did our work, the five hours of so-called manual labour every day, which might be anything from sewing to sweeping or making shoes), and then on the ground floor, the kitchen, pantries and the recreation room. The latter was where, for a designated period once the day's work was done, we met as a community and, for half an hour, the custom of silence was lifted. Unlike the rest of the day when words were held back, or weighed extremely carefully, at recreation time we sat in a circle and made efforts to converse. Our founder, St Teresa, had promoted the half hour of recreation as a safety net, a way to ensure silence was kept properly the rest of the time.

Over the months I was to learn new Carmelite ways of communicating, as well as ways of refraining from doing so. Naturally, a lot of this was strange at first. It was not so much the silence that was new to me, but the adapting of my natural way of speaking to fit with the wavelength of the group. Certain phraseologies had to be acquired: 'of your charity' was a way of saying 'please', while '*Deo gratias*' stood for 'thank you'. As hermits-in-community, we were not supposed to share our problems with others, nor to seek to offload emotionally, even to a legitimate superior, whether prioress or priest. Although there was a hierarchy, and, if you were new, you had an angel and a novice mistress to guide you in the practicalities, you were not meant to 'indulge' in easy talk about yourself, nor to use these other human hermits as a prop. They were there to point the way through example, and by helping you live your life according to the Rule and Constitutions. You certainly never shared anything heartfelt or deeply personal at recreation. You effaced yourself and gave priority to others. Every nun's first instinct, if ever she felt stirred or upset about anything, was to turn to God and take her problem to the cell, and to the uncompromising silence, the unflattering solitude that it represented.

What was it that kept us there, kept us going back for more? It was a mixture of beliefs and emotions, faith being the most important element in the mix by far, faith not only in the theoretical formulations of who God was and what he 'wanted of us', but as a staking of our lives on something unseen. The nitty-gritty of doctrinal belief can be read about in any Catholic Catechism, but we nuns took it much further than intellectual assent. Belief in God as creator, and consciousness of that historic and human misuse of free will traditionally called 'sin', and in Jesus as rescuer and redeemer, were taken as read. These and all the other articles of the creeds originally drawn up in the fourth and fifth centuries, and loosely based on scripture (and on Greek philosophy), were non-negotiables.

As a questioner and a convert, I'd had to swallow quite a lot of relatively unlikely stuff before I'd even crossed the threshold. Some of these assents were more hard-won than others. Certain Catholic devotions seemed off-puttingly fanciful, and it was only by the combined force of mental gymnastics and a willingly surrendered heart that I was able to get beyond them, to grasp the deeper meaning, taste the tender fruit within the rind. Behind each of the steps and decisions that I took there was this more-than-nagging sense that only in responding to all that faith asked of me could I grow to my full stature as a human being. Only by allowing faith to morph and shift and develop from being an option – one among many – to being a relationship, could I, daughter of a painter, soon to become Sister Catherine of Jesus, discover my true nature as a beloved child of God.

5. Little Jug

'We don't call it breakfast,' Sister Ellen said.

It was a sunny mid-October day, the sky suffused with glancing golden light.

'Breakfast implies a meal. Little Jug is nothing more than a gulp of tea and bread, which is why we have it standing up. It's all very simple.'

'Oh dear, I'm sorry,' I said. I had not always noticed the others standing in their places, usually being hazy with sleep at that time, and had eaten my own slice of brown with a scraping of margarine that morning sitting on the bench in my set place in the refectory.

'Nothing to worry about, Catherine – it really doesn't matter. Some sisters do take it sitting down these days, if they've had a bad night or are . . . you know. Indisposed. The great thing is not to spend too long over it. You should be out of the refectory by seven-thirty. There's work to be done.'

'So, Lauds at five-thirty, then an hour of silent prayer . . .'

'That's right. The meditation should set you up for the day. It focuses our minds and resets our compass towards God. Intentions have to be renewed again and again, Catherine, until whatever is otherwise unnatural become habitual. That's how it works. You'll learn. Although you won't be living the full horarium for a while yet. Mother has given you three late mornings a week for the time being. And the Little Jug should help.'

Little Jug, I soon learned, not only helped; it was indispensable. How the older sisters had managed on just a bowl of sugar water, in the days before Vatican II, I did not know. Tea had been an innovation in the 1970s, or rather a concession, and even now, in the early 1990s, a second bowl was frowned upon. I did not need to ask, I sensed it. Looking for refills or second portions was not done.

By my second week I was noticing the smell of baking bread that filled the empty passageways during our morning prayer time. Sister Mary Immaculata (a tiny, wizened creature who'd been a nun almost since she was a child) got up an hour before everybody else and kneaded dough, like the lay sister she once was, and got a batch of loaves into the oven. The yeasty scent that billowed down the corridor set my stomach rumbling. The cell was cold, and prayer was meant to sustain us, but the thought of bread was not always easy to dismiss. Bread was never just bread in Carmel. It was earth, it was grain, it was bounty, it was eternal-life-giving flesh. Echoes of the Eucharist were everywhere.

'No crumbs are to be left behind,' I'd read in the little manual for newcomers someone – I supposed Ellen – had left out on my desk to welcome me my first day. No crumbs, for the obvious reason that people all over the world were hungry, while we nuns had what was deemed enough to eat. But it was also because bread, even the unconsecrated kind, was always sacred on some level, and because 'even the dogs eat the crumbs that fall from their master's table.' Every crumb mattered, was potential nourishment and potential prayer (we thanked God silently as we ate it), just as every least detail of our lives carried not only material but spiritual importance. No mote of dust on a windowpane was without its significance, nor were these details without their lessons for us.

'Nothing is too small to offer up to God,' was a popular maxim, instilled early on, along with the portions of bread that lived in little cloth bags on our 'slate' (traditionally tiles used as plates) and tea, and other substances which, it must be said, rarely included anything as delightful as juice of the fruit of the vine. Only on major feast days did the cellarer – the sister whose job it was to watch over the hidden supply of bottles – come round and drip some potent dark-red liquid into our *creusets*, the shatterproof glass bowls we used for almost everything.

Slates, *creusets*, cellarer. There were not only new ways of doing things, there were new words to be learned, a whole new way of speaking about everything, and you soon noticed the very special intonation with which Carmelites enunciated, breathily and extremely carefully. Like crumbs, no word was to be lost or wasted. In fact, words were never just words in Carmel; they were reminders of the one true Word, the rational and creative principle that emanated, unstintingly, from the godhead from all eternity. That word was the one and only *Logos*, unique of its kind, but all words had their own logic that brought creativity and light and life. Both words and crumbs of bread were principles of life, and as such were held to be sacred, treated with the utmost reverence.

Wherever I looked, the spiritual and the material were intertwined. More than that, they were fused, remodelled into one interactive new creation. You soon got used to seeing life as one great intermingling of humanity and divinity, clay and light, body and mind, sense and spirit, and to attributing this glorious fusion to something that happened 2,000 years ago, a singular instance in history but one that affected not only the whole human species, but the very structure of the cosmos. Yes, our ways and customs may have looked insignificant, or odd, or merely fussy from the outside, but, if you understood them, and the thoughts behind them, you saw how they were all connected to a grand unifying vision.

To me, in my first convert's fervour, this was all intensely motivating. Meaning was stamped deep on everything. Purpose, too, which was what followed once you had grasped the first principles of faith correctly. London seemed far away to me, as I bowed to take communion (traditionally, on the tongue) or made the sign of the cross over my morning hunk of bread and reverently kissed it before eating – another custom. If ever I thought of the great city I'd left behind, I felt sorry for the people there, scurrying to and fro with briefcases and shopping bags, packed into Underground tunnels, breathing in the grimy air, risking their lives jumping on and off moving buses.

My father had fallen once, at the 30 bus stop outside our house, had cut open his left hand on the shards of a bottle of turpentine he'd been carrying. He'd crashed onto it, also injuring an elbow. For a while, his arm was in a sling. My grief for him still came in waves, and pangs of longing, but the memories of London as a place were dark and deadening. When Jennifer asked me, wide-eyed, whether I missed my active city life, incredulous that I'd disconnected myself from it apparently so easily, I was as surprised as she was. How was it, I wondered, that she still had hankerings for Outside? In this, as in everything, she and I were opposites, and felt everything as though through different pores, processed everything according to a different system.

In the silent refectory, where our places were laid out along the benches in the same arrangement as in choir, I saw her opposite me, pushing bowls of tepid tapioca away in disgust as I fell on the stuff, always hungry, always wanting more of everything. Looking back, I suppose I was drained of life, needing so much to be filled. Grief at the loss of family and of security and home had gnawed away at me, until I had embraced detachment, not so much by preference but out of necessity. I already knew I could not live on bread alone, or rely on others, but the early starts and the hard physical work of the cloister produced their own natural hunger. I was glad of anything that came my way.

After the midday meal – which was actually at 11.40, so early had our long days begun – and after supper, or 'collation', a few oddments of bread, soup and cheese, there was the ritual of 'dishes', done according to an ever-changing weekly rota. Although in theory everyone was supposed to take their turn, in practice there were the stalwarts, and then there were those important people who were always needed elsewhere, and who could not be expected to roll up their sleeves. Elizabeth, for example, never appeared at dishes – she was novice mistress and 'infirmarian'. But there were those who could be relied upon to arrive first where a bit of communal elbow grease was required.

One of these was Sister Judith. Tall and willowy, with sea-green eyes, it was her earnestness and kindness that stood out. She would scoot down to the kitchen, snaffle the first white apron from the communal hook, and then be found bent over one of the huge ceramic sinks doing the cutlery before anyone else arrived. Her way was always quietly cheerful. Dishes was in silence, of course, but when Philippa and the other novices arrived there was often a bit of nudging and cooperative giggling. I immediately liked the earnest Judith, and felt a connection with friendly Pippa – was it that she, like me and Judith, was a convert to Catholicism? There were not many of us. Or was it because she was a southerner? In a closed religious community, it is, ironically, the indicators of secular identity that rise to the surface and help you navigate between nun and nun at first.

Jane was one of the most inscrutable. She had a mouth that looked like it had never been opened, and hands as sleek and white as freshly washed linen, even though she took her fair share of the lowly tasks. She was 'Second' in the kitchen, which meant she was assistant to good-hearted Sister Ambrose. While we did dishes, Jane would be in a corner measuring out the double-diluted powdered milk for the morning – two scoops of the plastic shovel instead of four and a big yellow plastic bowl to whisk it in. The resulting pale liquid would be set out in jugs in the fridge, covered with sheets of card, alongside the blocks of cheese and the eggs and homemade yogurt. Fresh milk was a luxury, reserved for Sundays and special occasions. But when you were hungry even the powdered tasted delicious.

Little Jug was only part of it. We were all jugs, vessels, as easily shattered as filled, cracked earthenware fit for mending, but also adapted to become lanterns, with space and flaws enough to let the light shine through. That was one way of thinking about it, and the way that we were taught to see our frailty: to prize our wounds as battle trophies, and to glory not in ourselves but in the great, benign spirit that moved among us. Morning prayer started the cycle of redemption anew every day, and while we longed for bread and tea, God longed for us. There, in the cold cell, he stretched out his arms to us in love, stretched them out in pain on the unseen cross that hung above the world, stretched out his heart to us as a gift, and we reached back. Very soon it was clear that God was my true father and that the monastery was my true home.

6. The Grille

The grille, like many powerful symbols in our lives, was surrounded by mystique. There were grilles in all the places that we might otherwise have been seen by outsiders, which meant any one of the small rooms, called parlours, where priests and occasional visitors might come and talk to us. It was all highly regulated, and things like locks, and keys, and hidden drawers (for passing things through), and obscure hatches featured pretty heavily. In the old days, any nun receiving visitors had had to have a chaperone, a sister whose entire body, including her face, was shrouded in an extra layer of black cloth so that she appeared an incognito presence, hovering in the background, to make sure things did not go awry. Contacts with outside were traditionally viewed as dangerous.

In my day it was less spooky, but still some of the old weirdnesses lingered. There was the two-way drawer we called 'the turn', a deep wooden coffin of a contraption through which someone had once passed a baby (out to in and back again, you'll be pleased to hear), no doubt traumatising the poor thing for life. The child might have been briefly cradled in the scratchy folds of a big brown habit and a pair of chilly hands. Many of us had relatives who'd been fruitful and multiplied, and meeting our newborn relatives for the first time was one of the more exquisite jolts to our system that took place in the parlour.

How did we feel about such things as babies and fecundity? Difficult to say, as we soon got used to filtering our spontaneous reactions to events and reprocessing them in religious terms, so that, between the initial impulse of a thought or feeling and its acknowledgement on a conscious level, a whole active process of reordering had taken place. It happened fast, this filtering of feeling, a sort of lightning-quick adjustment, a 'conformity to grace'. The more internally intent and mortified you were, the quicker and more habitual was the translation from raw reaction to modulated response. If anyone felt sadness at the thought that she would never bring a new human life into the world, the answering thought that barrenness meant blessedness came close on its heels by way of consolation.

The other, more routine jolt administered in the parlour was Confession, a ritual that took place fortnightly with one of the black-clad monks from Kielder Abbey. The moist feelings that emerged and flowed freely in the confessional were of the permitted sort, mainly nagging displeasure with oneself, anxiety that one might have offended God, worry that any less acceptable feelings might have gone unchecked on occasion. Sorrow for sin was seen as a good emotion, and contrite tears a badge of honour, whereas sorrow over any sort of personal setback was something you had to sort out briskly, and, equipped with the virtues, 'work through'. Usually the monk would listen, hands clasped, head on one side, and then murmur gentle words of encouragement before offering the formula of absolution.

What kinds of problems might we have admitted to? If you were earnest, like Thérèse, you might have had a problem with religious 'scruples', as we termed an anxious or exaggerated conscientiousness. I certainly did, and Sister Elizabeth tried to put me right, saying I needed to 'loosen up' a bit. Scruples were a sign of good intent, but betrayed a lack of mature trust in God. Trying too hard to be good was something sternly disapproved of. This was a shock, and a sign that life in Carmel might not be all I had imagined. No one wanted a miserable saint around the place! Common observance, the keeping of all the ways and customs, was all that was required, and we were told that such unspectacular (and unthinking) simplicity and obedience was all we needed to become good nuns. If you expected anything more of yourself or of others, you were expecting too much, and were called a Pelagian.

It was Father Gregory who first explained the term to me. A contemporary of St Augustine's, the monk Pelagius's alternative teachings had been a foil to the Bishop of Hippo's lofty words. Augustine had had a problem with scruples as well as sins of the flesh, before reaching maturity, becoming bishop and casting off the yoke of spiritual self-reliance. Pelagius, on the other hand, was the sort to embrace that yoke with full accountability, to work out at the treadmill of applied endeavour and personal effort. No easy pleasures or unmerited spiritual satisfactions for him. He was a disciplined character who looked for discipline in others.

In time I was to learn that being too disciplined, or too overtly good, was a short cut to unpopularity in the Catholic Church. Pelagius had been labelled a heretic for his pains. Elizabeth was very much an advocate of humdrum conformity, an average approach, and had an eagle eye for anything she deemed unusual or 'singular'. As the one entrusted with the task of 'forming' novices, even if she did delegate many of the duties to our angels, Elizabeth waged war on characteristics that might attract positive attention, and any tendency that made people shine or stand out from the group. Singularity, even if it went with excellence, was the enemy of her

firm maternal rule. When faced with fine feelings and tremu-
lousness in her charges she brought out her watchwords, Just
Get On With It, and Do As You Are Told. But you could
always hope for an opportunity to take your more subtle soul-
searching to a visiting priest.

They did not come our way very often, these wandering
sages. Once a year there was the community retreat, a week
of intensified silence and solitude, when a new male face
might appear, a Franciscan friar, perhaps, or a Jesuit on
retreat from London. They would stay in the extern quarters,
immersing themselves in the quiet, but would also material-
ise to give us talks in the choir or parlour, always standing at
some distance and delivering their pearls of wisdom through
the grille. Obviously, you weren't meant to fall in love with
them. I never did, and only after years wondered whether I
was quite 'normal' in this. Given the hothouse nature of our
lives, and the fact that the only men we ever saw were the
chaplains – mainly older monks who appeared daily on the
sanctuary to say Mass – and the odd city parish priest, you
might have expected feelings to have been stirred when
someone younger or more 'interesting' turned up.

But no. I had no desire to bond with these lofty birds of
passage. The year everyone went quietly crazy about Father
Simon, because he was tall and blonde and wore Birken-
stocks (the first time any of us had seen them) and taught us
to sit in the lotus posture and watch our breathing, I steeled
myself against infatuation. A novelty, yes, but ultimately not
my cup of tea. No one was, I decided, because no man could
ever live up to my father, or replace him as the man who held
my heart. Dad was everything, and he was in heaven. He was
also by my side and at my centre. Every fibre of my being
bore his imprint. My vocation sometimes felt like nothing

more than a way of honouring him, of saying definitively to
the world: My heart belongs to Daddy. And what was wrong
with that? No other arms would ever hold me. On one level
it was still all about the grief.

Grief was certainly the backdrop to everything at this point
in my life, and it gave me the kind of recklessness and purity
of intention that might not have been possible under easier,
less drastic circumstances. After Dad and so much else that
mattered had gone, what was there left to lose? Only the
money a kind aunt had left me, and wasn't part of Christianity giving away one's possessions to the poor? My share of
worldly goods went to the monastery, as was customary in
those days. With grief had come a natural detachment from
the world. What was the point in clinging on to life if it was
only going to be taken away from me? I was young, but I'd
seen the reality of transience close up, and it had made a
deep impression on me. Once God had entered the picture,
I'd let go, one by one, of all my other interests. First, I'd given
up the boyfriends, knowing I'd suffered useless damage at
their hands, then the smoking, then the experimental music
and the hefty Russian novels which I replaced, gradually,
with measured tomes on philosophy and theology. I even
stopped playing the piano in the evenings, and spent my free
time kneeling before statues of the Virgin Mary, muttering
rosaries, lighting candles in dusty side chapels off the Kentish
Town Road or in Victorian churches in West End Lane.

I was searching. I was embracing self-denial. I was becoming prim. My sister Frankie moved away, to try out life
somewhere new, smaller and more affordable than London.
She needed to shake off old associations. Thanks to one or
two connections in the area, she decided to try Newcastle,

where she worked as a china restorer, and had a pottery studio in Jesmond. Rob was away travelling in Asia, still incommunicado, still untraceable since our father's death. None of us blamed him; it was easy to imagine how much he'd needed to get away from London, and from the family expectations. As the youngest, the loss of our home and family unit, and the lack of any adult support at such a time, must have been particularly galling. We'd just been left to ourselves and our own devices.

When people failed me, books came to my rescue; and when I failed myself, the unseen rescuer stepped in. The power of that first meeting, at my father's body, the sense that someone was with me, accompanying my every breath, my every step, was impossible to shake off after that. Like Francis Thompson's Hound of Heaven, my pursuer was not only behind me, he was ahead of me, he was staring me down. His eyes were everywhere, and I succumbed to a love that felt more powerful than any earthly, bodily infatuation. There were times when I honestly think I would have lain down in the road and consented to be run over, sawn in two, torn limb from limb to prove my love. I was in the throes of an emotional and spiritual experience that some would later call fanatical.

Visits to the north to see my sister in her new-found niche soon became regular occurrences. She had always been my ally, and we were able to talk for hours about the difficult family times we'd been through. Her personality was very different from mine. While I was naturally demonstrative and emotional by temperament, she was extremely reserved. She was also focused on the practical. But the support we gave each other was so important for both of us at this time, and the bond between us was strong. When she introduced me to a new friend, Agnes, who happened to be a Catholic nun, someone she'd met through her restoration work in a museum in Hexham, the die was cast. I was soon asking Aggie for tips about local places of worship, and . . . was there anywhere I could go away on retreat? I needed some special time apart with God.

Kielder Abbey, where I headed the next Easter, was a step in a very important new direction, but nothing in my experience there suggested I was being called to be a member of their order. There was something that seemed measured, sedate, almost too comfortable in the air they breathed. They had armchairs, and meals that seemed, by my spartan standards, like feasts. Was there a whiff here of luxury or decadence? My tendencies were radical, and I wanted stark. The thirst for the absolute and for dedication was now screaming inside me, pounding like an insistent need, and was not going to go away, or be satisfied by creature comforts. And then somebody said 'Akenside'. The word dropped like a bright copper penny bang in the middle of my mind's wishing well. I knew what I had to do.

Akenside Priory, some forty miles away in the flat farmlands around Morpeth, was not any old monastery but a place of ghosts, a place of peace, a place where I was soon convinced I would find union with my heavenly – and somehow reconnect with my earthly – father. Here, I would encounter my unseen rescuer full on, and learn to think of him as my spouse. Here, I would be blessed by the fruits of constant prayer, while combating the forces of evil, as Sister Ellen warned me I would have to do. Prayer would not always come easily, as she'd said. Like all the virtues, like faith, like hope, like love itself, it would ultimately be a matter of the will, sometimes even a difficult, or unsatisfying choice.

The highest virtue of all was love, but *agape* was not to be confused with *eros*, nor was it to be mistaken for familial bonds or ties of friendship. Christian love, like the charism itself, was a supernatural gift, something capable of overriding natural feelings. I still had to learn that love in monasticism (or 'charity', as we more usually called it) was understood not as a feeling but as a choice, and that we were called to love – that is, to *choose* and *want* to love – all people equally, with no special affections harboured, even for one's own kin. It was difficult to plumb the depths of this new approach, to appreciate its strengths and its limitations, when Ellen first explained it to me. On entering Carmel I'd implicitly chosen a dedicated group of women, not for themselves, but as vessels of the divine, and as a tribe with which to align myself and unswervingly to serve. I was called to love each one as myself, which meant loving them no more nor less than any other human being.

At first I thought it would be easy, as my nature was an affectionate one, and there were some – a few younger faces peeping out from veils and wimples – who'd mirrored something of myself back to me when I'd first met them. Here was flesh of my flesh, bone of my bone, I thought in the early days. These were special people, people unlike others in a harsh and inhospitable world, people I could finally believe in. Perhaps it was just the way they smiled, or sang, or the way they'd welcomed me on my first visit.

This was not yet my official live-in but a visit to the guesthouse. I'd suspended all commitments in London for a while to explore possibilities. After the lonely grey streets of the capital, Akenside Priory was bright and luminous. It seemed ancient, permanent, self-sufficient; a city set on a hilltop. Sister Paula, who didn't know me from Adam or from Eve, was nevertheless expecting me, saw me coming from afar and burst out of the side door to meet me, striding down the gravel drive towards me with open arms and reams of bright white laughter. 'Now there you are!' she chuckled, welcoming me as a long-lost child. 'And what'll you be after wanting now? A cup of tea? I've made up the table for you in the guest room, and we are all looking forward to seeing you in the parlour when you're ready for it. Mother says she'll have a little chat with you after Vespers, but you'd better be liking flapjack, because today's baking day and Sister Ambrose has made some specially . . .'

She rattled on, and I looked around me, wide-eyed at the beauty of these sudden, new surroundings. High red-brick walls, made friendly with moss and ferns, extended in a generous arc, which – even from the gravel drive I could see – included acres of lawn and of wild meadows, and lush greenery all blooming, bursting, blossoming (it was nearly summer) and giving out fresh floral fragrance that made me start to sneeze.

'Now you won't be minding the cats, will you? I hope that's just hay fever. You'll be used to London, naturally, so of course it will all feel very different . . .'

To both sides of the drive tall trees rose up as though straining for the sky, and away and beyond them to one side, in the gaps where the light came through, an endlessness of fields stretched into the distance, taut and tended, a patchwork of green and brown and mossy yellow. To the other side the trees were so dense as to let no light through, a tangled wall of trunks and branches, all gnarled and weaving, spreading their leafy hands aloft, some of them proffering tall cream candlesticks, others buds destined to become pine cones, evergreen foliage prickly with the scent of fir. Soon I was standing in the shadow of what, by long-forgotten courtly standards, would have been a rather modest mansion. Here, in the late twentieth century, it seemed a castle made for magic, or for the fulfilment of dreams, gabled, turreted, topped by a bell tower and a weathervane.

The extern itself, where I was to stay, was a semi-detached, neglected wing of the old house with a sitting room and kitchenette, two bedrooms, a couple of very basic bathrooms and a spiral staircase to a landing with a single door marked PARLOUR. The word felt fairytale-like, and I imagined a medieval queen to be sitting in there eating bread and honey. When I turned the handle out of curiosity, I found it locked.

For the first twenty-four hours I only met and spoke to Sister Paula, the one charged with the care of guests. As a naturally chatty older woman, she fitted the bill for a guest-house sister. She was warm yet brisk, and not the kind to listen to any nonsense. I liked her, but kept out of her way soon enough, when the pull of silence from the other side of the wall made its weight felt, like a magnetic attraction. What were those papery footsteps that skirted near and then disappeared? What unseen figure was it that pulled the rope that rang the bell that I could see across a covered walkway from my window? Did I hear someone cough close by? What were these souls and spirits living like the dead, so silently yet so ethereally alive? Paula summoned me for flapjack and then bustled out, remarking on the lateness of the day, the heavy weather.

On my second afternoon there was a thunderstorm, and the women I saw from my window, flitting across courtyards in their long brown robes, were like ghosts. They barely spoke and their pale faces were as inscrutable as distant moons. I saw them as brave, extraordinary, martyr figures. They belonged to the same forgotten world as the moss growing out of the ancient enclosure wall, the ferns that grew, unchecked, at its base, and the dandelions and smaller flowers peeping from its crevices. They belonged to the fields and forests. Above all, they belonged to the silence, and to God. I opened the window. The smell of damp earth rose, reeking of something half forgotten, mixed with spring.

The next morning, once the rain had settled, I caught sight of a young sister, her face serious and long, lifting a churn of milk and easing it through an open door. When the door closed and she and the churn disappeared, I stood and thought. There was something incongruous about seeing someone my own age, a girl of about twenty-five, who might have been wearing jeans in any other setting, dressed from head-to-toe in a concoction of medieval cloths. And she was so silent! So sure and strong. The figure I'd observed was fully intent on her task and had not turned to look at me.

I'd stayed an extra day, basking in the silence of the guest quarters, attending the monastic Offices, marvelling at this way of life, so unlike anything I'd imagined possible, and feeling my stomach curdling into that hollow ache I remembered from the one and only time I'd been in love. Returning for my official live-in, a month later, I was naturally excited but just a little apprehensive, worried it would not live up to that moment in the thunderstorm. But it did more. It went beyond. I found a rainbow of smiling faces all around me, a bar of carbolic in my washing bowl, and a room with a wide-open view over lakes and fields, a room you didn't call a room, you called a cell. A cell, I realised, was all I desired. And having a cell with a view was even better.

The community was warm and encouraging towards me. The inhabitants of Akenside Priory turned from being ghost-women to exemplars of something just alive that I myself might become. The moon-like pallid faces spoke (occasionally, in unfamiliar, dipping accents) and their words were like arrows pointing to something precious just out of sight, a special cloud formation or a rare bird, something of such ultimate and overarching value that it was worth waiting for. The sense of expectation in the air was palpable. God and all he represented – the afterlife – was only round the corner.

Whatever denial of life was mixed in with my desire to shut myself away would soon be clothed in dreams of a crisp white wimple, of sandals and a floor-length robe like something the Elizabethans might have left behind. Or something even more ancient, I suppose, as I later discovered there was a sunken abbey, a relic of the dark ages, in the grounds. Augustinian sisters had lived and toiled there centuries ago, and, in winter, when the foliage was low and dead, the ruins of their kitchen sink could be seen peeping from between gnarled roots in one of the more distant woodland areas beyond the lawns.

How often I walked those grounds, and pressed on through the untamed woods and copses to the kitchen garden, drawn involuntarily in the direction of the Mere. The bell for choir would call me back, and, in the early stages, have me running, picking up my flowing newcomer's dress, wrapping close my winter scarf and allowing what was left of my hair (I'd cut it to a tidy bob, but knew that that, too, would soon have to go) flap pleasurably in the wind. I'd come a long way from Paris, had journeyed far from the London that was once my home. Certainly, a long journey still awaited me, one through a sometimes stony landscape. But for now I was glad to be in God's own house. One day within his courts, I knew, was better than a thousand elsewhere. The grille was the symbol of so much that I desired: separation from the world, complete dedication, and a life lived with a singular and sole intention.

7. The Mere

'Next time you'll have your own pair of wellies,' Sister Ellen was saying as we strode deep in moist grasses across the meadow to the lake. She was becoming more encouraging, almost conspiratorial in her humour. My attempts at breeziness had rubbed off. My wellies had skidded and split during a recent outdoor recreation, one of the irregular midday ones, while we were gathering kindling for a bonfire, and now I was in a pair much too large for me, comically wading alongside her in her neat-fitting rubber ankle boots.

'The lake, the lake!' she said, spreading her arms out before us as we made our way.

'It is so beautiful,' I said. 'Even in this season.'

'Well, Catherine, if you haven't yet glimpsed the reservoir, just beyond the woodland, you're in for a treat. It makes this look like a puddle.'

'Really? It must be enormous!' I replied. 'I mean . . .'

'Yes, this lake is about three acres. But the Mere is of a different order altogether. You can see it better when the trees are bare. But you might get a glimpse of it today. The air is clear enough.'

We walked on, keeping the conversation light, looking around us with wonder at the beauty of the natural world. Ellen was in a buoyant mood. She was even on the verge of joking. I'd arrived at the toolshed in advance of her, and she'd found me browsing the veritable jumble-sale of anoraks that represented at least five decades' worth of new entrants' wardrobes. There was the baggy eighties duffel, the seventies quilted nylon jacket, even a sixties Peruvian poncho. I'd slipped on my old donkey jacket and was glad of it, and the oversized gumboots, as we headed out into the chilly air.

'So you're in your Eeyore jacket today?' she laughed.

'And my Paddington boots!' I replied.

'I know you've been here a month now. But still, it takes time, doesn't it? To adapt to the cold northern outdoors. Not quite what you're used to, I expect.'

Ellen's voice was quizzical and gently probing. No one had asked me much about my background or taken an interest in my previous life up to this point, and I wondered whether she was now homing in, was going to wrench it all out of me. But no. We talked of mundane matters, as usual, and today's topic was a possible allergy to washing powder. With this we were on safe territory. Ellen and Elizabeth both loved talking about domestic and minor medical matters – although strictly privately, one-to-one. Group discussions skirted assiduously around anything to do with health.

The trudge across the gardens to the Mere was a welcome change from work and kneeling. Yes, at only a few weeks it was good and refreshing to be at a distance from the great fortress of the old building for a while. It was possible to open up and speak more freely in these open spaces. I already knew how easy it was to hear even the most subtle sounds in the halls and corridors and cloisters, since the otherwise unbroken silence made everything stand out, amplified by contrast. You never knew whether you were really alone. In the garden you could be less guarded.

Or so I thought. I coughed, looking out over the pale-green landscape from which the morning mist seemed never to have lifted, and an enormous wood pigeon shot suddenly from a pile of bracken, startled by our approach. I jumped back, shocked at the agitated rustling of leaves and feathers. Ellen said gently, 'Gosh, what a bag of nerves you are! You need to get used to this kind of thing in the country. Foxes, rabbits and, worst of all, what the cats bring in. It's not too bad when they're already dead, but I hope you can toughen up, Catherine, and manage to overlook such displays of untamed nature. It's going to be a big change for you after London.'

It was more a gentle warning than a reprimand, aimed at setting a certain tone, and I bit back a knee-jerk apology. Grace and nature belonged to different spheres, were seen as being opposed, sometimes at war, and, where basic instincts were concerned, 'grace' must have the upper hand. Thomas Aquinas had spelled out the concepts for us. It was expected that the lower animals be motivated by instinct and preda-tion, but we, *homo sapiens*, the rational animal, were called to have our mind on higher things.

'Look,' Ellen continued, 'I just wanted to make sure we covered a few essentials while we had the chance. It's not often we get these free afternoons. How are you sleeping these days? And how's your appetite? And, well, you know – you must let me know if you need anything from the medicine cupboard. For example, how are your periods? Regular? I expect you know how to find more towels, but . . . please don't hesitate to ask.'

I was mumbling something about not being due for another two weeks, when she cut in with a comment about the mornings.

'You can always ask for extra sleep at the time of the month, you know. Unlike some places, we really are quite understanding. At Truro or Sheffield, you wouldn't even get an aspirin, believe you me. Here, we have three days a month when you can sleep in until after Lauds. We call it being on the second call, those days when you can get up at six-thirty. It's a concession, I admit, but one you younger sisters do seem to need from time to time. Things can get so out of proportion in the early years, and, well – it can be difficult for girls these days to rise above their little aches and pains. But that's when the fight begins. The battle for detachment from ourselves.'

The motion of walking was a relief, but Ellen gestured to a bench, suggested we take a few minutes to rest our legs. Mine would have been more relieved by further exertions, I realised, after the long daily hours of kneeling and sitting. I had to admit to myself that I missed my long tramps through London streets. Part of me just wanted to jump and sing and run, and take great gulps of garden-fresh oxygen. Still, we settled ourselves, looking gratefully over the view in easy silence. I pulled my donkey jacket around me. Ellen's thick winter habit was tucked up bulkily under a wide-collared jacket, and seemed burdensome and unwieldy, sticking out oddly at her hips.

'A garden enclosed, a fountain sealed,' she was musing aloud, her voice strangely singsong. 'I often come and sit down here on this bench, and think how blessed we are, and how gracious is the good Lord to have put us amidst all this beauty, in this . . . this veritable Eden.'

Her voice was quavering, as though a tear were lurking in her green-blue eyes, or a vast unacknowledged thought, pushing up just below the surface.

'It really seems untouched by the modern world, doesn't it?' she went on, almost sadly. 'I can never thank Him enough for all of this, and for setting me apart.'

Ellen was far away now, and I observed her, gazing quietly into the space beyond the turrets. I longed to be set apart, too, vowed and dedicated once and for all, my future sealed. I wondered how I could express such thoughts to another, and began . . .

But Sister Ellen was coming round.

'I expect you miss your family, and city life? What a change of life this has all been—' She swept a hand briskly across the extended view '—so different from anything you can have known before. How do they feel about enclosure? And the contemplative life? Do they very much oppose your being here? So many of our dear ones find it very difficult to accept the choice we make. They find it so, er . . . so unnatural.'

'Yes, they do think it a bit strange, I suppose. But they don't really mind. They're not the kind of people to stop me doing anything I've set my heart on,' I said.

Ellen looked blankly at me, as though I'd said something completely mad.

'They aren't against it, then?' she practically whispered, leaning in. 'They don't mind your having converted? They don't place any pressure on you to . . . ?'

'No. Why should they?' I said, but immediately realised this would make no sense to her. It was taken as read that most families hated 'losing their daughters' to a convent. Some did everything they could to stop them from going ahead with their vocations. Some of the sisters had come here in the face of feuds. Seeing the surprise behind her eyes, I added: 'They just don't feel strongly about faith or religion. It's just not part of the way they see things. It's not that they think it's wrong, or oppose it, it's just that they—'

'Ah, I see,' Sister Ellen said, leaning back. She sighed a

little, and brought her hands back to a folded position on her lap. 'I see. I see. A liberal family.'

It took me a moment to understand, to realise there was a gap opening up, a positioning of me as other, or different from what she expected. Then she went on: 'And of course, I think you said you had lost your father not so long ago? And, er, what did you say he did? I think he was a non-believer.'

'He was a painter,' I replied.

'Ah, a house painter? As in—'

'Oh no—' I laughed spontaneously at the mistake '—no, he taught art and painted pictures.'

I thought it best not to mention that he was a professor of Fine Art and a leading figure in his field. Nobody had heard of him here in Carmel. We were encouraged to hide anything that might draw interest. Dad had been recognised for services to the art world before we, his younger family, were born. I'd grown up knowing this, yet simultaneously thinking nothing of it. Dad and Mum were Sir William and Lady, but that's just what it said on the envelopes. It was our normal. Now I was going to make sure I kept perfectly quiet about my difference. I would hide myself away. I would make myself the lowest of the low. This is what St Teresa taught in her treatises. This was the way of *The Imitation of Christ*. Nevertheless, it struck me as odd that no one here drew me out or asked about my past experiences. We were called to be New Creations, our previous lives half-irrelevant once touched by grace.

'I see. You mean he was an *artist*?' Ellen rephrased emphatically, as though putting me right. 'An artist, not a painter. Is that what you mean?'

I nodded. It seemed pointless to quibble over redundant vocab.

'Ah, Catherine. I see. An *artistic* family.'

I'd noted the change in her tone, and was disappointed at her lack of fellow feeling. The traumatic reality of Dad's death and all I'd gone through was skimmed over, while our secular family culture was something she lingered on, making much of the difference, as though it were far more significant. Gnats and camels. An age-old matter of perspective. I knew what to do, and inwardly turned to God. That was the way everything could be resolved. Grace would be forthcoming, if only I lifted up my eyes to the hills. I'd tried it enough times and it usually worked.

Sister Ellen got up, brushed herself down vigorously, as though of something unclean, and suggested we move on. The afternoon would soon be getting late.

We made our way through the narrowest part of the woodland path. Overhanging branches lolled languidly on either side, dripping and brushing against us as we walked. It was not often sisters had the time to wander this far beyond the vegetable garden, far from the shadow of the house. The Mere was legendary, like the Loch Ness Monster. Sightings were rare. Although it was outside the enclosure wall, it was not regarded as part of the outside world. In fact, it was unique in being neither inside nor out of enclosure. It was a third dimension, like a black hole in our imaginations, or another galaxy, made of a different stuff, beyond what was familiar but not so far beyond that we could not occasionally visit it. Now we were getting close, pushing onwards through the decaying brown-red copse.

The ground was squelchy underfoot, my feet moving around within my unstable wellies. My toes were cold. On the really muddy patches I was tending to skid around. 'Oh, do be careful, Sister Catherine,' Ellen said. 'It's quite slippery.' She laughed, and in a flash the kindly Sister Ellen was back.

Before long we were rounding a curving pathway through the trees and then crouching, pushing our way through the dripping moisture of low foliage to the other side. I ducked a large, low-hanging branch. Ellen put out her hands, straining for balance. I giggled, enjoying the cold slap of oxygen. My cheeks burned icy and my lungs tingled with the exhilaration. And then there it was, wholly before us like an enormous grey-green whale. The Mere glinted darkly, reflecting low clouds and the blurred trunks of trees. It was stretched out, still and secretive before us.

Everything seemed to be serene and quiet as we stood there, staring. A plane crept noiselessly across the distant sky. Time passed like plainchant, slow, pulled long and taut to its limits. Two deer appeared, visible between tree trunks on the other side, then shook and shifted into evergreen foliage beyond. The silence settled and stood still. For a while we were like dancers, poised off-stage, holding our breath. I wondered how much longer Sister Ellen would keep us there, what she was waiting for, the two of us quietly alone amid the low, wet branches. Finally, she moved to one side, but immediately lost her balance and was wincing, reaching out blindly for support. I steadied her with one arm.

'A concealed dip!' she said, more irritated than embarrassed, while pointing to the offending trough. 'Do be careful yourself, Catherine. It's very easy to miss these traps. They're everywhere; we don't have enough able-bodied sisters to keep up the gardening as we used to. Everything has become overgrown.' She gazed around her, made a generous sweep of the hand. Nature had, indeed, taken over.

We talked about music as we inched our way back to the house, her arm around my shoulders while I served her as a crutch. The physical contact was slightly disturbing, already a novelty. She was glad at least that I was fit and strong. 'If I had been alone I'd have had to find a good long stick!' she commented. Search parties would have been sent out.

She asked me finally about my viola-playing, and how I'd settled on it as an instrument, and whether I'd ever played in an orchestra.

'Oh, yes,' I said. 'I used to love youth orchestra, learning all those symphonies, and then my years in Paris when I played in a more experimental band.'

'Oh, fancy that!' she said. 'I forgot about your time in Paris.'

'I loved it for a while. Paris was like a more exciting version of London. And full of novelty. But as a Londoner born and bred I've always appreciated the countryside. There were times when I just wanted to get out and away. You know, sometimes you just long for space and silence, and fresh air. You long to get out into the hills.'

Here she stopped and laughed out loud, looking me full in the face.

'Just like Julie Andrews, then?' she exclaimed. 'Or rather, like Maria! Everyone here, of course, sees a bit of Maria in themselves. We've all had fanciful longings in our time. And all that singing! Well, several of us have already noticed how *very* like her you are. Perhaps it's the music. Or perhaps the bone structure? But, of course, looks are immaterial when it comes to the interior life. And a good job, too – for most of us!'

She laughed and we hobbled on, me supporting her, our

roles blurred as I gave her my steadiness and warmth and felt the distant blood pumping through her wool-covered arms. I glanced over, and saw her round cheeks flushed. She smiled across at me. How odd, or rather unnerving, I thought, that they'd already spoken amongst themselves about me. Or was it perhaps an angel thing, and she and Barbara had to report back in full to Elizabeth, and comment on how they saw us. How odd, too, to feel suddenly a little closer to Ellen than to the others, just by virtue of walking round the garden with her, away from the community for a change. This was much better than novitiate! This was a chance to breathe a fresher air.

The walk had been physically refreshing, and I'd welcomed the opportunity to become more at ease with my angel, but the conversation itself had been a little disappointing. Everything important seemed to have been danced around. Her questions were so tentative. As for me, I'd wanted to ask some bigger questions, like whether our time in our own clothes would soon be over. Normally newcomers received the Carmelite habit after six months. I had toyed with the idea of confessing to my allergy to apples and pears (inconvenient, considering we were practically living in an orchard) but some inhibition held me back. Now I was focusing on offering her my strength as she weaved and wobbled on, talking about her love of the Scottish Borders.

Soon we were coming in sight of the grand old house once again, and voices needed to be faded out, or lowered. The community clock-tower showed quarter to four, and the sky was darkening, ready for Vespers. The weathervane was almost indistinguishable in the gloom, but I could make out the delicately carved shape of the crossed keys of Peter on it, fluttering high above the turrets. And then I heard an unfamiliar, rising sound. A throaty squawking preceded an approaching flock of geese that dominated the skyline, a low formation moving closer on heavy wings. They moved with solemn grandeur, slow and calm towards an invisible mark. The desperate cry (for they sang mournfully, as one) rose, and rose further, distorting until it reached a point of blazing intensity overhead, skimming the house before receding, echoing sadly over the darkening trees. Later, I would grow to love the long cold afternoons smelling of leaf mould and the autumn damp, even when my legs and arms were tired. The passing of the geese. The failing of the light. And then the bell for Vespers.

8. The Hours

Our days were divided up into neat compartments by the Hours. If you've ever seen an illuminated manuscript with lots of gold-leaf detail and things like ladybirds and butterflies wandering all over the margins, the chances are it was a Book of Hours, an ornate private prayer-book that once belonged to a late-medieval gentlewoman. Our prayer-books were very plain, and they were called breviaries, an essential resource for navigating the continuous round of public services that went to make up the Divine Office, or the prayer of the Church. Thick as bricks, there were three leather-bound volumes, each for a different time of the year (the Church's life was divided into seasons), and their pages full of psalms.

Unlike those pious gentlewomen, we did not say our Hours in private, reciting them over needlework in genteel turrets. No, the Liturgy of the Hours was the main thing we did in the choir. It was also where we did a great deal of silent prayer and a lot of singing. The choir formed an L-shape with the smaller public chapel, meaning we could not be seen from the outer seating area, a slightly desolate place where visitors could come to Mass. Our area was on a different level, up a series of steps and securely cloistered behind the grille, in this case an arrangement of floor-to-ceiling wooden bars.

There, in our separated space, where no one from outside was allowed to enter, we sang our way through our days. Lauds, God's morning praises, at the crack of dawn was usually something of a dazed affair. '*Oh God, come to our aid!*' we croaked, kicking off the day as we meant to go on. The feebleness of the croak was not a problem, because whatever was lacking in our execution was made up for in intention. That was where true virtue lay, we were taught, and the will – that invisible faculty, counted by St Augustine as the chief power of the soul – was where the action was. Everything in our lives came down to it. We chose God. We chose virtue. We wanted to Do Our Best. If at times it was hard, it was enough for us to '*want* to want', the highest good. Wanting God was like opting for the best thing you could possibly imagine, in the world or out of it, and *wanting to want* – because it was a choice – was the equivalent of *really* wanting, as opposed to merely desiring.

The only catch about this stark form of wanting (that was sure to catch you out eventually, no matter how fervent you were at first) was that it was at the expense of literally everything else. The order made a point of really enjoying this, cranking up the tension, imposing extra sacrifice and discomfort by contrivance. The best cook in the community, for example, would never be given the job of kitchen sister. We all knew that Sister Jane had been practically Cordon Bleu outside, but did she ever have a chance to exercise her skills? Well, obviously no. Nor were we, the brethren, given the chance to enjoy the fruits of her expertise. Thwartings were carefully arranged in other areas, too, because ease and pleasure were the enemies of the spiritual path. There was an equation whereby 'wanting to want' God meant not wanting anything else, at least not for the pleasure of it. In one's first fervour one gladly accepted things that later on might become hard to bear.

In between Lauds and the late afternoon, when we sang

Vespers (or evening prayer), there were the 'Little Hours', sweet little services which we knew by heart. The Little Hours were definitely worthy of ladybirds and butterflies. They were made up of the same hymns and psalms and prayers day after day, with only the scripture readings changing from one to the next. These services – Terce, Sexte and None – contained the Psalms of Ascent, songs associated with the ancient Jewish times of pilgrimage when the original People of the Book would go up to Jerusalem, perhaps with their caravans or on their donkeys. I imagined Jesus, Mary and Joseph singing them in Hebrew, or their own dialect of Aramaic, and the many centuries stretching back in time, echoing the same range of sentiments, the same human need for meaning, purpose and protection.

Having said that, there was nothing sentimental about the Little Hours, and, because the Office of Sexte occurred in late morning, it would often be accompanied by distracting thoughts about what was for lunch. Typically, that would be one portion of vegetarian protein (usually cheese or eggs – we never had meat and rarely fish) served alongside as much vegetable bulk as possible. We nuns needed fuel! Piles of scrubbed potatoes as white as stones. Soft pale-green cabbage leaves as watery and slithery as seaweed. The invariable baked apple. And, before all of this, the monastery soup, chunky and globular, made up of the leftovers of the day before. We ate heartily, but very simply, with no luxuries other than our delicious homemade bread.

The names of the Hours were derived from the Latin for 'third', 'sixth' and 'ninth', those Hours so darkly referred to in St Mark's Passion Narrative. I found it uniquely satisfying to discover that these references were to the ancient Jewish day, which began at 6 a.m., meaning that Terce, the third Hour, fell at 9 a.m., Sexte at midday and None at 3 p.m. In practice, our times were all a bit earlier, given how early we got up in the morning. It also meant that, under the 'old dispensation', we nuns literally got up before dawn (and cried for help, as the psalmist puts it in one translation) even in summertime.

The most solid of the Hours seemed to be Vespers, because, even though it mirrored the formal structure of Lauds, we were more awake and firing on all cylinders by 4.30 p.m., and there seemed to be a bit more commitment to the music. 'Oh God, come to our aid!' we sang again, and bowed, according to custom, during the doxology. The jewel in the crown of the Liturgy of the Hours was the *Magnificat*, Mary's song of gratitude and joy when she had begun to take in the most unlikely fact that she was to be the mother of the Messiah, and decided to share the glad tidings with her cousin.

The fact is, the liturgy was unfailingly uplifting, and one of the great perks of living an otherwise spartan life of self-denial, from dawn to dawn, from year to year. I loved the release that came from lifting up my heart and soul in song. I loved the words. I loved the thoughts behind them. I loved the music. The Offices all got a bit quieter in the evenings, after recreation, with the Office of Readings (once called Matins, when it was sung in the early hours) and Compline, the last Hour of the day, rounding things off before bed. They both seemed sober, even gloomy gatherings, the former being the occasion of lengthy theological readings, mainly drawn from the early centuries, the latter of candlelight and holy water, and the public examination of conscience we called the 'examen'. For five minutes, anybody who 'felt so moved' was allowed to declare her failings of the day out loud, in the dark, while we all gathered close in a resounding silence, facing each other on our knees on the chilly floor. There were those trusting souls who regularly declared their faults. Inevitably, there were also those who rarely did so – Elizabeth, for example, who guarded her own boundaries with a special vigilance. Sometimes nobody said anything. Then Reverend Mother would raise her arm to carve a huge sign of the cross in the air, sprinkle us with holy water as she did her rounds of the stalls, her great stick thumping on the hard floor, and we would curl deeper and deeper into our inner shells. Finally, the Great Silence began.

The Great Silence is an ancient monastic custom. In a silent way of life such as ours, it did not make a great deal of difference. But it did carry connotations of antiquity and loftiness, and bring to mind those grand old Cistercian abbeys where the cold cloisters just went on and on, and footsteps would vanish into the middle distance. What it meant for us was that, while daytime silence could always be discreetly chiselled away at and negotiated (if you really had to ask someone where to hang out the washing, there were ways of signalling you needed a word), once the Great Silence had begun it was a case of all heads down. Nobody so much as passed a note under a door between the end of Compline, and after daily Mass the next morning.

9. Winter

Arriving at Akenside in early autumn had been beautiful, but, as some had warned me, challenging. We postulants would have to survive a full monastic winter before receiving the habit and enjoying our first summer. And this was the Cruel North.

'Bricks before bedtime, and ice on your water jug in the morning,' Sister Ellen had said. I learned soon enough to wrap my jug in towels before sleeping, and to collect a heated brick from the Aga to take to bed with me – an alternative to hot-water bottles, although some went for the latter. 'And make sure you have a double layer of old blanket cloth wrapped round it. Those bricks can burn you if you're not careful.'

The monastery was indeed as cold as they'd all warned me, but, physically, very little worried me that first winter. I saw the gold of autumn creeping over the garden from my cell window, and watched the spiralling of russet leaves down onto the lawn, where they lay in clumps, or rolled, easeful with the wind towards the lake. I gazed into the massive bulrushes at the water's edge, wondering what messianic salvation lay hidden amid the undergrowth. Later I learned it was called leaf mould, something which we shovelled by the barrow-load, transporting it to the rose bushes and shrubs nearer the house. Ash from our weekly bonfires was put to similar good purpose, and I grew used to spending hours outdoors, working on the three dozen acres of half-wild, rambling grounds as one of the 'able-bodied', capable of double-digging, pruning, planting.

Sister Jennifer and I went out early each morning, when hoarfrost stood spangled on each twig and sheathed each blade of grass, and crunched our slow way from the house, via the apple-smelling, cobweb-windowed garden shed, across lawn and meadow, towards the lake, then over the small brick bridge, and through the entangled woodland area where a million bulbs of bluebell and wild garlic slept, biding their time until the spring. Eventually we'd reach the lovely high-walled kitchen garden, pass through its clapped-out wooden gate, one of us holding it open, the other following with the barrow, and all this in silence as tight and circum-spect as a November robin's beak.

It would be a while before my companion and I started falling about laughing at each other's gestures or ineptitude, or mouthing silly clues to each other about how to open the creaky gate while holding on to the barrow. In the early stages, like all newcomers, we were just a little overawed. But no one can keep that sort of anxious reverence up for ever. Jen's voluble and outgoing temperament would erupt, and I'd feel conflicted. She had a penchant for intrusive slapstick that, I admit, I found somewhat irritating. And it was the silence and solitude that drew me, an imperative concern that overrode all human connection.

I was glad when Sister Ellen came with us, always super-vising, pointing out the tasks that needed to be done, correcting and directing in sentences of few words. Then we'd gesticulate if necessary, raising eyebrows, avoiding breaking the new day's rich curtain of deep quiet. Only the punctuation of the Divine Office separated the early from late morning, midday from afternoon, with its ritual procession of sacred words, its psalmody sung in sometimes ragged monotone, and spoken prayers breathed into the air by half-hushed voices. The pad of our felty feet would then withdraw, as we moved between indoor and outdoor tasks as seamlessly as did the outdoor seasons with each other.

Life was ordered, sparse, and so materially meagre it would have been prohibitively harsh had it not been for the palpable love and presence I felt beating at the heart of it. God was as real and alive to me as my own beloved father had been, back when I'd had a human family and a home. *Our Father*, the words rippled, comforting, helping, explaining everything. *Our Father* . . . the repetition gave an airy symmetry to the world. Here below, and especially in Carmel's cold cloister, the spirit of paternal protection still lingered, or could be accessed by something as simple as a heavenward glance or an unspoken prayer. All it took to connect with the fountainhead of life was an intention. Privations that would have been daunting in the outside world only added to one's sense of purpose, purifying intention to a peak, a pinpoint that stretched, like light itself, across the abyss.

In the early days getting up was easy, just throwing on the secular clothing we could not wait to exchange for the monastic habit. Later, we'd be formally Clothed, and that would mean pins and layers of serge and linen, and the hit-and-miss of getting your coif and tocque just right without a mirror. All creature comforts and indulgences were put behind us, as was vanity and anything else that might encourage us to focus on ourselves instead of on God and his sacred image in others. Only in the Green Room, a dingy space we rarely used, was there a tarnished mirror on a chain, hanging between wigs and breeches and the old curtains that served as robes in our nativity plays. But so irrelevant were mirrors to us that it might as well not have been there. I am sure no one ever looked.

As the early months wore on, I sometimes glimpsed my reflection in a darkened window and got a fleeting shock. Staring back at me was a bob-haired boy-girl in a baggy cardigan, a stranger hurrying down the central staircase on the way to the Office. She was someone 'recollected' and intent, not the girl who used to love to dance and cartwheel. Gone was her outgoing exuberance and her instinctive self-expression. Not that this worried me in the slightest. The more subsumed I was into the monastery, the greater my sense that I was doing the right thing. Later, when in the habit, my reflection would become virtually indistinguishable from the rest. But not entirely. I was of average height, rather slight ('elfin' in another setting), and had a balletic bearing, instilled in childhood.

Height and gait were the main ways we told each other apart from a distance. At close quarters, it was the feet. What united us was necessarily so much greater than what kept us apart. That was the theory, anyway, and unity was a virtuous intention, one we tried to put into practice, in spite of inevitable forces acting to the contrary. But even in the early days I was aware of flickers of difference, tiny jolts, and of the waves of surprise that rippled when you, or someone else, slipped up and betrayed something of their human background that did not quite sit with the general expectation. It was never a deliberate thing, that blank look, or mispronunciation, or reference to a surprising preference, or something no one else had any experience of. These little jolts would usually come at recreation, the period each evening when silence was lifted after the day's hard work, and conversation was attempted in a spirit of charity and mutual forbearance.

I went up the back staircase to my cell. There on the wall opposite my bed was an imposing black cross that loomed high over everything in the room. When I had once asked Ellen why there was no figure depicted on it, she had replied that we ourselves were to provide the 'corpus', that is the sacrificial human figure. Her look at me was straightforward and direct. We were the victims who had come here to give our own lives, and to save souls, surrendering our whole beings to God's purposes. In this way we would glorify him. Glorifying him was much more important than receiving comfort in prayer, and was the real end towards which all spiritual incentives were meant to move us.

Focusing on the death of Jesus, as we did for hours each day, was bound to do something funny to you after a while. It did not take me long to notice that our cell crosses were of the same design as those in the monastery's rustic cemetery. Big, black, unadorned, empty enough for the addition of your own body. If I'd lain it out flat on the floor and clambered onto it – something entirely inadvisable, of course – my small frame would have fitted neatly over it, my large musician's hands and size four feet just dangling over the edges. I was not particularly morbid, and did not often think of things like that, but in the silence and vast expanses of unmitigated solitude it was odd what popped into your mind.

The refectory crucifix was much more disturbing. The one piece of devotional statuary that had not been white-washed over, it most definitely had a corpus, and one that was dripping with red paint at that. I would go so far as to say that it was genuinely shocking. Perhaps it was to ensure we kept our eyes down, always gratefully, on our bread and vegetables. I was extremely squeamish and averted my eyes, in keeping with the practice we'd been taught of harnessing all our powers so that we focused only on the immediate matter in hand, offering it to God. The thought that Jesus had died for me was still pretty amorphous, more a general sense that it was proof of his love than the real, messy, horrific process that it must have been. He'd died for me, and therefore I would die for him. I said the words too easily, vocalised them to tunes of favourite hymns. There were all kinds of things we said by rote. Then, walking in the cemetery, and finding replicas of our own cell crosses there, you realised that death was not only all around us, it was — strange to say it — a way of life.

10. Clothing

The first big milestone was upon us. In the olden days, Clothings were seen as the most exciting of all the rites of passage, since it was the moment that a visible transformation took place. The postulant, by then six months in, would be dressed in a traditional white wedding dress, complete with train and tiara, and appear briefly (and for 'the last time') outside the enclosure – that is, outside the grille – with fellow nuns playing the role of bridesmaids, and would then make a splendid entry, accompanied by festive singing. It was a grand public ceremony, modelled on that of marriage between man and wife, and typical of the show and drama of the pre-Vatican II Catholic Church.

We'd all heard about its disadvantages. Anticlimax for one, because, after all the fuss, the subsequent swapping of the wedding dress for a plain brown habit – not to mention the resumption of the daily grind – made monastic life all the harder to get on with. Dry bread after trifle. There was also the fact that no canonically binding promises were made by the newly Clothed sister, now an official novice, whose 'request' for the habit was more an expression of aspiration as she embarked on what was meant to be a testing and training period. Binding promises were reserved for 'vows', up until which point novices were, in theory, free to engage with the training and 'discernment' process.

Discernment covered a whole gamut of things, including listening, sifting, weighing and prayerfully working out what

God's will might be, as well as – oddly – making up your own mind what to do. Confusion was naturally bound to arise here, because the premise underpinning everything in our world was that, in adopting monasticism, you were giving up your own will, as opposed to consulting it. Once a sister had got to the point where she was able to say, with any degree of conviction, 'Not my will but thine be done', and was perfecting her renunciatory techniques, it was somehow conflicting to be asked whether or not she 'wanted' something. It puzzled me that no one else seemed to see the glaring contradiction here, or to find it odd when other values promoted as core were casually laid aside, as happened occasionally without explanation or rationale – but in this as in everything, it was not done to object to the standard practice. So, when we were told that we were 'free to leave' after Clothing, up until we made our final vows, no one acknowledged or so much as hinted that we'd been given a mixed message.

Psychologically, of course, things were far more complicated. No one felt genuinely free to leave at any point, however nominally enshrined the possibility might have been on paper. In this the order was no different from those other closed communities one reads about, those vortex-like cults where loyalty to the inner sanctum and the inward-looking status quo trumps every other consideration. Being free to leave in such scenarios is a technicality. Once you've crossed the threshold and been admitted to a sacred, special-seeming world, anything beyond its walls is apt to become hazy, unreal, insubstantial. Yes, we prayed for the world and for those we'd left behind, but, in an immediate sense, it was the prayerful sweeping of the corridors that counted. Even admitting to thinking about leaving, once you'd entered, was seen as a fault, a giving-in to distraction and temptation.

Unless the newcomer was proving manifestly problematic, and better off discouraged, any thoughts she might have of leading a different kind of life were seen as coming directly from the devil. Fighting his advances, and countering them with self-abnegating acts of faith, was essential to our weaponry.

There was a sense of our, as a community, being perpetually under siege and of fighting back, and this applied from the moment that you crossed the threshold. Once you were Clothed you had so markedly put on a new identity, so completely aligned yourself with the group, that it seemed your whole future, your whole life's purpose and validity, rested on it. It would be impossible to overstate the extent to which staying was esteemed and seemed to count for everything. The Life was a battle, and we were called to don the helmet of salvation, and to learn to wield the sword of the spirit. We would rather die than give in to the tempter! We would shed our blood if necessary in the fight for faith. You were a bride of Christ from the moment you put on the habit.

By the 1990s, Clothings were more modest affairs, as the Church had by then declared too much triumphalist show and presumption a bad thing. The rite of admission to the novitiate was now a private, intimate ceremony, the main adornments of which were a posy and a woven crown of freshly picked wild flowers. It was the symbolism and transition to the state of novice that was important. The cutting of the hair was no longer the stuff of theatre, but a mere practicality, carried out by one's angel beforehand in the privacy of the cell. After that, you'd be given the habit: a tunic (like a long Aertex nightie), a dowdy skirt with added pockets, and the main item, a big brown sack that covered everything from neck to the floor. Then you'd be taken down to the antechoir for the conferral of the head-dress (composed of coif, tocque and two layers of veil) and the scapular, the outer layer of the habit that hung, tabard-like, from the shoulders. And there was the all-important leather belt, symbolising the harness of John 21:18 that foreshadows the sacrificial death by which followers of Christ would bear witness.

How had I, a north London girl from a bohemian family, got so far? On one level there was nothing miraculous about it. The long hours of silent prayer to which I'd been drawn had begun intuitively, as a survival skill, mysterious meetings with my father, but had ended up exerting an irresistible force. The relief and peace I found in it made it addictive. All I wanted was to lose myself in this larger-than-life relationship. I wanted to give it my all. God's presence was so real, so overpowering and inescapable to me in those days of heart-felt searching, that the slings and arrows of monasticism seemed a small price to pay in return. What was a bit of cold and sleep deprivation? What did it matter that I felt all alone, and was continually hungry? None of this was of any consequence. The act of kneeling had drawn me in, deeper and deeper, until it was enough for me to recollect myself, close my eyes, and I was as though bathed in light and love, inwardly strengthened and attuned.

Jesus was my spouse, my everything. I was giddy with the power of it, head over heels in love. I closed my eyes and listened to his voice, a softness and a murmuring like the babbling of a brook. He assured me of eternal love, told me he had conquered the world. 'Abide in me,' he said, and deep down I knew that that was all I wanted. I opened my eyes and saw his own, burning green and brown, fixed upon me, everywhere. His heart was aflame with tenderness for me.

His arms reached out, kindly offering me a home for ever in his bosom. And so it was that life as a Carmelite got bedded in and took deeper root, and as the days passed, my earnestness and intensity only increased. I was not going to let anything, no transient upset or emotion, stand in my way, or stop me from responding to the call. God had shown me his love, and I owed him everything.

My ceremony of Clothing came round slowly, like the spring. It was Easter, and the bluebells were carpeting the woodland slopes around the monastery. The cooing of the turtle dove was heard outside our windows. During the sunlit ceremony I recited from a customs book, one that creaked open with some difficulty (Clothings being uncommon even then), and knelt before our prioress, Mother Julianna, waiting for her prompts.

'Why have you come here, my child?' Mother Julianna asked in her low, croaky voice.

'Because I was called, my Reverend Mother.'

'And what do you request?'

'To become one with Christ Crucified, a living sacrifice of faith.'

'And what do you ask of the community?'

'The holy poverty of the order, the mercy of the sisters, and the grace to become their servant in all things, great and small.'

At this the gathered sisters rose in a circle from their rigid kneeling posture, and joined together in saying: 'We offer you our mercy and our love. In the name of Christ Jesus, who rose triumphantly from the dead, may you be strengthened to endure whatever he sends you, a faithful witness to the end.'

Mother Julianna then leaned forward, placed a crown of

woven primroses – still pert and dewy – on my newly white-veiled head, and said, 'Sister Catherine, we admit you to the state of novice. Follow the path that is laid down for you, and never swerve to left or right. With the grace of the Lord and the assurance of his Holy Spirit may you accept the lot that has been marked out for you, and may you come, at the end of your novitiate, to the happy profession of your vows.'

'May you come to the happy profession of your vows,' the gathered voices chimed, while Mother struggled to her feet. I saw only a blur of brown and white, the movement of habits, veils and sweeping scapulas around me, while one swaying form grew larger, coming closer, and Sister Elizabeth stood over me, a figure of gaunt austerity.

'I entrust the task of your formation to your novice mistress,' the old prioress said, gesturing towards the looming figure. 'Greet her as a true model and daughter of the order, and take her as your guide in all things, great and small.'

And then Sister Elizabeth was there, beaming, extending a cold, thin hand in my direction. I rose from my knees to stand before her, my head almost level with her own. I knew what I had to do. I threw my arms around her, sensing her surprisingly bony frame, noting the prominent angularity of her ribcage, the icy smoothness of her cheekbone, and then heard her say, in purring yet husky tones:

'Sister Catherine, congratulations! You are now one of us.'

So, it was official. The habit had conferred a special kind of new identity. Other sisters now opened their arms, each one smiling, as Jennifer and I toured the room, greeting and hugging each one in turn, the unfamiliar burden of the habit dragging heavily from our shoulders. Naturally, there was quite a lot of giggling. The ceremony was a festive occasion, and, at times like this, the usual customs around silence did not apply.

'It will feel quite strange at first,' Elizabeth said, pointing to the yards of cloth that seemed to be hindering my simplest movements, 'but you'll soon get used to it. You'll need to learn about tucking up – there are hooks and eyes for securing the material in place when you're working.' She bent and lifted the thick, heavy hem to reveal two huge brass hooks, then dropped them, allowing them to clank coldly against the floor. 'The sooner you get the hang of it the better – indispensable when going to the humble office.'

A couple of nearby sisters tittered. The 'humble office' was the lavatory (H.O. for short), the word 'office' being a generic name for almost any of the rooms, as well as for the tasks that typically got carried out within them.

'I think Sister Catherine has enough on her plate today without learning about tucking up!' Sister Ruth said. 'I mean, it took me ages to get used to it.'

'Oh, I don't know, it's never too soon to try to get it right. Remember Sister Mildred and the time she sprained her ankle going upstairs her first week in the habit?' another voice piped up. 'Tripped on her own hem. We had her on crutches for six months!'

'Well, Mildred was Mildred,' Sister Barbara said, somewhat tartly. 'Sister Catherine looks like a sensible person, and she can't say we didn't warn her!'

Behind her, Sister Jennifer was joking with Mother Julianna. The old woman was frowning with confused concentration as Jen tried to explain what it meant to feel like a character out of *Nuns on the Run*.

'On the run? What is that?' old Julianna was stuttering.

'Oh, they were just dressing up as a disguise . . .'

'Disgraceful! Who would think of doing such a thing?'

Julianna leaned on her stick and smiled tolerantly and politely while Jen chattered on.

'Well, I admit it is a bit far-fetched,' I heard her saying as the old prioress began to hobble off. Thump, thump, thump, went her stick on the parquet floor.

'Manage as best you can for now,' Elizabeth went on, with a half-laugh.

Naturally, I knew I'd manage somehow. But even the smallest actions at Akenside needed to be done according to the customary ways.

'Now, let us get you safely to your cell. I expect you'd like some quiet time to make your thanksgiving before lunch,' she said, unusually attentive.

'Yes,' I said, secretly pleased that Elizabeth was acknowledging me, something I realised I could not take for granted. Hers was a character that blew unpredictably hot and cold. I knew it would be foolish to allow myself to enjoy her attention too much; it could just as quickly be withdrawn, and it would be better by far not to get used to it.

The cell, as always, was my refuge. Its quiet folded round me, paper-white and perfect. In the cell you could feel the solitude closing round you, warm and supportive, like a bathing, an embrace. In the pale solitude the presence of your spouse was kinder and more powerful than when you were with your sisters. Your mind could unlock, unspool, breathe a deep sigh of relief, and rest. In the cell you could think whatever you liked. You could stand at the window and stare, stare at the dark trees, the curve of shaggy grass that skirted the lake, at the lake itself and at the brick bridge over it, and the woodland beyond. Your eyes could follow the line of flight of any number of birds, or, in springtime, watch the ducks nesting near the bulrushes, or, in autumn, the low formation of the geese as they drove low and loud across the darkening sky in military formation. Each season had its own beauty, even the whip of winter which brought bright berries and holly round the laundry door.

Time passes in the monastery like ghosts that move through walls; it seeps through cell doors and stony archways, through bone and marrow, imprinting patience and endurance at every touch. With the shifting of the seasons, and by our second dusky-coloured autumn, we'd turned from eager novices, excited by the novelty of monasticism, to heavy labourers, hands chapped from toil, lips cracked with cold and faces raw.

It was the mornings that were hardest for me. The *matraque* still burned fleeting horror into me, like sacrificial fire each darkened dawn. And yet I woke and worked and grew to love the silent spaces of our routine lives – the shelling of peas by an open window, the solitary sweeping-out of chicken coops. Even the communal diligence of the chant, which threaded broken psalmody throughout our days until Compline saw us lighting the encroaching night before an early bed, was calm and unifying. This flawed exigency brought with it a sublime loveliness of sorts. The faltering reading and recitation of the nuns was no obstacle to transcendence. I lost myself in Gregorian monody, stretched out my inward arms to the invisible God, and fed on the mysterious nourishment of the scriptures. There was enough food for thought here to occupy me for a lifetime. I cannot stress enough how strongly I felt this impression. How strongly I felt the pull of heaven in those days.

11. Father Gregory

Sometimes we were visited by Father Gregory, a senior figure from Kielder Abbey. Gregory was at the top of his game. The bishop's chosen delegate, he held the cumbersome title of Episcopal Vicar for Religious, meaning he was charged with overseeing the diocese's communities of nuns, monks, friars and the like, and reporting back to episcopal HQ. His voice was smooth, and he had smooth white-grey hair, and the kind of features that looked as though they'd been scrubbed and washed to perfection. He reminded me of a superior kind of pumice stone. He was also shrewdly perceptive.

Gregory's order, the English Benedictines, was part of a yet more ancient tradition than our own, founded in sixth-century Italy by St Benedict of Nursia. Unlike us Carmelites, called to be hermits-in-community, these 'cenobitic' or more sociable congregations aimed for balance in their lives, blending liturgy, community and manual labour with learning. Their influence on public life from medieval times had been enormous. Unlike us, they did not shut themselves away (at least, the monks didn't, although the nuns – once they were invented – usually did) and often undertook tasks of education, translation, and, in the old days, illumination of those lavish, genteel Books of Hours. That was something they did in their *scriptoria*, I imagine, with quill pens.

Carmelites had never been very interested in quill pens or education, other than the sort carried out directly by the Holy Spirit, who would speak to our hearts if we would but listen.

Listening was largely why we were there. Listening and waiting for a glimmer of response, a sense that someone was reaching out to us from the other side. We'd all read those lines in the Hosea where God says: 'I will block her way with thorns and *lure* her, and lead her out into the desert, and THERE I will speak to her heart.' To us, this seemed scintillating and persuasive. Nobody said so, but I think many of us felt it as quasi-erotic. Perhaps it was the word 'lure'. Some translations actually went further: 'I will seduce her, and speak to her heart,' and at that we all swooned, and panted, and felt the light touch of the invisible hand against our necks, the sweetness of the Beloved's breath just above our faces, the closeness of an energy that could sweep us off our feet. High and aloft, high, high, high into the clouds it could sweep us, like Elijah, who we knew had been carried up into heaven.

As for the blocking of our ways with thorns, that bit was taken as read – we all knew it was a precondition of any holy courtship. God was a determined lover and we Carmelites had all known blockages of some sort. How else had God got us there? Most people in their right minds didn't wander into deserts, even if they had a water flask. I was definitely flask-less when I entered that shape-shifting desert-garden and stumbled into a mysterious sleep that fed me at a deep level, and – most importantly – brought me a very special kind of healing. The Life was an intensive-care unit for the spirit, and a detox centre for the soul. It was a place where we, the damaged, flawed and wounded, would be reordered and reorientated, put back together again brighter and better. You had to rely on the process. As Elizabeth reminded us, we could not minister to nor heal ourselves.

The Trappist monk and writer Thomas Merton memorably

described an abbey as a hospital for wounded souls. I liked the description because of its honesty, and because it let me off the hook, somehow, made it acceptable that I often felt so sensitive, so raw. You could not have imposter syndrome when the norm was to be a flawed and failing human being. I cried easily, and all it took, if I was cold and hungry, was the beauty of the liturgy to set me off. Add the turmoil of a painful monthly period, and 'My Song is Love Unknown' into the mix, and I'd be a blubbering wreck for half the day. No one knew why I was crying and nor did I. It was not that I was unhappy in the usual sense. I was delighted to be in Carmel. Akenside was heaven. I had no complaints. But tearing at me from the inside was a loneliness I did not know how to acknowledge. I did not even know it was there.

I suppose it dated back to childhood and to the deep seams of trauma in my family, the instability of my mother, the fragility of my dying dad. It went back to the loss of our house, our unique and precious home, and the displacement that followed. It went back to our father's black depression and decline. It went back to the loss of Aunt Winnie, and the stability she represented. And certainly it went back even further, to my mother's sudden vanishings on acting tours and other derelictions. I could still let out stifled howls of agony in my cell. My whole body could still shake with the impact. There were times when I could not contain the still vivid anguish of my late teens and early twenties, still all so recent. We'd been abandoned by everyone and everything that should have stood firm. Mum kept herself apart. Letters once or twice a year and sometimes a (certainly welcome) cheque were all we got. She wanted to be free of us. We'd tried to reach out, but as often as not she would not answer the phone, let alone open her door to us. In Carmel, no one spoke about such things. We all have troubles of our own, Sister Ellen told me chidingly, and like everyone else I needed to 'take myself in hand'. That meant developing a cross between a stiff upper lip and a manner of remote dreaminess and poise so that no raw emotion ever slipped through the net. You kept it in. You 'offered it up'. Above all, you kept your eyes on the cross.

It was odd. We were meant to be suffering, uniting our pains with those of our spouse, the great Redeemer of the world, but if ever you let on that you were in pain you were told to Pull Your Socks Up, and Get On With It, and – Elizabeth, I had now begun to notice, loved the words – not be such a Cry Baby. Her face would take on the expression of a taunt. Shame on you! Goodness me, anyone would think you had something to cry about. Now, go back to your cleaning and your polishing.

Knowing there was a nice, safe monk to talk to was reassuring. Or rather would have been had we been allowed to see him when we needed to, or had free access to him as we should have done, since he was the bishop's delegate and above our Reverend Mother in the hierarchy. Technically, she should have provided a free channel of communication between us and our legitimate overseer, since he, too, was responsible for us. What actually happened was that everybody, including the priests and bishop, deferred sycophantically to someone whose position placed her inviolably apart, seemingly above reproach. And so we saw very little of anyone from outside, and the longing for someone kind or wise who might understand one had to be suppressed. The idea that young sisters might need help, or counselling, or any sort of warmth or moral support, went clean contrary to the spirit of the order as Mother and her assistants in the novitiate understood it. We were there to help purify each other, not to look for friends. Our charism was one which taught that character was refined in the furnace of affliction. You stood firm when the flames were raging all around you. God was with you. You did not reach out for other props.

We knew it was meant to be tough, although no one thought of it as overtly cruel or inhumane. Instead, the kind of words we used were 'austere', 'ascetic' or – just occasionally – 'penitential'. You were not only supposed to 'overcome', you were meant to ensure that others did the same, and so were not supposed to show anyone any sympathy, to the extent that doing so was considered a fault. Pandering to feelings of any kind was a 'womanly weakness' worthy of Confession. Such softness was linked to sensuality, and to pathetic cravings to give and receive affection. I was surprised to find how highly the quality of 'toughness' was rated, far more prized than things I thought important like purity of heart and a good intention. Sadly, this perception of virtue meant that in most closed religious communities there were always bound to be a few really hard-bitten individuals, or boisterous bullies, women who had adopted the 'rough manners' (it seemed to me) of men, and whose insensitivity to others was rewarded by approval. I certainly found this perplexing. Behaviour that, outside, would have been seen as lacking in kindness, was a mark of someone who really was Getting On With It, Doing As She Was Told, and making a difference – a military kind of personality. Naturally, I shrank from this kind of thing, thus relegating myself to the category of the oversensitive.

Father Gregory would have understood what Elizabeth dismissed as my 'aches and pains'. If she noticed you were feeling 'low' she simply told you to snap out of it. Emotions were essentially base animal instincts, not of God. Gregory, however, would have proceeded with nuance, and taken time to listen and work out what was behind the emotions. He would have spoken with me as human being to human being, not trying to humble, chisel or chide. Certainly not trying to shame. There was a world of difference between the Carmelites and the Benedictines, I was slowly seeing, but any thought of changing ship now, between the milestones of Clothing and vows, of looking to move to another order, or even a different Carmelite monastery, was so stringently disapproved of that I discounted the idea. I was a Carmelite now. I would persevere. I would stay the course. You're in it for the long haul, people would say, and we knew that they admired our dedication.

One day Gregory brought a cello out with him on a pastoral visit, and delighted us by playing a movement from one of the Bach Suites. His tone was so beautiful, the memory of music, and its proximate vibrations, brought tears to my eyes. Reciprocally, Jennifer and I were asked to play something, and I dug out some adaptable duos I'd brought with me, slipped in among a pile of choral music. Music had always been central to my life, humanly, emotionally and now also spiritually. I had come with a little harp and a viola; Jen had coincidentally arrived with a French horn and a guitar, a fact that bolstered the community's tendency to talk of us as 'the Twins'. I'd been studying for an external diploma at the Guildhall, and Gregory had immediately responded to and connected with me on a musical level. From then on, there seemed a special friendliness between us, even though I rarely had the chance of speaking to him.

Like many of the priests who visited us, either as confessors or simply looking for a bit of peace and quiet, Gregory trod a fine line between familiarity and warmth towards Our Mother, and a respectful distance. Far be it from him to interfere, his attitude seemed to say. The bishop's delegate he might have been, but even the bishop would have known there was no point meddling in what went on behind closed doors. There was the Carmelite charism to be borne in mind. No one knew an order's charism like its own proponents. From a distance, however, I could tell that this mature and educated priest understood a lot more than he let on, even the extent to which Jen and I occupied different spiritual planets and had different comfort zones (her musical attempts were awkward and mechanical, for example, but she was brave and did her best, while I was expressive and imaginative, but totally impractical). Who knows, he might even have felt some sympathy for me, a convert and a Londoner trying to blend in to this no-nonsense, anachronistic world.

In the novitiate we young ones sat round and submitted gladly to our lessons, while Barbara and Ellen talked us through the basics of the monastic life. Sister Elizabeth, as the long-standing novice mistress, would occasionally drop in. She liked to talk about Carmel being a powerhouse of prayer. Our sequestered lives had enormous voltage, she told us, and had the potential to change the world. Jen had looked round and asked why, if that was the case, there were still wars. Was it that we weren't praying hard enough? Ellen had commented tartly that 'we were not to look for results'. Wanting results was a form of grasping. Looking for evidence for faith was a secular and shallow way of thinking. In Carmel we acted in naked faith alone. I smiled sweetly and sent up a swift, sharp prayer for light and patience. I was careful to fight against, and to conceal any incipient stirrings or doubts. But we all had them. As the months passed it was inevitable that shadows should start to fall. Nothing was as it seemed in Carmel. You had to go deeper, to rely on unseen sources.

A garden enclosed, a fountain sealed. We lived a hidden life for a higher purpose than ourselves, and an all-consuming life it was, a way of singlemindedness. As the days wore on, through all their changing moods and seasons, the cycle of psalms went up not only from isolated Akenside, but from sociable Kielder, and every convent, priory, abbey, friary and monastery, the whole universal Catholic jamboree one big party, or one big lament, a human drama but also a divine comedy, the essential element of which was the flame we cloistered women were called to guard behind our grille. And guard it we did. But fire is dangerous; there were obviously going to be casualties.

12. The Cats

They prowled the forecourts, scarpered at our tread, terror-
ised the sparrows, and were what Sister Elizabeth called
semi-feral. The Cats. Coming in from the farms was a no-
brainer for them, as they knew the whiff of a good bowl of
chicken liver, finely chopped, from far away. Walls were no
obstacle to these travelling companions, dustbin-savvy, alley-
slick, claws as sharp as goblins' knives. The one big rule – since
we weren't supposed to have them, or any other pets – was
to be sure not to give them names. It was imperative they
remained incognito, most definitely not pets. The other
important rule was never to touch them. They were visitors,
they could come and go. They had no lasting city among us.

What they did have were eyes. And tails. And sometimes
fleas. The 'sometimes' was to do with how often one actually
found them in one's cell, tiny little hopping things on top of
the pillow, or dancing around between the sheets. How they
got there, given that no cat ever entered the cells, was unclear,
and my mind was too occupied with non-feline things for me
to stop and brood on the fact that my own body may very
well have been their vehicle. I was so itchy anyway, for various, not unrelated (cat-allergy), reasons the odd flea bite
would not have registered. But fleas there were, and bite they
did. Still, that was all 'part of the penance'.

At what point our straw mattresses, called palliasses, were
singled out and identified as a problem I do not clearly remember. Surely some time early on, judging by the abundance of

white veils that crop up in the photographic bank of memory. It was certainly before anybody had left. Elizabeth had told us to take all the old mattresses downstairs for a bonfire. We dragged them from our beds, and went sliding down the great staircase on them, each of us young ones whooping with delight on our improvised toboggans. At one point Suzi and I shared a palliasse, sliding down together, giggling, the whole thing swerving, bumping, thrashing against the sides, while she said – in her best 'fancy that!' tone of voice – 'Oooh, this is just too exciting!' Her normally pallid cheeks were flushed, and I sensed a double meaning in her words, felt her relish of the speed and of our closeness, but batted it away. We were two young women on a stripy mattress that was being eaten from the inside by bugs, and Elizabeth had told us they had to go. From then on it would be horse hair, a more reliable material on which to sink our exhausted bodies after Compline every night. The stately wooden staircase had never seen anything like it. Nor had the leaded, stained-glass panels.

As for the cats, they were in hiding, incubating their next batch of fleas, or generally keeping out of trouble, which was their speciality. They knew when to make themselves scarce. It's funny how no one batted an eyelid when the incontinence began. Perhaps I should say 'the litter tray issues', but – same difference. The fact was, there crept up on the community a weird phase when poos were appearing all over the place. And their more fluid counterparts. They'd show up, betrayed by their smell, in alcoves and on landings by the dozen. Did I say 'by the dozen'? Make that a baker's dozen. A score. We weren't only overrun by fleas.

It was typical that what began as an irregular phenomenon, to which everybody turned a blind eye, ended up going to the bishop. It was one of those concerns that seemed too petty to mention and no one wanted to make a fuss about (minds on higher things and all that), but after a certain point took on a life of its own. Overnight it went from being completely taboo to being a massive problem. It wasn't just the smell – almost worse when half covered up with cheap pine disinfectant – and coming upon and nearly skidding on these manifestations while innocently en route to choir. Whole patches of antique floor varnish were being stripped away in unsightly splodges wherever the cats had made it their business to frequent. Something to do with the acid content.

Why were there no litter trays in evidence, you might ask. The answer was that they were in the infirmary. There, unlike us, the cats bred prolifically and lived in harmony with their innate biology. Potty training had never really been applied. Perhaps they never sat still for long enough, but skittered off to the farms and fields and back again, up and down the stairs, shadows, the silent daemons of our own community. What was remarkable was their status as Sister Elizabeth's feline bevy. She fed them. She watered them. She attended to their needs in the spare cell that was set aside for them, equipped with such things as baskets and balls of wool. Away from the main body of the monastery, she could call and coo to them. Sometimes, however, she also fed them in an alcove off the hall. There she wore a nice blue overall for the task, a rather lovely shade, secured to her habit with pins, and was always busy shaking mini biscuits out of bags, scooping jellied meats onto saucers, bending over, elegantly as was her wont, to fill little rows of neat enamel bowls. You walked past quickly. You tried not to notice things that were exceptional, like the special cuts of meat. If, however, you were a novice looking for a word of support, she would straighten up and tell you to run along – shoo, shoo, and don't stop me now – because it was Time. And then, the hall clock would chime delightfully, miraculously, on cue. It was always Time to Feed the Cats.

Things were definitely getting out of hand, but it would be years before the bishop got involved. By then there were other, far more serious things to be dealt with, all seemingly different but all springing from a single source. Sister Elizabeth's twin foibles – indulgence of those who, like the cats, seemed to eddy round her looking for food, and her intolerance of those stronger characters who were able to stand in their own integrity, and think and feel at all independently – would one day grow out of all proportion, and spread their branches like a poison tree, far and wide. They would go from being completely taboo to being admitted as a huge concern. They would divide our community, casting different people in different lights, because, once something is out in the open air and everyone is aware there is a problem, no one can afford to remain neutral or on the fence.

The bishop was not yet involved, however, and our lives went on as they'd always done. The hierarchy left us to our own devices. Mother knew best. The idea that, one day, an outsider might come and hold us to account seemed improbable, but more than that – completely inappropriate. We were a city set on a hilltop. We were a fortress, defiant of the rest of the world. Each Carmel was autonomous, and each house of the order, while subject to a common Rule and set of Constitutions, was free to implement these as the canonically elected prioress saw fit. And, since she was God's elect, the one chosen to rule over us, whoever she might be, the idea that she might be challenged was unthinkable.

It was therefore something of a surprise to learn that a local government functionary was coming to check up on our standards of health and hygiene. What right had they? The question trembled in the indignant air. Suddenly the word 'autonomous' was the latest slogan. It cropped up everywhere, at recreation, in the novitiate, and in all sorts of contexts. Sister Elizabeth was most energetic in reinforcing the term, driving it home before anyone got any ideas to the contrary. Autonomous. Self-directing. Still, it was all hands on deck, and bottles of Dettol spray appeared as though from nowhere. The kitchen was unrecognisable once we'd finished with it, Sister Ambrose's hay box (the rustic equivalent of a yoghurt-maker, hangover from her wartime days) stowed safely out of sight, and the Aga stripped of years of debris. The bumpy flagstone floor was almost dangerously clean.

The morning of the inspection, we were all present and correct, no one missing from the Office. On any normal day, there would be a couple of empty stalls where sisters, usually the Infirmarians, had excused themselves 'in the call of duty'. Elizabeth and Barbara rarely attended all the Hours or took prayer and reading time like the rest of us. That day, however, the voices that rose in song at the prioress's knock were fuller and more determined than usual, and the enunciation of each word of the psalms seemed to carry special force and meaning. The bidding prayers included a special mention of 'those working in local government', and Sister Ambrose asked specifically for 'the gift of wisdom for all those in authority'. Ripples of sympathetic understanding were felt all round.

Standing in the refectory after Mass for the bowl of strong tea we called 'the cup' – a tonic that was optional but that I never refused – I heard the sound of manly and 'worldly' women's shoes clattering along the corridor. It was a jarring sound within our walls, so different from our stealthy, sur-reptitious padding. Voices, too. Elizabeth's husky tones, in a stage whisper, alternating with something less distinct. The voices and the steps got closer until the refectory door was opened a crack, and a scuttering could be heard from the vestibule outside. Two small animals shrieked at each other, and a bird flew off. I heard its wings and then the familiar sound of an airborne body colliding with a window.

'Let's let it out, shall we?' Elizabeth's throaty voice surged into the refectory through the half-open door. 'Poor thing...'

'It's a good job they've got wings,' a woman with a strong local accent said with a half-laugh.

'And how many cats have you got at Akenside?' The man's voice boomed in the echoing corridor.

The door to the refectory swung wide open and Sister Alison walked in, only slightly flustered, holding a notebook and a pen. Then the door clicked shut behind her. The foot-steps and voices moved away. In the dimness of the enclosing quiet nothing very definite could be heard, although one clear word kept rising above the rest. A word that came so naturally to Elizabeth's lips. It was easy to mistake it, the voices sucked back into the encircling hush, but I am pretty sure that word was 'ferals'.

PART TWO
The Way

Adapt yourselves no longer to the pattern of this
present world, but let your minds be remade and
your whole nature thus transformed. Then you will
be able to discern the will of God, and to know what
is good, acceptable and perfect.

Romans 12: 2

13. The Toolshed

If the cell was a high sanctuary, a sacred space apart, the toolshed was its polar opposite, a shadow to its luminescence. Across a flagstoned courtyard it stood, close by the outbuilding where the altar breads were baked, a creaking and extended shack. The toolshed was a place of secrets, of scuttling creatures and of ancient implements, of medieval scythes and spades and forks and rusty shovels. There were the heavy-handled sickles we called billhooks – apparently erroneously, and what a real billhook looks like to this day I cannot tell you. But ours were huge, theatrical things you needed to flex your muscles to lift and slash with. By day, they were hoisted in and out of the toolshed, reminding us that we were called to live like peasants, poor, and weary, and self-sufficient. At night, they lived pinned to the apple-smelling walls, exhibits in a derelict museum.

Entering the toolshed felt like walking into a memory, an arcane deposit where, for all its cold, there was a kind of mustiness that felt like warmth. It was a friendly place, a dim confusion of enamel buckets and outdoor clothes and wellies that got stuffed away, any old how, at the end of an afternoon. We each had our own hook and cubbyhole, some filled with packets of seeds and clumps of roots, some with encrusted gardening gloves, but, with just the one lightbulb overhead, nobody really bothered about what went where. As I said, it was the polar opposite of the cell. The roof was buckled, and the dingy gloom went on and on, with room after room – each cubicle a former chicken coop – leading to a point of total obscurity in the murky distance. I loved its cracked and cobwebbed windows. I loved the mossy decay around the edges.

While time passed stealthily in our clean cloisters, it hung, like the bats, upside-down, a perfect eternity, in the toolshed. There you could not hear the ticking of the clock, although you could see the weathervane if you craned your neck out of the door, or cleared the dirt from a patch of rattling, window. In the toolshed the Office bell could startle you, too, being so close by, and then you'd throw off your overall and run to take your turn at the courtyard tap to rinse the mud from your hands and implements before processing into choir. Spades were left standing in great troughs of sand, and wheelbarrows of wet weeds abandoned until after supper, when – at least in summer – you could fit in a visit to the compost heap before recreation. If you were lucky a murmuration of starlings might surprise you. If you were less lucky, it might be a rat.

For all its simplicity, there was a beauty in the rustic aspect of our lives. No one interfered with what was not their business. No one spoke after Compline, or in the corridors, or out of turn. Some never spoke at all, unless it was to confess their faults, or agree with others, or join their voices to the common chant. Only at evening recreation were belly laughs emitted by the young, titters by the elderly, and anecdotes repeated tirelessly for the benefit of the newcomers. Oh, how did we ever manage without tea, or pyjamas, or night-storage heaters (albeit on the 'miser' setting) in the olden days? Can you believe we did without bras, until we learned how to make our own stretchy nylon underwear? How strict things used to be! Do you remember feeding the chickens before Little Jug? And gathering the eggs in the afternoon? These reminiscences, like refrains, were passed from generation to generation, a testimony to resilience and good cheer. And all the while, the garden grew thick and heavy, and the fruit ripened on the burdened apple trees.

There were wide-spreading orchards to the distant west, and then, by the kitchen garden walls, the plums, apricots and espalier-trained pears. Like the mistletoe far up in the treetops, or the frogspawn in the bulrushes, other life proliferated all around us. In the undergrowth it burgeoned. Under the bridge there were flickering fishes. Toads appeared occasionally, one portly fellow dragging himself along a path, another floating – was he moving? – in an open water butt. The mists came, and then they cleared.

We lived surrounded by farmland but with never a farmer in sight. The fields worked themselves magically and produced their crop, each according to its kind. Seasons came and went. We saw rapeseed blaze bright beyond our upper windows, and distant hills merge apologetic into the far horizon. At other times the red of maple and sumac trees enlivened a backdrop of evergreen and oak. No visitors ordinarily came our way, except a few sturdy pilgrims to Mass, a clutch of villagers who kept alive the old traditions. There was Connie from the Lodge, the former gatehouse, big Ken from the foundry, and Cecily, a distracted old lady who sang to herself in the chapel when she thought no one was listening. But other than these flitting presences, we were alone with each other, and ourselves, alone with the haunting presence of our spouse, who as time passed might prove an increasingly elusive companion.

'So, how's the morning shift in the kitchen going?' Ellen asked me at one of our routine chats. We still met, although less frequently now I was deemed to have mastered the intricacies of the grounds and of the horarium. I told her I was doing all right, that I felt very peaceful preparing veg in the mornings and was happy to be working in the open air in the afternoons. It was a pleasure to feel oneself in contact with the earth, and so lovely to stretch my legs a bit. We were sitting in the bower near the toolshed at the time.

'And you are still regular?'

'I'm afraid I don't always notice,' I replied. 'But I usually know when it's coming because of the pain. You know, for a day or two before . . .'

'Oh yes. But it all seems quite normal?'

'Oh yes, sister. I mean, it's never easy. I do get quite tired and low with it sometimes.'

'Well, that's something we all have to cope with, Catherine. None of us is immune. You can't control your biological functions, but you can control how you respond to them. Or at least can learn from and accept them. Which, of course, you should.'

The nettles were ripe and high around the edges of the meadows, and pollen seemed to creep like prickly sand into my eyes and all over my skin, at times. I pulled my hankie from my habit pocket and shuddered with a spasm, expecting to sneeze.

'And I see your hay fever is as bad as ever!' Ellen said.

'Yes, sorry,' I said. My sneezing fits were well known by now, and I always felt bad when they seemed to crumple and incapacitate me. I needed twice the quota of monastic hankies (enormous grey-white cloths) as everybody else.

'All this grass! So different from your life in London.'

'*Aa-a-aah* . . .' The sneeze decided to slip away. 'Yes, sorry!' I half laughed.

'It's not your fault of course, and having cats everywhere

can't be helping. Do they set you off, as well? Are you all right for antihistamines, or will you need to see Dr Gill next time he visits? You know he comes in weekly to see the invalids.'

'Oh no, I'm fine. I've got a supply . . .' I replied, blowing my nose and regaining composure. So far, I'd got away with rarely seeing the doctor, apart from our routine flu jabs. Like the workmen, he was allowed inside, but only as far as the infirmary, where the bedridden aged waited for him, and Elizabeth beamed and offered tea.

'That's good. I'm glad you're feeling better. But what I really wanted to talk about – Catherine – what I wanted to have a word about was Sister Philippa.'

'Oh? Pippa? Yes, of course.' I was taken aback. Pippa, the most balanced of my fellow novices, seemed the least problematic. In many ways she was also the most likeable. Wondering what this could be about, I looked for signs on Ellen's face. Then asked: 'Shall we talk here, out of doors, sister, or . . . or, should we go to the novitiate?'

'I think this might be the time for a little walk, Sister Catherine. Just to the hornbeam and back. We've got time now, while the others are at spiritual reading. We have permission. And it's good to take time to sort things out.'

I wasn't aware things needed sorting. But I happily set off with my mentor across the lawn, past the near, well-tended flower-beds, and diagonally across the meadow to where the foliage became wilder, and swallows darted this way and that. As far as I could tell we were alone. Meetings with angels happened not in work time, but while others were in their cells poring over the scriptures.

'Yes,' Ellen began, once we were halfway to the bridge. 'Yes, I expect you've noticed Philippa has been a little unsettled.'

I hadn't, and I said so. 'Pippa has always seemed so cheerful,' I added.

Sister Ellen took her time to respond. A question mark seemed to hang in the air between us. 'Cheerfulness is a lovely quality, Sister Catherine. And Pippa does have such a lot of it, and many of the right dispositions. It is a pity; she still has a great deal to offer. But I am sorry to say she does seem to have, er . . . have got herself into a muddle.'

'Oh?' I said, aiming at cautious curiosity. I'd noticed the term before now, the way the word 'muddle' was used to cover a range of perceived shortcomings. To be muddled was to lack a grasp of clear-cut dogma. To be muddled was to think differently from Reverend Mother or Elizabeth. To be muddled was to be deficient in the one thing necessary, the quality of submission required of a perfect nun.

'A certain lack of understanding seems to have crept in, as far as Philippa's concerned. She seems, by her own admission, to have become confused. We have suggested she take time to talk things over with Father Gregory, but in the end . . .'

'You mean?'

'I mean Pippa will, sadly, be leaving us.'

A cool breeze tugged at my veil. Two large ducks quacked loudly not far away. In the distance, a tractor was crisscrossing a field, the thrum and hum a characteristic backdrop to our early summer walks. The landscape surrounding us was a constant, one that followed predictable patterns, moved and changed only with the seasons. But nothing else in our lives was supposed to move. Not really. The hands of the clocks crept round the dial of their neutral, staring faces, and the weathervane fluttered, but all else stayed the same.

'You look surprised, Catherine. But surely you remember

Philippa talking about her interest in the community at Mellerby? Her desire to take up some sort of, er, yoga? And now it seems she's made up her mind . . .'

'I see,' I said. 'So, is she actually transferring?'

Ellen looked across at me with an expression of concern. 'I'm sorry to say she is.'

The summer unspooled, bright with birdsong. The ivy grew and the moss crept round our walls. The fields blazed and flamed and flowered, then faded. And the lake slept. In autumn the geese flew low towards the horizon and the sound of them, impersonal though it was, was a kind of friend to me as I tilled the soil and worked the garden. In spring, the ducklings brought charm, and the wildcats sprang their traps on unsuspecting birds. The summer hay piled high, and September heaved with it.

The year darkened and there were few things that unsettled our routines, apart from vague threats of visits from other Carmels, actual visits from the bishop, and the occasional flicker of interest in our life from outsiders, one or two a year at most. Father Brendan, an old friend of the community, sometimes brought out a student from the university chaplaincy, with which we had a tenuous link, or a small prayer group from a nearby parish. They'd sit in the outside chapel, and we'd hear their limping, unfamiliar voices, an afterthought to our own – the time-lag between the extern chapel and our stalls was like a bend in a very long road. But occasionally a young woman might make a formal request to come inside, and we'd chatter about the prospective candidate at recreation, excited at the possibility of a new recruit. *She plays the flute, you know.* That kind of thing.

Comings and goings were rare in as settled a world as ours.

The grille itself, and the walled enclosure, gave expression to the fact that Akenside was a world apart, a place where different rules applied. There was nothing vague about our separation, not only from the world, but also from other religious houses, even those of our own order. Although we heard plenty about Mellerby Hall – another northern Carmel – and Greenford Priory and Norrington Grange in chatter over knitting or card-folding in the evenings, few if any of us had been to any of these places, or met their inhabitants.

When Pippa vanished, the waters closed over her memory. She became a shadow for a while, something we were all aware of both as a presence and a gaping lack, but were not allowed to discuss. Letter-writing to former sisters was not permitted (bad example for us, too unsettling for them) and all temptation to follow suit was discouraged by a range of comments and recreational asides, mainly from Barbara, all part of the mental machinery that would keep us settled in our places, tireless, dedicated, rejecting all but Akenside.

Whatever the real reason for a sister's departure, the explanation was always couched in formulae that hinted at some fault or deficiency on the part of the departed, even when the reality was far more complex. Even when a sister was progressing on to a meaningful new life. Oversimplifying was convenient, just as segregating other monastic houses into camps was a standard resort. There were the orthodox and the observant, and then there were the progressives, liberals who were, by definition, lax.

As for the other Carmels, those to which former sisters may have transferred (or defected) in the past, they were disparagingly labelled and dismissed. Exceptions were made for a few select monastic communities or friends – the odd sister at Greenford, for example, or an old friend of Sister Barbara's who'd ended up prioress at Norrington, one of the southern houses. But other than that, the collective mindset that saw them all as potential competitors found ways of reducing other monasteries to houses that were 'failing', or 'sinking', or 'in danger of going off the rails' . . . Coming from a liberal sort of background, some of these attitudes surprised me at first. 'Poor old Birmingham,' someone might say, at recreation.

'Oh, yes?'

'Well, you know they've had terrible trouble implementing their formation programme.'

'Yes, well of course they have. I mean, unlike us they don't have any suitably able formators. Who is their novice mistress these days?'

'They've had to bring back Sister Ludwiga, there's no one else really up to it.'

'Well, I always thank the Lord for giving us such a strong cohort of young ones to help in the novitiate. I mean, aren't we blessed? We're flourishing! When you look at the other Carmels, you have to pity them . . .'

'God knows how some of them are coping with the decade of evangelism.'

'You know in France they've actually got a federation?'

'What, instead of an Alliance like ours?'

'Yes, I know. It's like the French Revolution. Everything made into a kind of central state. A Federation of Carmels . . . honestly! Such a betrayal of the charism.'

As time passed, I felt more uncomfortable at some of the things I heard said of our sister monasteries. It all seemed so unthinking. We hardly knew these women. And yet there were the 'dwindling' ones, the 'ancient' ones, the 'misguided', and the 'rather self-important' big ones, who were in danger of becoming more like the Benedictines.

Good for them, I couldn't help thinking, and felt just a glimmer of curiosity to know more about them. Was there anything wrong with the use of the zither in the liturgy? Or with icon-painting and bookbinding instead of making altar breads?

'Oh dear. Holton Priory really won't be able to carry on for much longer.'

'Holton! They're just not viable enough to pull their weight any more.'

'I know. They don't attract the young, you see. Too irrelevant.'

But on the other hand, someone else might declare, almost triumphantly: 'Oh goodness! They've gone crazy up in Glasgow, have you heard? It was in Sister Marcia's Christmas letter. They even remove their veils for housework! I don't see the point. And have you heard about Sister Zelda?'

We'd rarely, if ever, met any of these characters, but we talked as though we had, and the prioresses all swapped newsy Christmas letters, cards and gifts. Sometimes a photo might appear on the hall table, for us to gloat over.

'Gosh, they haven't got our grounds, have they?'

'Imagine living the Life without a proper vegetable garden!'

'Or a lake!'

I kept my counsel. But as those early years wore on, I became more aware of the complex dynamics swirling around me. Beyond the aura of quiet and the sense of specialness, darker energies were at work. Silence and solitude allowed for a serene surface, but could not negate the less palatable aspects of human nature. Even within our supposedly ideal community, there were covert loyalties that owed little or nothing to the divine. Some people were regarded as more acceptable and mainstream than others, while some were inexplicably dismissed as inferior. What was it that made the crucial difference? Why did Sister Barbara tell us not to take any notice of the (to my mind, shining) example of Sister Judith, she of the lowly washing-up sink, and why should we 'disregard the example' of the other 'in-betweeners'? They were neither young nor old (young, in Carmel, was anything under forty) and so were never included in the activities of the novitiate, but neither were they venerated as those who'd fought the good fight. They stood on their own two feet unsupported by infirmary or novitiate. Was it that, rather than being Elizabeth's dependents, they were in a category that made them potential rivals?

Walking to the hornbeam was a good way of clearing one's head and finding space away from the house and other people. Its branches were testaments to life and growth, and symbols of all that we as a community might be. The shade it gave to small woodland flowers – wild garlic, aconites, bluebells and crocuses – was generous and protective, the architecture of its limbs against the sky magnificent. Far around it, its own and other tree roots lifted the dry earth, forming knots and channels, sinuous and strong. Trunks rose to the sky. Ivy pushed and pulsed, pressing up towards the light. Halfway to the Mere, within striking distance of the kitchen garden but far enough from the house to feel secluded, the hornbeam offered another kind of oasis from the cell, a place apart under the sky, a place where your thoughts could not be heard by others. How often I ran there and stood in its shade.

Then, it was back to the toolshed, and deep into its apple-smelling darkness, the moisture of the afternoon upon you, its ferns stuck like transfers on your wellies. You'd leave your overall hanging, wet with mud, an elbow prickly with burrs, remove your gloves and adjust your veil, perhaps sad for a moment to leave the world of must and mess. The cleanness of the cloister courtyard lay before you, and then the covered walkway that led, by way of the kitchen, to a low flight of steps and into the wood-panelled corridor, and on and on, until you reached the chequerboard hall and then the huge oak doors, twin portals that opened noiselessly to reveal your place in the choir.

The cell, the choir, the novitiate, the recreation room, the toolshed. These places were all separate worlds, and all had their own modes and atmospheres and rules. It was the silence of Carmel that had attracted me, the liturgy, the sense of God's presence pervading everything, and the faith that, in a life of absolute focus, seclusion and prayerful service of others, I would find my role. But mystery was also everywhere. In dark corners. In the floodlit infirmary. In the chequerboard hall. In the cell I was most securely alone with God. In the garden I was the most emotionally free. In the toolshed, however, you never knew. There were surprises among the decades of accumulated dirt and dust. There, standing in the dark, you might find yourself alone not only with nature, but with yourself.

14. The Novitiate

The novitiate was both temporal and spatial. It was a process, whereby the raw material we newcomers presented was to be knocked, kneaded and moulded into a specifically Carmelite character, and it was also a place, a rickety annexe to the main building, semi-soundproofed by virtue of being semi-detached. It also had some special features, such as a cassette recorder and a bulky harmonium that had been donated to the community by a popular actor who had moved to the area. The instrument had great wheezing foot pedals and two manuals, the one mild and muffled, the other strident and raucous. The novitiate also had a supply of Plasticine, some rubber balls and a collection of skipping ropes, things beloved of Sister Elizabeth who swore by their therapeutic properties.

While nominally in charge of our formation as novices, Elizabeth was a remote figure who only occasionally graced our gatherings. She glided around the main house, and padded in and out of the infirmary, but more often than not communicated with us by note, telling us she was busy and would not be able to make it that afternoon. Then we would be told to get on with 'little works', which was our name for crafts and so-called hobbies, things like knitting that kept our hands and eyes busy during recreation.

We younger ones were a mixed bag, a rag-tag and bobtail of innocents and desperados, all intent on the same end – whether we thought of it mystically as 'union with God', or practically as 'service of the Church' – and of making it to final vows. Some exuded piety, others a desire to be approved. Some were active and outgoing, looking for tasks to carry out, others self-effacing, drawn to voluntary obscurity. The unlikeliness of us as a group could partly be explained by the fact that all that was required of a new entrant, apart from being (or having become) a sincere Catholic, was availability, good health, and the 'right disposition', which boiled down to piety and good will.

There were five of us before Pippa left. Now we were just Felicity, tall, pale and angular, Emily, a bewimpled beauty, then Jennifer and me, the youngest in the community, the so-called Twins. Sister Emily was the kind of person you were bound to notice in a group. Like a faun in a farmyard, she was far too pretty to pass muster as a regular nun. In another life she might have been a muse or a fashion model. She walked the choir like a catwalk, head held high, hips inappropriately relaxed. Some of the older nuns tut-tutted and shook their heads. You knew what they were thinking – that this was an example of today's sensuous and easy-going youth. Not quite stern enough to do battle on the field of the Church Militant. Not quite solid enough for the spiritual warfare Carmel required. Whatever others said, I could tell that Emily was secretly feisty – not the brightest button in the box, but quirkily determined. According to the 'order of religion', dictated by the date of our entry, I was at the bottom, then Jen, then Felicity and Emily, both already in first, or 'temporary' vows. This was a provisional stage, only to be confirmed for life at the ceremony of solemn profession which was the desired end of the formation process.

The person charged with the lion's share of our formation was Sister Barbara, a steely character, alternately jolly and acerbic. She was in her late thirties, which seemed quite old to me at the time. In addition there was a smattering of younger chapter sisters who also frequented the novitiate. These included Sister Suzanne, a powerful character, and lovely, gentle Ellen, both of whom were seen as responsible and, at around thirty, close enough to us in age to make a relevant impression. Along with the authoritative Barbara, they took it in turns to lead the sessions in Sister Elizabeth's place, teaching us about the history of the Church, the order, or Catholic doctrine. We'd read a point from the Rule or Constitutions, talk it through, and then 'discuss' it, we newcomers being coaxed into an explicit understanding of each fine detail that accorded precisely with the 'Mind of the Church'. The latter was a mysterious entity that hovered somewhere above the Vatican, but that also drew on the *sensus fidelium*, a sort of holy collective consciousness among the faithful.

Sister Elizabeth was more like a figurehead than a real-life novice mistress. It would be easy to imagine her sticking out of the prow of an old-fashioned sailing ship, chin forward, pale blue eyes set calmly on the further horizon. Carved in wood, of course. And yet she had a strange and silent power about her person, something difficult to define. You did not need to talk to her to feel her influence. Already, when I entered, she ruled the roost. She'd been understudying for the real prioress, Mother Julianna, for years if not decades as her unofficially anointed successor. As for Mother Julianna, she was so much more than a figurehead, despite her age, her walking stick and her stoop. She had bright white beams that shot out of her eyes when she looked in your direction, and her words resonated tremulously, in a tenor register. She seemed to look into your soul, and even to care, although she could also do chilly, ethereal and remote.

Mother Julianna hobbled laboriously about in a cloud of sanctity. Although I'd wondered about the term before, I now knew what it meant. Mother was holy. I'd never known any other Mothers in the order, but we were told very early on that all Carmelite Mothers were the same in one hyper-important way: whatever their human character and individuality, they were all God's elect, his chosen representatives among us. Through her, we pledged allegiance to the unseen spouse, specifically when we took our all-encompassing vow of obedience. This required that every action and decision in the community be determined by this one chosen and trusted person alone. Obedience was woven into the fabric of the order at the level of the warp and weft. Pull at one thread, remove another, and the whole thing unravelled.

The prioress was God's representative in such a fundamental way that some of the older sisters had been known to assert that they had 'only ever had one prioress'. It was the office not the office holder that was considered important. The human appearance of the prioress might change, but the sacred essence of the office remained identical, its divine anointing an unvarying benediction from the heavens. To be elected in the formal voting ceremony we held every three years, the candidate needed to have either an absolute majority, or, if she was the outgoing prioress, two-thirds of the votes. Hanging around too long in office was not supposed to be a good thing, although it used to happen all the time before Vatican II. The anomaly of the perennial prioress had been known to blight more than one community. Put one person at the top and give them permanency and a nice shiny pedestal, and no one else got listened to, not even the Spirit with his rushing winds of holy, beatific change. Having regular elections was meant to counteract such complacency and stagnation. Once the name of the new prioress was announced by the bishop (or his delegate, in our case Father Gregory), the 'spirit seized on her', and she received something ineffable called 'the grace of the office', which meant she was now enabled to lead the community according to the will of God.

The new Mother was henceforth a subtly different being from the rest of us, by virtue of her role. The anointing she received and the grace of the office, together with the faith we placed in her, meant that her authority was unchallengeable and unchallenged. To people now, only thirty years on, this might ring more than a few alarm bells. But in the late twentieth century few people thought they had any reason to mistrust authority. Due deference was part of the package. If you were a Catholic, hierarchy was important, and roles and offices mattered very much indeed, and were nothing if not clearly defined. But substitution was also part of the wider culture of transubstantiation, where shapes could shift, and masks could fall. There were layers within layers, within a classic community, and sometimes the roles people played were not quite identical to those officially accorded them.

An illustration of this holy mystery was the fact that Elizabeth was understudying for Julianna, and that Barbara was understudying for Elizabeth, while Father Gregory was understudying for the bishop, and both the bishop and the prioress were understudying for God. Even within the novitiate, you got the feeling Jennifer was understudying for the position of 'senior novice' from the beginning, indeed she had once said as much. Although I was a couple of natural years older than her, it was 'age in community' that counted, and I supposed it was partly because the nuns had known her since she was a child that they'd arranged things that way when we entered on the same day. They'd kept me back waiting for her so that she could cross the threshold first. There was definitely sleight of hand involved on Mother's part, although it mattered not a jot to me.

It was important to look at things through the eyes of faith. Being vessels of God's grace, all of us bore his image and were his representatives in small ways. One great art in the life of any Christian – an art agonised over in a monastery – is that of seeing God in all his creatures, however humble. This meant even, and perhaps especially, that one recalcitrant sister who didn't immediately strike you as the repository of the Most High. There were bound to be some who seemed less than inspired. We all had our bugbears, things that wound us up. Some sisters had natural charisma, style, immediate appeal. Others lacked obvious charm, and maybe had irritating habits instead, things that came to seem like crimes if you looked at them (or could not avoid looking at them) too long and hard. As happens in all groups, there were hidden loves and buried antipathies. Not everyone had the aura of Mother Julianna, or her immediately detectable sanctity.

Sister Elizabeth was one of the few blessed with natural charisma. A generation younger than Julianna (Elizabeth was around fifty when I entered), she had arrived, all smiles and ringlets, at the age of nineteen, from an old Catholic family in Louth in Lincolnshire, a place for which she retained a deep affection that often came out in jokey disparagements of the area further north. Our Mother's doting on her was perhaps the old woman's only foible. But Elizabeth was tall and smooth and slender, and blessed with innate elegance and poise. Airs of authority and good looks often go together. Elizabeth had both, and a voice like a fine reed with just enough husk in it to make it viscerally compelling. (Slightly sexy, in truth, although we never would have used the term.) Sometimes she added an extra layer of frisson to her enunciations, as though pulling out a special organ stop, especially if she was trying to be particularly persuasive. People succumbed readily to her aura and her influence. She had power, and knew how it worked.

By the time I entered, Mother Julianna was approaching eighty, venerable, huge and misshapen like a twisted oak. We young ones did not often see her, but one day it was announced in the novitiate that she would visit us. In a few days, her large frame, which was barely supported by her walking stick, would lumber through the lean-to walkway, and we'd all stand and bow deep at her appearance. Our little monastic schoolroom would be graced, and she'd tower within it, fill it like a shining light that would cloud our eyes with indefinable emotion. We all loved Old Mother, or said we did, and would half tremble, half well up at her approach. Her long head would rise from its half-slump to greet us, and the great brown eyes, bright behind her spectacles, would momentarily meet ours.

When the awaited afternoon arrived, one late summer's day a few months after Jen and I were Clothed, there we were, all spruced and dusted, our veils pulled straight and early for novitiate. We'd gulped our bowl of tea in the refectory after None, and got there in time to brush the pencil shavings off the main table, light a candle on the smaller table next to the order's rule book, and to open the shutters and let in the sun.

'Ah, the little flock is already gathered!' Julianna croaked as she heaved herself through the door. Jen rushed to hold it open. Felicity coughed. Emily looked down at her carefully trimmed nails, then up again. Emily was the one currently under scrutiny (even I could tell, for all my custody of the eyes) and it had occurred to me that it was – unfairly – because of her aura of unwitting glamour. Poor Emily – this must have been the last year before her disappearance. The old woman advanced heavily on her stick, then slumped into the big teacher's chair at the head of the table. We all smiled and waited for her to give the signal. Her chest heaved for a few moments, and she held up a hand for patience. Only after her opening blessing and invocation were we allowed to speak. After the nod and prayer we could relax our vigilance, wait our turn, then talk a little of our lives as novices, and, in return, expect something special. A blessing or a tiny token of encouragement.

She asked us how we had been getting on. As prioress she was not only the holder of the grace of the office, she was an ardent believer in the supernatural spirit of obedience. It worked both ways, a quality of reciprocity that is a property of any covenant relationship. According to the teaching mere human nature was, or would be, overcome by grace, particularly where the vow of obedience was concerned. If we gave full rein and assent to the mysterious workings of God in our lives, he in turn would enable us to have the kind of faith that defied natural limitations, even to the moving of the craggiest of mountains. Yes, the gospel saying employed metaphor, but in Carmel metaphor was far less important than stark belief. You held firm. You did not doubt. Essentially, we were taught that, with God, 'nothing was impossible'.

Mother Julianna exuded everything we ourselves wanted to attain and embody. She had both loftiness and humanity.

She smiled even when she seemed a million miles away. She was firm (severely so, when she wanted to be) but also sweet. How did she do it? Grace of course was the answer. She sat and spoke to us about God's goodness and the joys of heaven. There were simple smiles and nods all round. Then she changed the subject and talked about the old days, when she was a young sister. She recounted an anecdote from 'before the Council' and another one about sardines. She reminded us that we had come to the community to serve the Church, and in order to do that we must forget all about ourselves. Offer ourselves up. The model of the monastic life was that of martyrdom.

'Can anyone give me a definition?' Mother Julianna asked.

Jen and I both had a go, mentioning witness, persever-ance and the lives of the saints. Ellen threw in a bit of early Church history, Tertullian and the spread of Christianity in the Roman Empire, lions and amphitheatres. Then Emily repeated something about 'martyrdom', tying her tongue in knots as she did so. Emily, who was much too charming to be taken seriously. 'Matradom' is how she always said it, and no amount of listening or correcting seemed to enable her to get it right. Matra ... matra ... *No, Mar-ter*, Our Mother countered. Eventually we all laughed.

By the end of the session we were enlivened, buzzing from the rarity of the contact with Our Reverend Mother, a group session with our saintly leader, someone whom every-one implicitly revered. Felicity looked briefly radiant, as though she'd shed her cloak of worries, and stood tall. Emily blushed and hid her nervous hands at last. Jen gabbled some-thing indistinct, then put her hand to her mouth, comically shushing herself. I closed my eyes and prayed. The bell sounded, a signal to us all to bow low as Mother prepared to exit, before we moved on to the practical tasks – our manual labour of the afternoon.

One night when everyone had gone to bed after a long, hot afternoon of hay-raking, a slow bell began to ring. Such a sound at that late hour was unheard of, and yet there it was, a distant, deliberate tolling. It crept into my sleeping consciousness like a convent cat. Meow, it pawed at me. I looked out of my cell door, ragged in my tunic and night veil, sensing strange creaks and movements from unexpected quarters. People were rustling and gathering somewhere far below. Soon I was putting on my slippers.

When I reached the ground floor, I saw a huddle of bodies in night caps and dressing gowns by the passage leading to the infirmary. All were even paler than usual, and some were yawning. I was surprised how different people looked without their daytime habits. Then Sister Jane appeared from the passage, fully dressed and business-like, signalling sisters through to the new wing where only the infirmarians normally ventured. I followed and was soon passing through into the electric brightness of the breeze-block modern wing where, somewhere beyond a half-open door, Sister Elizabeth was softly speaking.

'Father will be here soon,' I heard her say. 'Father will be here . . .'

And then she appeared in the full light of the corridor. Oh, so this is it, I realised. This is it. People were wiping their eyes. It was all happening so quickly.

Elizabeth held up both hands, palms out, signalling calm and prayer. 'Yes, sisters,' she said. 'It is Mother Julianna. Already unconscious. Slipping fast. It came on suddenly this afternoon. But now it seems the Lord wants to take her quickly. The Lord is merciful.' She blinked for a few seconds, her own eyes red under the strip-lighting. 'Come now, sisters. Come, let us keep her company. Two at a time by her bedside. And two at her feet, praying the rosary. Come, come . . .'

The sight of the dark infirmary cell dotted with candles, and Sister Barbara bustling around with posies of geranium, was deeply affecting. The scent of roses hung sonorously, like a great gong in the air. The night emitted its smells of velvet and the heady breezes of the garden. There was a glint of moon just outside the window. Our Lady of Perpetual Succour was surrounded by flickering night-lights, and a framed saying of St Teresa's was propped up on the moonlit mattress. A spray of lilies spreading from an urn on the floor amply filled the area around the bed. Hunched bodies were praying on all sides, anonymous and wordless in their unfamiliar hats and dressing gowns, the room silent but for the click of beads, Old Mother's husky breathing and the sound of someone's on-off sobs.

I took my turn at the foot of the bed, recited my decade of the rosary in utter silence and passed on. Then Barbara was ushering me to take up a position at close quarters, and I felt a rush of dread as I saw Old Mother's face, as hard as granite, nothing about her mobile or responsive. I had to look, but simultaneously did not want to. She had become a staring, empty mask, a rigid carving on a totem pole. Already she seemed gone, and I closed my eyes. *De profundis clamavi . . .* I thought. Then I said the words, '*De profundis . . .*'

Then I was out into the clean, artificial light of the corridor, standing under the strip-lighting. Elizabeth came over, speaking in kinder and more human tones than I had ever heard from her before. She, too, seemed changed dramatically, visibly shaken and emotional, addressing us through the pressure of wholly unfamiliar tears. How much she must have loved the old prioress, I realised with start-ling clarity. How long she must have known her for – three decades, I supposed – and how random this all feels. Sister Elizabeth, grown suddenly human, and dear old Julianna as strange in the cold moonlight as a creature from another planet. Sisters moved past me towards the connecting pas-sage. Elizabeth padded away, looking oddly broken. As I reached the door between the old monastery and the new wing I heard a harsh electric bell seeping through from the extern.

'That will be Father,' I heard Sister Barbara say. 'That will be Father Christopher.'

It was a summer funeral, a mingling of tears and joy. I remem-bered Old Mother's words: 'I am old now, and I'll soon be gone, my daughters, but God will be with you. He will always guide you, no matter what happens, through your prioress. It is not the human figure of your Superior you should focus on. It matters *not one iota* whether it is me, or Sister Elizabeth, or another sister. A prioress's personal characteristics are of no account. What matters is that you accept her as God's chosen one, not whether you happen to like or agree with her. No, all those human judgements and characteristics are irrelevant. Whoever is chosen by the Spirit is a vessel, set aside for a specific task. Chosen and consecrated, she will become God's representative in your midst. But I'll still be praying for you.'

How deeply these principles had been impressed upon us, driven deep into our souls. The prioress was God's elect. The elections were guided by the Holy Spirit. Obedience was a choice, made in the power of the Spirit, a naked act of the will to submit one's judgement to another. And when the inevitable happened, and Elizabeth stepped into Julianna's shoes, it was as though the old woman was still guiding us, still talking to us about the 'supernatural spirit of obedience'.

15. Only Human

With a new prioress at the helm, life continued virtually unchanged, only that there was now more emphasis on the preparation for taking vows. A great deal of explicit formation to this end went into the years between Clothing and first Profession, as the public promises of poverty, chastity and obedience – even when made for three years in the first instance – were understood as weighty, life-defining undertakings. Sometimes likened to the nails piercing Jesus's hands and feet, sometimes to 'self-immolation' or 'human sacrifice', the vows loomed ahead of us in those early years both as threat and promise, punishment and reward. It was difficult to know how I really felt about them. I'd got so used to whipping up my enthusiasm and conforming my behaviour and words to reflect what was expected of us, an unconditional 'self-giving', that any contrary feelings got pushed down, sometimes even deliberately, to the bottom of one's boots. You knew not to think about the ifs and buts, knew to categorise them as 'temptations'. Still, the faculty of reasoning, like the shadow side of the psyche, cannot be kept down for ever.

The phrase 'manual labour' had begun to strike me as excessive. I did not say so, of course. But surely 'labour' was the word for heroic acts like giving birth and building railways, not for sweeping tidy corridors and weeding flower-beds, even if it meant slashing neck-high nettles at nine in the morning. But I silenced that thought. I would not quibble.

Independent judgement was among the worst of monastic faults, we'd learned, and you knew instinctively to suppress it. My keen energy seeped through, though, and I soon began to see that my desire to take things to logical extremes was viewed with suspicion by my elders, those whose job it was not to foster exceptional zeal but deeds of common submission. They had a stable tradition to pass on, not anything as unpredictable as inspiration. Perhaps I should have known better, but it came as a shock to learn that idealists were seen as undesirable.

'What you want in community is practical people,' Father Brendan had said. Brendan was a Carmelite friar and a friend of Sister Jennifer's family, all of them dyed-in-the-wool, as Catholic as they come. Based at one of the order's friaries in the north-east, he'd been sent there from one of the Lancashire parishes, and Jen had known him for half her life. While I had arrived an unknown quantity, a recent convert from Islington, Jen had evolved over years into what everyone hoped might turn out to be novice material, implicitly sponsored by Brendan, who kept a close eye on her. He had also evolved into something like an unofficial advisor to the community.

He was a rough diamond, ruddy-faced and 'simple' in the way that Mother liked, and it was deemed fitting for him to continue to act as a support for Jen. The rest of us had to manage with just the Holy Spirit, or 'without props', as Mother Elizabeth liked to say, the word 'props' being sharply emitted, as though it contained a hidden poison. We were not meant to lean on anyone or anything, or to admit of basic human needs. Certainly not if we were to avoid the extremities of our novice mistress's scorn. But for reasons that were, perplexingly, never clarified, my twin was someone who needed special support in a range of surprising ways, and to whom general expectations did not seem to apply. For example, in the early stages she was allowed to phone her family every evening during the Great Silence (and did so in such a way that the conversations could be heard all over the monastery), when the custom was that only Mother ever used the phone.

None of this was her fault, of course, but it naturally posed some unanswered questions for me, and raised the stakes where keeping one's eyes down and applying super-human strength to Minding One's Own Business was concerned. Perhaps my own silly fault was that I was secretly rather pleased with myself for never mentioning any of these painful discrepancies. If ever Jen had thought about leaving, she would of course have had a warm and supportive family to receive her. I could not but reflect that I had none, and doubly so now that I was expected miraculously to manage without a trace of human encouragement or help. But I must have been one of those annoying novices who persevered in silence, kept quiet and acted as though they noticed nothing. An attitude of composure was not that difficult to maintain. Custody of the eyes and constant prayer were my refuge.

'Ordinary, down-to-earth pragmatists are the best sort for keeping the communities going in this day and age,' Brendan had said. 'What you don't want are enthusiasts,' he'd smiled. I'd expected at least someone to laugh. But then I realised it was not a joke. Now, in the late twentieth century, with voca-tions being so few and far between, communities faced a stark choice: compromise on ideals or die out. There were not only the unseen spiritual traditions and beliefs, but large build-ings and extensive grounds and goods to be taken care of. Religious orders all had their own equivalent of the Church's 'deposit of faith', which referred to the body of teachings and beliefs accrued like capital over the centuries. The phrase made my blood run cold (wasn't faith meant to be alive and active, not something to be ring-fenced and stashed away?), and even when it was explained to me as something of eternal value, a timeless treasure, the word 'deposit' had far too worldly and material a connotation to recommend it to my youthful and demanding mind.

'You need people who will protect and maintain what you already have. Your traditions. Your stable heritage. What you don't want are airy-fairy people who aim too high and . . . oh, I don't know—' Here, at least, he hesitated '—young firebrands who don't know their own limitations. What you don't want are dreamers.'

Ouch. Was that dig intended? But more importantly, his words made me wonder – what had I stumbled into? Was it not just this sort of complacency that Jesus had come to earth to challenge? Wasn't the Church founded by Jesus Christ meant to be bringing fire, and even some well-aimed fury to the earth? The firebrand in me was piqued and stirring. Applying an extra level of perfectionism (now redefined as submission), I suppressed it. I was learning to hold things in, to smile instead of scowling, and to hide my reactions under the veil of silence and serenity the Life required. Still, it was painful to hear these comments, knowing by now that I was seen as both airy-fairy and idealistic. Jen's occasional jibes had already made as much clear to me.

New and surprising realities were suddenly impinging, things I hadn't noticed at first. My convert's enthusiasm – the one thing I'd thought I had in my favour – was, I now realised, destined to work against me. You'd think they'd have been glad of it, given the order's motto – 'With Zeal Have I Been Zealous of the Lord God of Hosts' – but in practice, having someone so keen she had already read St John of the Cross, and was into things like fasting and Marian apparitions (I'd been particularly fired up by a pilgrimage site in former Yugoslavia) was perhaps more annoying or unsettling. No one wanted to be shown up as lukewarm, and leaders naturally defend their decisions and priorities, not necessarily from the highest motives. Be that as it may, my perception of the community of which I was now a fully active part was becoming more informed, more granular, less abstract and idealised.

Is it not enough, Ellen asked me some time the next spring, for us to have given up our freedom and our futures in order to live in this way, in lowliness and poverty? She was worried I was finding the Life insufficiently radical or challenging. I did not say: Do you mean, is it not enough for us to live protected in a grand old country house, with thirty-five glorious acres, the stuff of privilege, with orchards and kitchen gardens and mullioned windows and panelled walls, while people are sleeping on the streets in Kilburn? Is it not enough for us to have 'given up everything' and shunned a harsh and hostile world in return for being fed and clothed, and having all our most essential needs taken care of?

She more than read my thoughts. 'You don't need to go looking for heroics, Sister Catherine. You will find it hard enough to live the common life as we do, day to day, after a while. Mere regular observance is all we ask. Year in, year out. Anything more than that is a vehicle for the self. The self, as you know, is the enemy and something you must get used to shunning. Self-love and self-reliance are the essence of the sinful state. Having spiritual ideas of your own might seem good to you, but is really something you must be very wary of. Seek the level and the down-to-earth. No one should stand out of the common herd.'

I went back to my weeding and my raking. The peas were in, and new tight leaves were unfurling on the trees. The wind blew strong across the lake, and new life fluttered in the shallows. The ducklings crisscrossed the dark water, following their mother from shore to shore, and birds' eggs warmed and cracked open in the overhanging branches. High up, there were rooks nesting in the trees, and their larger, more mottled eggs would soon be hatching.

As I learned more about the interpersonal dynamics in our world, I became more aware of the little eddies frothing around Elizabeth, the undercurrents that were later to come to the fore. Her twin domains, the infirmary and the novitiate, were semi-separate spaces, places apart, where things were done differently. Even by her own admission, Elizabeth had her 'funny little ways'. But nowhere did she rule as fully as behind these two sets of closed doors within closed doors. In the monastery proper, people expected unwavering 'observance' of the Rule, and for the writings of the order to be studied, and for silence to be kept. These were the principles that had attracted many of us to Carmel, and it was the attentive spirit of recollection that was traditionally the key to all things monastic. But within the orbit of Elizabeth a different set of priorities applied.

I was still too new to realise the extent to which her methods of engaging the young, and of ensuring their loyal adhesion to her person, were unusual, even anomalous. The middle sisters knew better – although, being dutiful, they kept their counsel. Many of their number had long since defected to Mellerby, where secret tea parties were not used to foster cliques or buy the loyalty of the eager young. The Mellerby sisters were more interested in theology and engaging in community discussion. They also knew how far the Church had moved since Vatican II, and how strongly it now discouraged an exclusive or autocratic style of leadership, and the repeated re-election of the same nun in a way that fed a club mentality, with absolute power ceded to a single charismatic individual. Sometimes I wondered what it would be like to be among their number, but any thoughts of leaving and re-entering there (or 'transferring') were ones you knew not to entertain. They belonged to the category of 'temptation'.

With us, there was the novitiate, dedicated to the initiation of the young, and there was the infirmary, a sanctuary for the old and infirm, two domains, two apparent opposites, that were segregated areas for the more vulnerable elements of the community. As a novice, you needed an extra layer of guidance; as an invalid you needed an extra layer of protection. Mother Elizabeth had both areas completely at her fingertips. In any other Carmel these offices, as stipulated in the Constitutions, would have been shared out among a range of capable nuns, and we certainly had plenty of those at Akenside. Only much later would I realise that the exceptional circumstances under which a prioress might also hold the roles of novice mistress and infirmarian simply did not apply. Instead we had a situation that revolved around a single dominant but all too human and powerful personality. She was not only intransigent, she was at times utterly charming and attractive, and it was in this paradoxical grey area that many threads and covert community dynamics came together. It was a classic, if a toxic situation.

The subculture fostered by Mother Elizabeth was

disheartening once a pattern emerged and the situation became impossible to ignore. Well-meaning Barbara and Ellen were part of it, and somehow managed to swing between the mainstream – being stiff and starchy when required – and then relaxed – when, say, our new prioress clapped her hands and brought out a donated box of Black Magic chocolates from underneath her scapular. 'I don't expect anyone feels like doing any work today,' she'd say, arriving for a session on Carmelite spirituality, and then beam the more brightly, the more giddy and enthusiastic our response. What she wanted was a coterie of the like-minded. What she wanted was for you to shout and cheer. I suspect she also wanted confirmation of her own bias, which saw serious reading, study and discussion as a waste of time.

One day when Jen was finding things heavy-going, Mother Elizabeth laughed and told us not to bother reading John of the Cross, as he was far too 'difficult'. At this Jen beamed. She was glad to be let off the hook. John was weird. He was obscure. His writing was all poetical. How were we supposed to understand it? Naturally I sat squirming with discomfort, not understanding what was going on. Wasn't John one of the foundational teachers of the order? Wasn't it required reading? What was wrong with it? When Mother Elizabeth heartily agreed with her and pronounced John optional – an acquired taste, for 'enthusiasts' – I could not avoid feeling more than a pang of disappointment. John and Thérèse were the two Carmelite writers who had attracted me the most before I entered. They were my adopted guides. What was the problem? And surely they were our role models, our mentors, supernatural sisters and brothers in the order. But it was no good. My own preferences, even my most apparently spiritual and zealous ones, had to go, had to be sacrificed on the altar of acceptance, community conformity if you will. And here, certainly, John of the Cross would have agreed! While Jen was manifesting some of the traits associated with unruliness and rebellion, I was guilty of spiritual gluttony and excess.

Months passed. The novitiate sessions went on, seesawing from tense to untethered in a heartbeat. It was in these closed sessions, apart from the main body of the community, that I started to notice the extremes of Sister Jennifer's behaviour. At the word 'chocolates' she'd tilt back her head and roar with laughter, and start banging the table with her fists, sometimes even screaming with excitement. I found this sort of thing so perplexing. At the words 'I don't suppose anyone feels like doing any work today,' she'd say, 'Yeah, great. Let's have some extra recreation.' Elizabeth could not have been more delighted. Her own approach favoured the letting down of our metaphorical hair, if only with herself and strictly behind the closed doors of the novitiate, in keeping with the tenet that we were 'only human'. It seemed to follow that we weren't meant to enjoy solitude and silence, or any of the attractions of the monastic life for their own sake. Everyone needed a change of mode now and then.

Up to a point this was clearly true and made absolute sense, but what was beginning to grate was the sheer excess and lack of balance in how it was applied. Since the curtailing of our critical faculties and any sort of independent thinking was part and parcel of what was required of us, I made sure to keep my perceptions to myself. Preventing oneself from thinking about and judging things instinctively would, ironically, have made us really inhuman, far more so than reading John of the Cross or trying to keep the Rule in its entirety. But there we are. In closed groups you do not always get a choice about how to best express yourself. Mother Elizabeth seemed sure that we were doing enough already just by being here, just by showing up for work and recreation and the Office. It seemed not to have occurred to her that some new entrants might be looking for a bit more.

In the 1990s the dominant model at Akenside was still very much a pre-Vatican II approach, with absolute, unquestioning obedience being top of the list of requirements, and with words like mortification, immolation and martyrdom being cheerfully bandied about as though they were completely harmless, along with talk of the virtues of humility and self-effacement. This was the bread-and-butter of our lives, and, in theory, I was fine with all of that. After all I'd been through before entering, I was looking for some strong and effective medicine. I was already used to self-reliance. I was used to emotional privations and a certain degree of material austerity: ten years in boarding school, for a start, as well as the years living on a shoestring abroad. But at the same time an altogether different philosophy was being promoted by Elizabeth, as though we were not in fact expected to embrace the theories put before us. What was going on? Was it mere lip-service that was required?

The modifications Elizabeth introduced when she was alone with us, her young charges, were unconvincing to my mind. They seemed more a reflection of her own hot-and-cold personality than anything more generally applicable. There was also something slightly sinister about the way she played with us, and the heady reactions she inspired. I tried so hard to understand what she really expected of us, tried to read her mind through the smokescreen of piety and absolute control. On the one hand, steely rigour and self-denial were required – yes, genuinely inhuman at times. If she didn't approve of it, you got away with nothing. On the other, she was intent on 'forming' us young ones to think and feel like small children towards a nanny. Were we being infantilised or punished, or both at once? It was impossible to say. We were certainly being moulded into a group that would reflect her personality, reinforce her influence within the community, and be ready to do her bidding without consulting our own (or anybody else's) judgement. The fact that it involved setting aside much of what had attracted me to monasticism was beside the point. We had come to Akenside to put both our bad and our good desires aside.

But I hadn't spent the years since my father's death straining every nerve to accommodate myself to Catholicism only to be told none of the things I had embraced and thought so important really mattered. John of the Cross, for example, and his poetry about the journey of the human soul, the so-called 'Ascent of Mount Carmel'; attitudes and beliefs I'd had to force my will to, things I'd found difficult at first but had persevered with, were not things I was lightly going to downgrade to 'optional'. Otherwise, why had I tried so hard? I'd read all the standard books on Catholic doctrine, thinking I was doing merely what was required, only to find that I'd somehow gained more knowledge of these areas than was expected for a convert, even more than some of those born into the faith. I had been uncompromising with myself, trying to detach myself from the affective consolations of a mother-figure. Was I wrong? Surely I was not going to be one of those novices who lingered too long chatting to Elizabeth in an alcove after she bent the rules, conferring smiles all round, of some exceptional community exercise she had instigated in the hall? I would live not for Elizabeth but for God alone.

I had to ask myself, had my eagerness really been

misplaced? Jen, with her dismissal of the niceties of fine feeling, and her casual attitude to things like silence and detachment, seemed more in line with what Mother really wanted. Someone who could be easily led into the 'coterie mindset' of dependence. Someone who did not take things to logical extremes. But what was wrong with the poetry and inspiring teachings of John of the Cross? What was so threatening about reading and thinking and studying? What was so irrelevant and dangerous about good art, and self-expression, for that matter? And why were the standards of detachment set for Cradle Catholics so much more relaxed than for those of us who were newer to the Church? Was there some vestige of Reformation suspicion lurking in our corridors, an undercurrent that still regarded us as inherently suspicious?

What was hitting me now were the mixed messages. On the one hand we were meant to be offering ourselves up as living sacrifices, mortifying ('putting to death') our natural instincts, fighting tooth and nail against 'ourselves' and putting the ascetic traditions and values of the Carmelite order, as set out by St Teresa, before all else. Yet we were simultaneously being told it was important not to be too serious, or keen, and to be more like unquestioning children. Naturally, 'only human' as a phrase sounded good – didn't we all want to be ourselves, and retain some elements of our own identities? But the reality was that only certain people were allowed to be themselves, and only certain characteristics counted as 'human enough' in Mother's book. Being sensitive, introspective, 'artistic', emotional, creative, questioning, or philosophically inclined, just didn't count.

Elizabeth had the power to enforce not only silence but its opposite, and sometimes she did just that. Then the contemplative quiet that characterised our corridors, the silence I felt mattered at a cellular level, was cast off like an unwanted cloak. People became harsh and rough. Overt infantilism took over. Different temperaments and backgrounds (things we were supposed to transcend) began to make a painful difference.

A gulf soon appeared between how I actually felt about Carmel, and the reality of the community, and how I was 'supposed' to feel about a life of dedicated prayer. Apparently my ascetical enthusiasm was 'not normal'. Ellen told me as much. My outward and evidently easy acceptance of the Life's material privations (on the level of food and other comforts, I barely noticed them) was an anomaly. It seemed I needed to be taught lessons to humble my lofty-mindedness, and to counter my 'spiritual' inclinations. I was already seen as not being 'simple' enough, and with the application of another label – 'not ordinary' – I knew I'd touched a raw nerve with Elizabeth. What she wanted were no more than average levels of engagement. Whichever direction your failings lay in, whether towards deficiency or excess, you were raw material that needed to be broken in.

Jen's natural boisterousness could take verbally scathing forms. This crept up on me slowly, and was eventually very upsetting. Sometimes she'd shout from behind a tree, pounce out, then run away laughing while calling me a namby-pamby if I jumped. It was meant to be a joke, and Mother loved this kind of play, but I was left feeling acutely alone and puzzled, unable to reconcile it with my expectations of Carmel. The playground at my London primary school came to mind, and the enclosed Shrubbery behind our house where we'd been beaten up by older local children when we were small. At other times I was labelled a 'posh southerner', a rejecting term that was sure to condemn anyone it stuck to, although

Elizabeth was exempt. Being posh, it seemed, was OK if you were not actually southern or if you were the Mother Superior.

The garden at least was full of loveliness, even of poetry, and it was full of God. I recalled Marvell's lines: 'Two paradises 'twere in one / to live in paradise alone', and secretly wished myself more solitary. The knocks and bumps of community, the unexpected gulfs between sister and sister, the lack of sympathetic resonance, were jolts to my system, odd forms of hardship in a cloistered world. Physical renunciations were not a problem for me. But the othering, mental and emotional distancing by others was painful, and, to my open and trusting mind, completely incomprehensible. I'd always been naturally affectionate. Holding it back, keeping myself in in the name of chastity, and then seeing others trample all over my natural sensibilities, was more agonising to me than any number of early mornings and portions of dry bread. Was I not doing as I was told? Was I not wholehearted and sincere? Where was I falling short? Why did Elizabeth hate it if you felt too deeply or tried too hard?

If, as a postulant, Carmel had given me answers, now that I was a novice the questions were proliferating. What had seemed so simple, a charism based on the hermit ideal, a life secluded and apart, one of dedicated prayer and self-offering, was now revealing its mental dangers, occupational hazards of a life strung between two extremes: the human and the divine, the material and the spiritual, the hard and the soft. In theory these opposites were supposed to blend and intermingle, as in the mingling of God and man in Christ. In reality, we lived a community life divided between those 'too spiritual to be any earthly good' and those who prided themselves on their ordinariness and practicality. These latter, rugged characters, were not always above expressions of scorn, and, as time went on (sad to say) of spite. I had been brought up to be conciliatory and turn the other cheek, even without Catholicism. As a result it could not but hurt to find among these exemplary believers people who had been pro-grammed to do the opposite. It was deeply confusing. I had come among them looking to their shining lead.

Circling the lake, crossing the brick bridge, staring at the unending sky, listening to the wood pigeons in the trees, all of this was a way of unplugging the mind from an increas-ingly claustrophobic human landscape. Sometimes my tears would fall, and I'd shudder with repressed emotion in a woody copse. Sometimes I'd reach out for divine love among the trees, but end up sobbing, realising how much I still missed my father. Was it just 'Dad love' that was at the hub of my vocation? Nothing but a way of coping with grief? Was I merely making a virtue of the fact of recent loss and loneliness? Was I looking to an eternal horizon, or was I just running away from life? If the latter, was it too late to turn the clock back, to have another go at being fully human?

16. Lemonade

It was the week before Palm Sunday, and we were preparing to go into community retreat. Every year at Holy Week the atmosphere in the main house, already hushed but for the odd bell, drew itself in like a cat curling itself into a basket and falling asleep. At such a time, the softness in the air could feel like balm, an invisible unction you could almost touch, or breathe, so comforting was it to our sometimes raw and jangled nerves. Even contemplative nuns need times apart in deeper solitude and silence than the daily grind permits. Even novices need a break from their instructions.

'Oi, Sister Catherine!' Jen burst into the novitiate. 'Oi! Coo-ee! Sister Catherine! Cathy! Fliss! Ems! Anybody there?'

I looked up and smiled. There'd been talk of Jen's family visiting in the parlour that afternoon, and today she was in one of her cheerful moods, which was a relief. You never knew whether you were going to get her jolly side, which – even if it felt a little forced – was preferable to her moodiness. And we all had our ups and downs.

'Have they arrived?' I asked.

'*Deo gratias, Deo gratias*, sister, cake ahoy! Dad's brought some custard doughnuts and my sister's just gone back to her car to get some cake and lemonade! She's brought five bottles. Yeah, yeah, yeah . . .' She was crashing about, making banging noises with the furniture.

Mother Elizabeth appeared in the doorway, laughing. Two

of the cats were playing in the interconnecting yard, chasing a ball of yellow wool she had put out for them.

'Oi, you!' Jennifer addressed the smaller, more skittish cat. 'Leave off!'

'It's good for them to interact,' Elizabeth murmured.

'Go on, scarper!' Jen said, rushing at them with her arms. She loved a joke, did Jen, even if it was not funny. But the novelty of a family parlour put most people in a slightly exalted mood.

Mother Elizabeth hovered, waiting to accompany her for the event. 'I'll be spending the first half hour of novitiate with Jennifer's family, today, Sister Catherine,' she said. 'But then I'll leave her with them for a while. I'll be along after that, and the two of us can have a little chat. It's been a long while now, hasn't it?'

This was a first. A touch of warmth. The recognition I might want (or need) to see her. A reaching out. She even seemed to smile right at me.

'A chance for us to catch up!' she added.

Yes, she meant it. This was indeed light on the horizon. I was pinching myself at the thought of having Elizabeth all to myself for a proper conversation, after so many thwarted meetings, so many disappointing weeks and months. Usually, she only had time to see the other novices on the Saturdays when we'd line up outside her office in order of religion for our slot. The queue would go down, until the bell would ring while Jennifer was still in there, and Mother would realise she would have to put me off until next week. By the time next week came, anything might have happened, and it was usually a case of back to square one. My own efforts at self-effacement were taking their toll.

I took out my copy of *The Interior Castle* by St Teresa and

looked up La Madre's classic account of her own inner struggles, her battles with the world, the flesh and the devil, those
enemies we were all called resolutely to rebuff. But the possibility of vows was all I could think about, given the season
and the sense of anticipation I'd been feeling in recent weeks.
It was nearly a year since our Clothing, which meant, according to the Constitutions, that the junior novitiate period in the
habit was up, and that we should now be eligible to take our
temporary vows, to be 'professed'. I turned over the satisfyingly neat word: *vows*. So small and crisp and clean. So potent
for its tiny size, like the point of a sword. But it was also a
word of heft and unknowability, and of massive implications.
In some ways it was a frightening word.

'Obedience is by far the hardest of the vows,' Barbara had
once commented. 'You might not notice it at first,' she'd
gone on, 'being new and fervent – ha ha! At least some of
you are! – but those comfortable early feelings never last.'

Jen had shrugged and murmured, said it was 'bad enough
already', and then a long discussion kicked off about the transience of the honeymoon period of the religious life. Sister
Barbara was testy, repeating the refrain that it normally gets
much harder later on. And then I'd thought, *this* honeymoon
period will last. *This* honeymoon won't wear off. My love
affair with God will last for ever. Barbara had then skimmed
over chastity and poverty, the other two vows, which were
seen as dependent on obedience, the primary and 'most difficult' one.

At last, I heard brisk footsteps in the covered walkway,
and looked up as the door was opening. Mother Elizabeth
swished in, her soft brown habit as mobile as a ballgown,
her face hot and pink from the novelty and excitement of
the parlour. She was brushing herself down, ensuring it was

free of crumbs, and straightening her veil as she approached, then took up her place at the big oblong table. Her demeanour was always so poised, so different from that of bustling Barbara or soft-spoken Ellen. In spite of myself, and of my best intentions, I found her fascinating but also completely unfathomable. She was both hard and soft, both friendly and reserved. How did she manage it? Something in me wanted to rush towards her, to get beyond formalities and to befriend her, to know her as she really was. But that kind of naturalness – was the word intimacy? – was contrary to the spirit of the Life. She was always telling soft people like me to 'stand on their own two feet'. If I dared show any emotion I would be rebuked. So no, I decided, I would make efforts to control myself, hold everything in, and present as serene and perfect a face as possible.

'Ah, well,' she began, as though following up some prior thought, while looking around. 'It's all very tidy in here, Catherine. Well done. The novitiate is not looking too bad at the moment. Is this your Sweep?'

'No, Mother,' I replied, surprised she didn't know it was Emily's patch. It was she, Elizabeth, after all, who allocated all our jobs. 'The antechoir and the top passage are my Sweeps at the moment.'

'Oh yes. That's it. The antechoir. And – how's it going?'

'Oh, it's fine. I have to allow a lot more time for cleaning on Saturdays than I used to, as it can take quite a while, and the tom-poms get clogged very easily.'

'Ah, the tom-poms! You've got used to our traditional cleaning implements by now, I trust?'

'Oh yes!' And I went on to explain how happy I was to be using such wholesome old-fashioned methods such as these primitive rag-and-stick brooms, and what a relief it was not to have noisy things like Hoovers banging around the place.

'Oh yes. I think they have Hoovers . . . at Mellerby,' she said. 'Hmm. And, and – how's the asthma?'

'I'm managing OK, although it's always worse in warmer weather, with all the pollen in the air. And on cleaning days, with all the dust . . .'

The clock ticked loudly as the half hour allocated to our chat neared its close.

'Anything else? Anything worrying you?' Elizabeth tilted her head. Her manner was more amenable than usual, and something suggested it might be all right, after all, to ask about the plans for our profession.

'Well, yes, Mother. I was just wondering about . . . um . . . wondering whether there was any news about our vows,' I said, looking up. It was a risk, but I had to get this out there. 'I've been wondering whether it might be quite soon? This Eastertide, perhaps?'

There was a horrible moment when I thought I saw something like shock, or fear, and strange changes move across Elizabeth's wary, sapphire eyes. She looked down in some confusion. There was something wrong, I could tell.

'I know, Mother, of course, that we have to be voted for by the chapter,' I said, 'and . . . and I do realise it has to be God's will, and that we can't take it for granted. But . . .'

'But you didn't realise?' Mother Elizabeth flushed quite violently. 'You mean . . . you didn't know?'

'Didn't know what?' I said.

'Has no one said anything?'

'Said what?'

'Do you mean, Catherine – do you mean you *have not been told*?'

My heart was banging loudly now. I'd worked ruthlessly at the art of continual restraint. But naturally it was all in there, the emotion, swimming around under the surface. Swirling. Storming. All those normal, natural human feelings. My eyes were prickling. Everything in me yearned for even a flicker of Mother's friendly interest, her humanity, or at least some token of her acceptance. I'd prayed, I'd waited, I'd dared to hope . . .

'Oh dear, I am so sorry,' Mother said.

'Sorry?' This was another first, Reverend Mother looking apologetic.

'I'm so sorry you've not been told about this, Catherine. It . . . it was the decision of the voting chapter, you see, some months ago. We discerned it best to keep you both back for another year. Sister Jennifer was not feeling ready for it, you see. And she—'

'A year,' I said. It was already a statement, not a question. 'I see. Another . . .'

Mother nodded. 'A year.'

'I see,' I said again, more quietly.

'Oh dear. Really, someone should have told you, of course. I thought Sister Ellen or Sister Barbara, perhaps, might have passed it on. Or even Sister Jennifer, as she's over you in the novitiate, isn't she? I assumed she'd have told you. But, er . . . yes, there we are.'

I was blinking hard by now. So, there we were.

'Since you both entered together, and then received the habit on the same day, we felt that to split you apart now might not be the best way forward. Sister Jennifer needs to be egged on and encouraged. She needs to feel boosted up, made to feel valued and important. You see, Sister Catherine, she doesn't have your poise and confidence.'

Now, this really was confusing. I wondered what on earth Our Mother was talking about. Confidence? Needing to be boosted up? What did any of this have to do with anything? Weren't we supposed to be making ourselves small and insignificant, the 'least of all'? Wasn't Mother always pushing us away, testing us for humility, teaching us lessons about not getting above ourselves? As for confidence, Jen was the noisy, bossy one, always putting herself forward, always demanding attention. Anyway, what did the word even mean, and why on earth did it matter to us as Carmelites? I had barely given 'confidence' a thought.

'Yes, Sister Catherine, you probably feel you are ready to take your vows. And, who knows, perhaps you are. We all know that you are keen. But if you'd gone ahead of Jen it might have made her feel outstripped, you know . . .' Elizabeth looked round as though searching for the right word. Then she lowered her voice to a croak: 'She's very easily discouraged, you see, and it wouldn't do for her to feel she's not doing well. Not everyone copes well with playing second fiddle.'

For a few seconds my world was spinning. I was utterly incredulous. I'd swallowed Thomas à Kempis, and all the classic teachings. I did not congratulate myself for trying to 'imitate Christ', on the contrary I believed I was fulfilling a simple instruction, one that applied equally to all of us. Had I misunderstood something? Mother Elizabeth was looking red-faced and uncomfortable. For the first time I'd seen her acknowledge a dereliction of her duty. Yes, she'd always been deeply uninvolved in anything to do with my progress, appearing totally aloof. But God works in mysterious ways, I'd always told myself. And now . . .

'It went to the vote before Christmas,' she added. 'The

outcome is determinative, of course – as you know. And, given what we knew about Jen, we all thought . . .'

Yes, I didn't need her to complete the sentence, I knew what they all thought. And who could blame them? I had demonstrated an unvarying and smiling acceptance of every-thing from Day One, had hidden all my natural thoughts and feelings about these things so successfully, they must have thought I'd be bound to smile and say nothing. Must have thought I'd be no trouble, would go along with whatever was decided or asked of me. Yes, I was seen as tearful and emo-tional in many ways – a cry-baby – but not in those ways that suggested a lack of acceptance or compliance. My emotions were seen more as the euphoric or constitutional weaknesses of an 'artistic nature'.

'Be accepting, sister, and you will save souls,' Mother finally said as she got up to leave. 'I know it's a disappoint-ment, but make a clean sacrifice of it. Offer it up, as you've been taught, and as Our Lady would have offered her own setbacks in her life at Nazareth. By accepting this setback you can purify yourself, can cooperate with Christ in saving the world. That's how it works. And then we can look at your situation again next year. Until then, just keep on praying and working. Just keep on keeping on.'

And so, it seemed my prayer had been answered. I'd wanted to live for God alone, and now I was discovering what that tasted like, all support denied, all warmth withheld, while so manifestly given to another. With this reversal began a new phase in my monastic life, a more decidedly inward-looking one, during which I'd make sure to take my innermost hopes and feelings far, far away from everybody, to become more truly insular, a hermit, alone with God. I would use this extra year as a time of deeper dedication, and of more decided solitude, and would ask God to bring me through it as whole-hearted as ever, by his grace.

'Do not try to understand or to question the vote or the decision of the chapter,' Ellen said later that day. 'Mortify everything within you that is not of God, and let Him alone show you the way. No one and nothing else should matter to you. Hand your will over to the Lord, and let God decide your future for you. Just as Emily and Felicity, who made their temporary vows before you entered, are now awaiting providence to decide their futures, let God alone decide yours. Remember no one can run before they can walk.' She smiled one of her elusive smiles, flushing as she did so, and started gathering up some brown cardboard boxes full of altar breads. In a corner another sister was writing a note, not acknowledging our presence, all exactly as was normal during working hours. Outside, I could see Sister Alison working the edges of the meadow with a strimmer, while in the distance an older sister slowly pushed a wheelbarrow. I thought of Fliss and Emily, and of how much they said they hoped to make their final vows, those that would bind them and keep them here for life. What did it feel like, I wondered, to be like them, almost on the brink of the point of no return? Was it a bit like getting married, full of joy, or more like a slow procession to the guillotine?

That night we had lemonade at recreation. People were busy with their little works and the room was thrumming. Everyone knew that Sister Jennifer's family had visited. The banging door and bursts of conversation from the parlour had filtered into the corridors during the afternoon. There'd been some cause for hilarity, but only Mother knew about it, as part of the gathering. People noticed irregularities like this, but no one commented. All kept their eyes down.

'Before the end of the evening we were regaled with

Mother's account of the day, including the impromptu tea party, cake with Jen's family, and various pieces of associated news. Everyone did their best to be polite and interested, and the day was rounded off with talk of 'those pests', the feral cats, of which Our Mother seemed so fond.

'They made a right mess of that ball of wool,' Jennifer exclaimed.

'But it's good for us to have them around,' Mother said.

'No need to encourage them quite so much, surely?' someone chipped in.

'They really should be house-trained,' said Sister Ruth.

'We can't keep tidying up after them,' said Sister Alison.

'I know, it's one of my foibles, but – I do like the cats,' Mother replied, 'and of course we need them to deal with rodents.' She shuddered, adding: 'Without them we'd be overrun!' Then she rang the little, tinkling hand-bell for silence and the procession to the evening Office.

'We already are,' someone whispered, putting away her knitting. 'With cats.'

But Mother was not listening.

In choir, ten minutes later, the chant was flowing softly. Heads were down, voices modulated to the simple psalm tone. '*Oh Lord, remember David, and all the many hardships he endured. The oath he swore to the Lord, his vow to the Strong One of Jacob.*' We sang it a cappella, the sound rising like an uneasy sea to the vaulted ceiling. It was still light outside. But now my voice was failing and my vision was obscured. It was the words that set me off, I told myself. The words and the undulating, soft music, the atmosphere of absolute perfection. It was all too much for me, such beauty, such happiness, such pain. My eyes and my cheeks were stinging. The tears were rolling down my cheeks.

17. The Vows

Poverty. Chastity. Obedience. The vows. We'd talked about them for months, dreamed of them for years. How many was it – two already? Soon the disappointment that I'd felt on being restrained, held back from running where I felt the wind of the spirit might be leading, waned and settled back into the gentle lull and exigency of our daily lives. The rhythm of the seasons, of the garden and of the Mere, danced with the patterns of the liturgy, the symbolic seasons of the Church's life. Interwoven with these two strands was the thread of our lives as a community, the nod of sister to sister in the corridor, the notes left lingering on the hall table, or passed under a door, the fingers raised to lips, the veiled expressions. Mysteries to each other, we glided past, eyes down, personalities barely touching except for the half hour of recreation, or the hour each day spent in the novitiate if you were still in, or involved in, the process of formation. The weeks and months flew past, yet at the heart of every-thing was a timelessness, a sense of being set apart, cloistered, listening for the sound of silence, looking on.

'You need to take the bull by the horns,' Elizabeth said one day, when she realised I was losing some of my initial élan. Until recently, the thought of vows would have had me feeling all legless and fluttery, in a good way, but now the prospect was looking just a little daunting. Mother, of course, was used to people wavering after a while (naturally you can't keep poised to dive for ever) and she had her catchphrases at the ready.

'This is what you signed up for, Sister Catherine. Total renunciation. Now you just need to get on with it. Nothing's changed.'

Objectively, nothing had. I was just a lot closer to the reality of vows, and everything looks different when seen from close-up. Stare at the back of your hand long enough and it will morph before your eyes. Now we really were in the run-up to profession, and to these three great surrenders that were supposed to cover every aspect and dimension of the human experience. The three vowed areas went deep, touching the marrow, but they also overlapped, creating one seamless network of supposed selflessness. The theory was that in giving up our power to possess or control things we were affirming our dependence on a provider God. This was poverty. In renouncing a disordered or exclusive love of creatures (mainly other human beings) we were saving our all for the creator, our spouse, loving him with 'all our heart and soul and strength'. This was chastity. And in submitting our wills to the highest good, mediated through the prioress, God's representative, we were making ourselves wholly available for God's inscrutable purposes. Becoming not only brides but slaves of the Most High. This was obedience.

It all folded together, like a beautiful, translucent piece of origami. Where one vow overlapped with, or faded into, another you could see interesting subsets of each category. Was refraining from stroking a cat poverty (not owning or having the right to touch the cat), or chastity (renunciation of 'luxury' and sensuality – those nice, silky, affectionate feelings), or was it obedience (we all knew we were not meant to touch the damn things)? It was satisfyingly all three. The lover of logic and symmetry in me, the lover of Bach, enjoyed the thought that my whole life could now become as integrated, as united and directed to one final cadence as the *Musical Offering*. Although I sometimes wondered whether I'd missed a trick by not joining the Missionaries of Charity, a radical order of nuns famous for their work with the homeless and dying on the streets of Calcutta, nuns I'd volunteered with in London, I'd somewhere along the line accepted that a life dedicated to God in prayer and sacrifice was a higher form of generosity.

The novitiate sessions were intensifying. Mother Elizabeth was now attending more frequently (thank goodness!) and making time to see us for sessions on Carmelite spirituality on Saturday afternoons, when she would expect us to kneel at her side and recite the list of our recent Faults. These breast-beatings were different from Confession, when we'd dig a bit deeper and the priest would give us absolution (the Church's official forgiveness, on behalf of Christ). They were more akin to the community examen at Compline, when people would announce to the world that they had dropped a bowl, or whispered in the corridor. One night Alison had set us all off by saying she'd lost the nozzle to the hosepipe, and the ripples of suppressed laughter ended up a tidal wave, sisters shuddering uncontrollably and mopping their eyes, unable to get another word out, until Elizabeth had disbanded the whole operation. There was always something suppressed, waiting to erupt. Random laughter was a wonderful way of defusing such emotions and it probably did us all a lot of good.

Listing our Faults, beating our breasts and saying we Would Do Better, was a way of life, intricately tied in with the virtue of humility. This was seen as the foundational virtue, the 'mother' of all the other good qualities we were praying for and supposed to be acquiring. Long were the hours we spent studying Mary, Mother of God, many were the prayers sent up to her, our Mirror of Perfection. Each morning we knelt before her whitewashed statue in the chequerboard hall, mumbling into our rosaries, each afternoon we called on her to 'show us' her beloved son, and each evening we entrusted ourselves to her purity and perfection.

Sexual inclinations, obviously, had to be most decisively rebuffed. Although we made a lot of the virtue of chastity (by public declaration) it was the least openly discussed of the vows, and the one most surrounded by awkward feelings. No one asked the really probing questions, but we all understood implicitly that any deliberate indulgence in carnal pleasure, of whatever sort, was so unthinkable that you'd rather die than succumb. You just did not go there. As with all the virtues, and their opposite vices, the first beginnings of an act, whether positive or negative, began in the mind – in thought, in will, in memory and imagination. It followed then that the 'purification' of our most natural thoughts was deemed necessary. John of the Cross wrote extensively on this, describing how the caverns of the soul would be filled with God once the consuming fire of his love had destroyed everything else. Nothing was to stand in the way of God possessing us. No love, no object, no other obstacle.

Mother Elizabeth loved the word 'loyalty'. It was a bright, sparkly word with a sapphire glow, perhaps because of its assonance with 'royalty'. Elizabeth would toss it up into the air, and we saw how it spun and how – glinting blue and purple – it caught the light. I have to admit, I had my doubts about it. It seemed to me a little too self-referential. The object of loyalty was always something proximate, socially defined, rather like medieval fealty. It was usually a club, society or person, and had vested human interests at its heart. It was not quite a case of loyalty for loyalty's sake, or that I felt it had gone out of date – people would always need friends and family who would stand by them – but that, in spiritual terms, it did not go far enough. As a virtue, it was less liberating than faith, less 'prophetic'.

Religious people tend either to be of the 'club-minded' or the 'heavenly-minded' sort, and a study of scripture and the history of the Church gives us exemplars of both. The prophets – literally 'mouthpieces for God' – are those concerned with the big-picture stuff, the building blocks like 'eternity' and 'transcendence', and are conscious of being called to speak for God. A prophet is concerned with uttering truth, whether of present or future concerns, and has the courage of their convictions, is prepared to speak truth to power. Many of the originators of and reformers within the great religions had a prophetic stance, which is why so few were popular with the higher-ups. The club-minded, on the other hand, speak primarily as approved by the human collective of which they are part. They may repeat truths learned or heard elsewhere, but there is always a cap on how far they can go in saying what they really think. The loyal are guided by human leaders. Prophets are guided by their search for truth. You could say they are loyal only to the truth.

In Mother's book the human quality of loyalty stood cheek by jowl with the divine habit of obedience. One sensed the two had almost been welded together to form an alloy, like one of those base metals that are so supple and convenient to work with. At times the alloy might glint as bright as gold, or look like silver, but the reality was there was another element running through it, a pragmatism and desire that things should function, merely 'work', rather than be authentic. It was more important for her that the community and its separate members should cope, manage, succeed, should keep afloat, rather than draw closer to the truth. Truth was not something she ever seemed interested in. To some extent we were all adept at pretending, since it was considered a virtue to smile if you felt sad, and to hide all emotional disturbance. If it was a lie to pretend you liked everybody equally, and to shower praise on the things you secretly deplored, we were all liars.

If I had felt held back intellectually as a novice, and if our mistress had shown little interest in exploring ideas, or talking with us in depth about the finer points and problems of theology, where the vow of obedience was concerned she was both forthcoming and implacable. It was a simple and straightforward vow. It was unambiguous.

'It's an unbloody sacrifice,' she said, conjuring up dreadful images of ancient Rome.

'It's a living sacrifice,' Sister Ellen added, echoing St Paul.

'It's about doing what you're told,' Barbara added, ever brisk and business-like. 'The main thing is, you are giving up your own way of thinking about everything, Catherine. Everything. You are not just giving up your life, you are offering up your will.'

In theory none of this was problematic for me. I'd devoured Kierkegaard's *Purity of Heart Is to Will One Thing* long ago, back in London in the fallout from the funeral. I had been searching, profoundly open, welcoming the light his writings beamed around my mind. I had always been drawn to strong solutions, had an innate streak of both rebel and philosopher in my nature. I wasn't ever going to be comfortable following the crowd. And so I'd run with the idea of total surrender, sought out every church and book and prophet to instruct me until all roads had really seemed to lead to Rome – and further yet, into the heart of the cloister. Now I was there, facing the logical implications of my choices, an unfamiliar wavering was beginning to shake me to the core. I looked around me and saw, not an obviously compatible group of people, a gathering of the like-minded or of the sympathetically attuned, but an angular collective, one with resistant areas and awkward bumps, a motley crew. Fishermen, Mother had once said. Fishermen. Remember the people Jesus chose as his first disciples.

Mother Elizabeth was having a dig at what, in her eyes, was my problematic background. It was liberal, it was north London, it did not count in her book as standard stuff. I had realised there was some elusive common denominator we were all tacitly supposed to be conforming to, but I also felt instinctively that this was an unsatisfyingly unexamined category, Elizabeth's own projection or mirage. What was 'normal' and what was 'ordinary', and were we meant to pick it up by osmosis? What if our ordinary and normal were different from hers? Did that make them any less valid? What if my life outside had been nothing like she imagined it? After all, what did she really know? Was ordinariness something to do with being unchallenging? Did she just want us to be intellectually easy-going and controllable?

When Barbara had said 'You are not just giving up your life, you are offering up your will,' she was enunciating a well-known principle, one of the core demands of monasticism. But how did this sit with the apparently contradictory insistence we should 'be ourselves', and again with Elizabeth's completely unexamined assumptions about what would go down well with 'the young of today'? She'd been in the cloister for decades! And if I'd spent my life before coming to Carmel being myself, wasn't I supposed to be doing something different now?

It was important I conceal any sudden waverings, that much was clear. If there were new understandings rushing in on me, vertiginous new perceptions of what it was that I was taking on, if things seemed stacked against me, so much the better. I could be a proper martyr now. It was too late to look back. It was too late to have second thoughts. I'd come, pledging myself on the altar of God's will. I'd done my best. I'd been disappointed at the delay of a year. Now the prospect of self-offering was really before me, everything now in the balance, it would be madness to turn and run. Our job, as dedicated religious sisters, was to stand firm, to remain with Mary at the foot of the cross.

'The will,' Sister Barbara went on, 'is the volitional centre of the human person. It is the most precious thing we have to offer to God, an offering that reverses the sin of Eve. By the surrender of it we glorify Him most fully and absolutely. Even though we failed the test when we opted for disobedience, in the garden . . .'

Her voice trailed off as I sat and gazed out of the window. Was my attention wandering? The afternoons were still dark and cold; it was the tail-end of the year, not yet Christmas. There were a few months to go till our vows, and the uplift of Advent and of the carol service ahead of us. All that wonderful music would be bound to lift me out of any temporary despondency. Something must have unsettled me, but I'd soon regain my poise.

A couple of weeks later, I was in the novitiate one black morning, scrabbling around looking for my outdoor shoes, when Emily burst in, her face red, her eyes streaming.

'I knew they were going to do this to me!' she blurted. 'I could see it coming.'

'Oh no!' I said, reaching out. 'I'm so sorry.'

'Too late for fine feelings now, Cath, they've dumped me. Voted me out. There's nothing anyone can do. Sister Barbara broke the news to me last night. Ice cold, she was. Said I was "not sufficiently surrendered" or "at the disposal of the community". Something like that. Some formality or other to justify washing their hands of me. "Surrendered" . . .'

She was in full flow, and just carried on emptying her locker, thinking aloud while throwing out her books. 'Mother Birmingham warned me, actually. You know, that time I met her at the Maryvale Conferences while I was still outside? She said, "If you know it's not going to work out, don't let them string you along. No point hanging around doing their housework for them if you know they're only going to reject you later on. That's unpaid labour. It's exploitation." Keeping me on right up to the last minute, without telling me. I had a feeling this was going to happen, but they should've told me earlier, let me walk free. But you know what – I've not forgotten Mother Birmingham, and what she said: "Emily, darling, your heart's in the right place, and you can always come to us if it doesn't work out at Akenside."'

'Gosh, Emily, I had no idea. This is so unexpected . . .' I was trying to find the right words. Trying also to imagine how she was feeling. While it was seen as a disaster, or last resort, to consider leaving, you could be thrown out at any time up until your final vows. The feelings associated with being 'sent away', not deemed adequate, were bound to be different from those associated with choosing to walk a different path. Was there a part of me that envied her? Saw her new beginning as an opportunity, a chance for her to flourish? If there was, I certainly suppressed it and offered her the most appropriate words I could find.

'I'm so sorry, Emily, so sorry – and we will miss you. The novitiate won't be the same,' I said. 'But you never know. God works in mysterious ways. Perhaps Birmingham is where you're meant to be? Mother Birm sounds really supportive . . .'

'Doesn't make it any easier, Cath. The rejection. Honest, if they'd let me go earlier, I'd have had a chance to sort my life out. Get on with it while I still had things going for me. Who knows? I'm nearly thirty-two. Birmingham may not work out, but . . . you know what, I'll give it my best shot. I haven't thrown away the best years of my life for nothing.'

I could see that Ems was galvanised, transformed, already practical and forward-thinking. She was in determined sur-vival mode. At the same time, everything about her was in a state of turmoil. Finally, I managed to calm her, and she heard my words of reassurance.

'I know they won't let you write to me, Cath, but . . . if you ever wanted, needed to find me, for whatever reason – try Birmingham Carmel.' Her voice cracked.

'I will,' I told her, and reached out my arms to hug her, in a moment of naturalness. What did it matter now? I could smell the salt on her, feel the wet of tears on her cheek as our faces brushed for a moment, then repositioned into a sisterly embrace that felt so strange, yet so natural and supportive. We held it for the length of a doxology, half a minute. Releas-ing was slow and awkward, accompanied by a soft relief.

'With any luck,' she added, choking back her tears. 'Fin-gers crossed.'

And with that we drew apart, sensing we'd crossed a small line, but that – given the circumstances, and the overriding claim of fellow feeling – it really didn't matter. I'd shown her kindness, and she'd spoken her mind. In an hour or two she would be gone.

Emily was too pretty, too concerned with small personal niceties – having the right kind of wellington boots, the right vests, that sway of the hips. It was all unconscious, of course, but then so was the prejudice of the stalwarts who saw her as lightweight because she couldn't help being charming or looking nice. We were all gigglers, but Emily giggled more giddily than all of us, even more than Jen (who didn't so much giggle as roar out loud). I felt sorry for her. Mother mocked her singing style – and Jen joined in – because it was a bit 'pop-py', it was true, and yes, it didn't quite fit in. But at least it wasn't loud or out of tune, and I felt the charity of forbearance should have applied here as it applied in other far more trying areas. Anyway. We all saw each other, and the facts and figures of our Life, through different lenses. The vows were meant to bring us all into one dedicated line, like an army, were meant to free us from singularity and self-interest. They were a high ideal, a narrow door, something to concentrate the mind. If the thought of them sometimes frightened me, I reminded myself that what lay behind them all was love, pure and simple. God's love for us and ours for him.

18. The Wishing

It was nearing the darkest point in the year, and frost lay caked on the toolshed roof, and the 'O Antiphons' had begun. As anyone familiar with the Roman liturgy well knows, the O Antiphons, sung in the run-up to Christmas, represent one of the most atmospheric and expectant moments in the yearly cycle of chants and readings. Sung to special Advent tones at Vespers, and so named because each day's text begins with the vocative 'O', they usher in a sense of grand and holy wonder mixed with pleading.

'*O Adonai!*' we sang into the candlelit dark, calling on the God of Moses to 'redeem us with outstretched arm'. He'd managed to appear in a burning bush for the benefit of his original chosen people, had done his bit with lightning and wild terror on Mount Sinai to set the record straight. Wasn't there anything he could do for us? Or even for weary little me, I wondered, as each of us had probably done at times. We all so much *wanted* to be cloistered, sequestered apart for him, wanted to be his new elect, brides set aside for his inscrutable purposes. 'Come on, Lord,' we seemed to say, 'we're counting on you to do your stuff. Come on, dear Heavenly Friend, and Do Not Tarry.'

But tarry he did. How much longer were we supposed to hold our breaths and wait for the grand unveiling, the promised moment when 'peace shall over all the earth its ancient splendours fling' – the midnight hour when our spouse and saviour would appear, illuminated among angelic trumpets in the heavens? Was the Second Coming ever going to take place? Would mere mortals like us ever live to 'hear the angels sing'? Sometimes you really wondered.

'Get me up there,' I heard someone say under her breath one afternoon in the darkened toolshed. 'Get me up there.' The words were weighted. Who was it, muttering under the scythes and billhooks? I coughed and made a shuffling noise to alert the poor sister to my presence. 'Get me out of here' might have been her more exact thought, but there were standard ways of filtering and rewording things, and choosing the correct nuance was important. 'Get me up there' was the other side of the 'mourning and weeping in this vale of tears' coin. 'Get me up there' was theological hope. I admired the sentiment, and made more effort to look forward to the end-point that was life after death. Wouldn't it be lovely? But there were times when you felt death itself would be happiness enough.

Still, the light shining in the darkness would come among us anew at Christmas, and the angels would sing over the humble stables of our lives. Jen and Fliss and I would put up the crib together, traditionally a novices' task, starting with our going out with wheelbarrows to collect holly and ivy from the many sprawling trees and bushes around the grounds. It was always an early start, after Little Jug, and we'd stop off at the toolshed and get trussed up. Anoraks, wellies and an extra layer of protection over our heads, a gardening veil. Out we'd go, the sky still half dark, the frost not yet melted. Back we'd come with barrow after barrow of greenery, bearing the odd wound, a scratch from the holly bushes, random bruises on our shins. The crib in the antechoir was the main one, taking up half the room and with life-size models of Jesus, Mary and the *bambino*, the holy child who'd come among us to calm our fears. Each year we'd try to do it slightly differently, with mounds of hay in one corner on one occasion, and yards of hessian from the loft, crumpled and arranged to create the illusion of a cave, on another. The hessian was an original touch. We were nothing if not resourceful. Everything would be topped off with tinsel and a string of fairy lights.

The celebration of the feast was preceded by the annual Christmas 'wishing', a formality when we all lined up and wished each other Happy Christmas. Wishings also occurred on other big events, most notably at professions and on Easter Sunday, amid candles and a blaze of blue and yellow flowers. We dressed up in our best ceremony *alpargatas*, the homemade rope sandals modelled on those worn by St Teresa of Ávila, and donned our heavy cream cloaks, normally reserved for Mass, the most sacred of all the sacred ceremonies.

I always spent far too long looking forward to the winter wishing, which was one of the two or three annual opportunities for a hug, however restrained. The rest of the time physical contact was entirely eliminated by a range of customs that saw to it that no sister got within touching distance of another. Even if proximity was unavoidable, everyone would know to avoid even the brush of a fingertip along the back, or arm, or shoulder. Each of us was surrounded by an aura and a sacred space that told others to keep well away. We fostered it. We cooperated with its demands. That was the hermit charism. I'd accepted it in principle, wanting to keep my heart pure and entire for Jesus alone, but that didn't mean that in practice it was easy. Living without any expression of human affection was something that got harder the longer it went on, until the surface of your skin felt somehow stretched and starved, and your heart ached for a kind word, a smile, some sign that you were not entirely on your own under the endless sky.

How far an occasional squeeze might have gone to help things along! But because personal touches, and particular friendships especially, were out, hugs also had to go. Mother always had to be there, presiding, and keeping a watchful eye on proceedings. If being human required that we do messy things like 'congratulate' each other, the least we could do was make it as inhuman as possible. That was all bound up with Carmelite asceticism. We were at war with fallen human nature, just as we were at war with ourselves.

At last, the day came around, and the expected lining up in order of religion had begun. There I was in my festive cloak and pristine footwear, now one space closer to Our Mother, since Emily's departure, although still at the back of the queue.

'Who's left?' she called out over the festive hubbub. 'Who haven't I done?'

Most had by now reached the top of the line, and been administered the chill clamp of the fingertips that passed for a hug in Mother's book. She was famously 'not a huggy person' but still had to do her duty as Our Mother. Once she had 'hugged' you, you were free to hug whoever you liked, and the sisters dissolved into a general melee with everyone wishing everyone else a Happy Christmas, laughing and chattering. It was one of the few occasions of the year when a party mode took over, and the recreation room filled to overflowing with simultaneous talk and random exclamations. It was meant to be a happy time. You were meant to enjoy it.

People were milling everywhere by now, passing on the greeting and generally getting into the mood. You were meant to hug every single person, from the oldest to the youngest, exchanging pleasantries, showing what a good 'community person' you were. Finally, the Advent waiting was over! It was time to celebrate! But hugging, in Carmel, was a stilted affair. There was quite an art to it, this going through the motions associated with warmth and human affection, while being sure to show no real closeness or natural emotion. You made sure the hug you gave was expressive of just the right degree of friendliness, while withholding anything that might be deemed too familiar.

Mother was pretending not to have seen me, and was still looking round, her chin raised as though scanning the room for stragglers. Everyone knew the ritual was a burdensome duty for her. Was it that she feared to show too much pleasure in the process because she feared whatever currents lay beneath the surface, or did she really hate it as much as she made out? In any other area where you were required to do something you didn't like, you made efforts not to show your natural distaste. When Mother Elizabeth squirmed flamboyantly at the mere mention of giving and receiving hugs, you wondered: was she protesting too much, or were we all supposed to be as cold and unfeeling as she was? Was hating hugs meant to be as natural to Carmelites as loving them was to nearly everybody else on the planet?

I was by now sandwiched between moving bodies. Comments were being traded across the room, the words 'Happy Christmas' being let off like corks. The awareness of how much I longed even for a fleeting sense of warmth and closeness was making me feel apprehensive. And then finally I was there, the last in the queue, standing right in front of Mother Elizabeth. I tried to master a whole panoply of feelings. Was she going to fold me kindly in her arms? Of course not, and

I had been so wrong to hope. Just as I held out my arms she swivelled her head in exactly the opposite direction and began talking to someone – Oh, it was Jen – and to laugh with her, making a brittle sound, while (it seemed to me, pointedly) making a big thing of ignoring me. I shrank within the circle of her non-embrace, shrivelled into a painful puddle, aching more than ever. Was she not human? Had she no courtesy or kindness? She had not even looked me in the face.

'Is that everyone?' she called out with steely determination and something like relief, looking beyond me. 'Is that everyone? All done? Have I forgotten anybody?'

Yes, all done. But she had not even registered my existence. It was a conveyor-belt Christmas wishing. In some ways it was a punitive one. Fake jollity was never a substitute for the real thing. Everywhere there were moving bodies, bulky cream cloaks, long black veils, the swish of habit hems and the familiar brush of semi-silent footwear in a labyrinth of movement around the room. All our usual restraints were ostensibly lifted while actually remaining as rigidly in place as ever. What was this charade? Soon Mother would be asking us to sit while she 'said a few words', and while she opened the cards that had arrived – from Mellerby, from Holton and from a smattering of parishioners – or been dropped off by priests in the extern. Soon she would be passing on news, and a selection of greetings from the other Carmels. She might even pass around a photo someone had sent in.

I vanished to the humble office to cry, and was not missed for the twenty minutes that I sat sobbing there into my enormous handkerchief. My mouth was dry. We had not yet had our Little Jug. My hands were raw, the chapped skin deeply cracked around the knuckles. Last year's tiny Christmas tub of Vaseline had almost run out. And there was still holly to be gathered from the garden. Then the blood came, a flood of sticky red, filling the vitreous china bowl. It was a miserable start to any Christmas. But the Feast of the Nativity was not so much about feeling good as it was about the mystery of the incarnation, God's self-emptying. It was about there being no room at the inn, and about straw pillows, and cold milk and a night full of distant stars. Yes, I thought, this is why I have come here. To be with Jesus the outcast. I am in the right place and doing this properly after all.

The reality was that I found the community festivities and recreations one of the most difficult areas of the Life to adapt to, emotionally and psychologically. For all our shared faith and convictions, there was a lack of emotional common ground, and I felt this deeply. Aspects of innate or previously formed personality had to be suppressed so as to interact 'recreationally' with people whose cultural reference points were very different from one's own. Being excitable, even exuberant by nature, I looked for warmth and connection with other people, and was pained when I failed to find it. The blank looks and dismissiveness could cause secret agony. Recreation was ultimately not a relaxation but an exercise in restraint, listening to oft-repeated anecdotes, laughing at other people's jokes, and taking an interest in their crochet, while observing the long list of taboos. Topics we were told not to touch upon included our work, our food, our families, our dreams, our preferences, and of course any sort of past distinction or achievement. Politics, former boyfriends and sexuality were obviously out of the question.

Not being able to meet others at a conversational level, or to share anything but the most superficial or formulaic interactions, felt very strange to me, and for the first couple of years struck me as stifling and depressing. On the level of sensibility and taste there were some major disconnects. Snatches of conversation – 'Oh well, they're *southerners*', said in easy, dismissive tones, or 'You know the new one, Father Stephen, he isn't a Cradle Catholic' – filtered through to me, breaking the seal of denial that had shielded me in the early stages. 'Not cradle' meant he'd 'come over to Rome' from a different background, and was therefore not as dyed-in-the-wool as he should be. A half-blood priest. 'Oh, you know them posh folk,' someone once said within earshot, and I winced. 'They've all got a finger in the art galleries over in Newcastle and Hull.' This followed by a concerted burst of laughter and scornful agreement. I began to notice, and to feel uneasy on hearing such prejudices being aired, while talk of all sorts of really interesting things was sternly discouraged. You were expected to stick to the weather and the garden, not to have meaningful or searching conversations, all in the name of a common denominator that was perhaps nothing more than a chimera in the mind of Elizabeth.

Not only other cultures but other faiths were denigrated; one evening when talking of 'the Anglicans', those poor creatures also known as our separated brethren, Suzanne – yes, good old Suzi of all people – came out with it straight: 'Of course, they're in error,' she said – apparently for my benefit.

'Error?' I replied.

'Yes, Sister Catherine. There is such a thing as error.'

Oh. Error. The word was like a pebble, a hard, intractable object landing on the ground before me. Suzi, whom I'd thought so modern and dynamic, that bold countrywoman who strode around like an unfettered farmer, was now dismissing other denominations on dogmatic grounds. I'd taken her for one of the more broad-minded. After all, she was the fun, outspoken one, the progressive member of a relatively timid group. She'd done something interesting at university. The woman whom I'd once seen lifting a churn of milk, and thought dignified and beautiful, was now casting anathemata about. And then Paula brought me up short by lamenting that one of the parishioners had married a divorcee. 'Really, how could he?' she exclaimed. Another pebble. At that moment I clocked the fact that I was one of only two converts to Catholicism now that Pippa had gone (Judith was the other), and the only Londoner in the room. I was processing the fact that I had lived a very different kind of life from most of my sisters before my entry to the cloister. But what was wrong with that? Weren't we all meant to be one in Christ?

Gradually the south was becoming even more distant, like an island that was drifting out to sea. Some spoke of it harshly, only to reveal that they had never been there (never been to London! That was another jolt, another pebble). Yes, I'd come to the Life ready to practise renunciation and detachment, but being detached from something was very different from denying or disowning it. Choosing Catholicism as something inspiring, something with a grand and higher purpose, surely did not require me to be ashamed of my native background? Who'd have dreamed that, in following my guiding star, I'd have found myself feeling so very alone?

Eventually I stopped looking forward to the wishings. I learned that they were nothing to do with genuine human warmth, or the welcoming of the helpless Christ-child in our midst, and in each other. They were certainly nothing to do with kindness. It was one of many hard lessons for my soft nature to learn inside the cloister. I learned it slowly. I'd taken to the life of the cell as though it was a second nature, but the emotional coldness of the community was a reality I had not bargained for. I soon realised I was in fact not alone.

It was after Mass one morning that Felicity came over to me as I said my prayers by the statue of St Joseph. It was immediately evident she was in what Mother called 'a stew'. She was looking wobbly, her normally parchment-pale face pink with tears. Her big grey eyes were brimming over. 'They've told me I need to go away and get some life experience, then reapply,' she said miserably. 'It's not for ever, just for a couple of years. But if I wasn't ready for solemn vows a year ago, and if I'm still not ready for it now, will I ever be? I've been here seven years – and still they think I am not ready.'

'I'm so sorry, Fliss,' I said. 'I didn't know they were voting for you this week, and I'll be very sorry to see you go. It won't be the same . . .'

She smiled a watery, half-hearted smile. I reached out to touch her shoulder, and was about to open my arms in a gesture of solidarity, if not a full embrace. But then I saw Sister Barbara peeping at us from behind a pillar, and pulled back.

'It's all right, Catherine,' Felicity quavered. 'I know you won't forget me, and that we'll be praying for each other. We'll always be sisters in Christ. Whatever happens. Please God, after my year out, maybe they'll let me come back and then we'll end up in community again. I know I still have some growing up to do. I know my health has let me down at times. I still need to put on weight. I'm still very weak. But Carmel's all I've ever wanted, Catherine. I'm sure you understand that.'

I said I did, and held out my hands as though to hold her

own. She touched them briefly. Hours later she was gone. The new year would be the poorer without her high, clear singing voice, and the mood in the novitiate would be that bit less kind and nuanced. Epiphany would come and go, and the talk was that there would be snow.

19. Resolution

Valentine's Day, my third spring now, and the house was quiet as an obelisk, a silence towering to the sky. I had never known the place so still, so deathly poised. It was as though the very walls were holding their breath. I'd come downstairs after my reading time, made my way to the refectory for my 'cup', and noted the absence even of the usual muffled noises, footsteps, distant movements, the odd cough. Today there was a different flavour in the air, a different wind in the trees. I gulped down my bowl of strong tea, wondered where everybody was, and headed for the toolshed. It was a Sunday, the one day of the week we could take free time in the afternoon and go for a walk, browse the latest selection of books from the county's mobile library, or do extra crafts or little works. Flower-pressing, calligraphy and embroidery were popular choices. You could even make music, as long as you did so away from the cells.

The courtyard was startlingly white in the cool spring air, something about it crisp with neglect. For a moment I felt myself as though within a ghost town, the cloister flagstones not having seen human feet for years. Then I saw a white veil bobbing along behind the bushes near the bonfire patch. It was Sister Jennifer. So, I had not awoken in a dreamworld after all. Still, I could not shake the impression that something out of the ordinary was going on. I'd circle the lake, perhaps make it to the Mere, and then come back and play my viola in the novitiate. That would take me through to

Vespers. After supper there was to be a short play rehearsal, something organised by Sister Suzanne. Let's see if she turned up.

Now Christmas was past, with Lent still ahead of us, there was nothing special on the horizon. Life was suspended briefly in a kind of lull. I rather enjoyed it, the lack of pressure and direction. It was like being held in amniotic fluid for a while, and part of me wished this happy and unhurried state could continue. I liked seeing the clouds moving gently across the sky. I liked watching as spring emerged, touching every aspect of the garden. I liked being left alone, carrying out my duties, praying my rosary. Why did anything need to change? There was a level on which I think I would quite happily have remained an unprofessed junior for ever, or at least indefinitely. I didn't mind being the lowest of the low.

The walk as ever worked its magic. I'd taken a detour on the way back from the lake and run down into the flat oblong meadow that we called 'The Deep'. It was much bigger than a football pitch, and with a surface so level and so close-mown it reminded me of a swimming pool. The temptation on reaching it was to jump and dance. No one could see you there, and the feeling of space and freedom was intoxicating. I threw my arms up in the air and began to swirl and spin. The sky scudded. The sun peeped through like a benediction. Very little else around me stirred. But I was dancing, leaping into the cloudy air, reviving my childhood gymnastic skills. I was laughing. Finally, I tucked up the skirts of my habit and began to run. When I reached the toolshed I was flushed, happily out of breath.

The monastery was as deserted as ever, but when I reached the chequerboard hall I was startled by raised voices from the choir. So that was it! The community was having a chapter meeting. Only Jen and I were rattling round the house and grounds, like children in a stately home. And now the raised voices were rising further. It dawned on me that what I was hearing was the sound of conflict. And then one voice predominated. It was Suzi's. Other voices fell away, cleared a space for her. Forthright, and now forceful, she was holding the floor. This was the Suzi I'd seen glimpses of, a strong and straightforward character, someone sure of her own mind. You could see it in her body language, in her unapologetic gait as she strode around. Now what I was hearing could only be described as anger. The words escaped me, but the fire was there.

It is impossible, when you know the community might well be discussing you (novices being under near-continual scrutiny), not to be a little anxious about what they might be saying behind those huge, creaking oak doors. At least there were two of us still in formation, and, who knows, the anger could have been about any number of other things. But it sounded real enough, the heat, a sound I hadn't ever heard in Carmel. Applying the usual vigilance, I moved on towards the novitiate, telling myself not to brood. But the day held other surprises. Ten minutes later, as I crossed the hall again to collect a music stand, I saw Mother Elizabeth coming towards me. Other black-veiled sisters were flitting here and there. Normal activity had been resumed. And then, surprisingly, she was beckoning me over to an alcove, her face grey, and rather tired and solemn. Already my heart was sinking.

'You have been accepted for temporary profession,' she was suddenly saying. 'You've done well, and had your extra year of novitiate. It was a tough test for you, Catherine, but you seem to have pulled through and to be flourishing.' In spite of the encouraging words she was saying, she had adopted her most forbidding tone, and seemed somehow hardened, tightened, like a shiny pencil point. I looked at her, looked down at the black and white tiles, sensed something swimming behind my eyes, and noted the complete mismatch between her manner and the ostensible fact of what was meant to be good news. Everyone wanted to be accepted for profession. Didn't they? Making public vows was all we had been working towards. I'd been wanting this for months, for years. But suddenly it all felt so wrong. What was Mother really communicating to me? Why wasn't she smiling, warmly welcoming? Why, only minutes ago, had there been anger in the air?

'You do want it, don't you?' Elizabeth said. She must have noticed something in my face, just as I had noticed something in hers. 'You do want to be professed?'

Now I was really losing my foothold. What was this novelty, this new tactic of offering me a choice, when we had been taught to renounce our own desires long ago, to do only the most perfect thing, only to obey God's will? What was this acting like it was optional? There was a horrid miasma suddenly, an awareness of something not quite matching up. Of course I had to make my vows. That was the whole point, wasn't it? That was Carmel. And Carmel was my life, my home. But now the prospect of vows was changing its character before my eyes. It was like seeing the colour drained from a face, the blood from a dying body. What had been so desirable last year and the year before, was now twisting and turning into something dreadful and distorted, something horrid and grotesque, a malignant threat. My stomach plunged into my socks.

'The official announcement will be at Vespers, Sister Catherine, but I will have to have your written request before we can go ahead. Just a simple paragraph formally applying to make your profession of vows. Signed and dated. Or perhaps that should be back-dated. You should have made your written request by now, in order to be considered eligible, as I am sure you know. But let that not detain us. We know you wanted to apply.'

The formal request to be admitted for profession was indeed overdue, on the assumption I'd actually intended to write it. But had I? Suddenly, I hardly knew. The validity of the request rested on its being written freely and not under duress. My failure to write it was now staring at me, an enormous question mark. Why had I waited so long? Had I even thought seriously of doing it? Why, when I'd thought and said I wanted it so much? What was the real reason, Sister Catherine? A storm of doubt was now raging in my mind. It was impossible to reach out for help, for a steadying hand from Elizabeth. She was a million miles away. And there was nearby bustle, other sisters passing by.

'I've had Jennifer's request for some time now, Catherine, so if you could just go upstairs now and get yours written, that would be perfect. I'll be expecting it.'

Ah, Jennifer too, I thought. Both of us bound in together for life. That was another revelation. I wondered how freely, and how long ago she'd asked to stay. The communication between us was so skimpy. But evidently she had made her mind up. Evidently she was now far ahead of me. As for myself, I was not going to let the emotional brainstorm of a moment overturn the years of training, of quiet deliberation and intent. I knew where virtue lay, had learned all about it, knew that it was in the naked exercise of the will to glorify God. It was the giving back to God the gift of my own freedom.

'Yes, of course,' I said, but in a way that felt all wrong, all jumbled up. Even the word 'Yes' felt odd and alien in my mouth. Like a dab of oil paint in the wrong colour, there was something false, something out of place about it. And then there was another colour, another word pressing up with terrible force towards my mouth from deep inside me. It was a word with a very different shape, a different colour, something so obvious I'd never even considered it a possibility. No. I heard the unspeakable syllable pushing up through the churning of my stomach. No, I heard – it was the sound of a stranger. No, no, no – a shower of words like pebbles now flying round inside my ribcage. No. It had a hollow echo.

This was a disaster. It was wrong, perhaps diabolical. An assault. I could, I *must* see this for what it was. I only had to stop this inner din. Make sure no hint of the dreadful word escaped. Mother must not be allowed to hear these thoughts. 'No' would be a disaster. 'No' would be finality. 'Yes' was the sum of all my training. 'Yes' was what it had to be.

'Yes,' I said aloud. Mother half smiled. Or did she? I could hardly tell what was going on now. The floor was tilting. Perhaps she was just asking me, again, to go and write that note. She needed it quickly. By Vespers. She held up her watch. Fifteen minutes. And everything was now out of my control. Everything was a blur.

Mother Elizabeth moved away. She had seemed completely emotionless. Sisters Suzanne and Alison walked past with a couple of guitars. I gathered up my habit hem and began to walk up the staircase, legs only slightly wobbly. Purple splodges of light danced beside me on the wall. The stained-glass windows loomed far above. No one passed me on the landing or the upper corridor. The dormitory cells were still. Finally, I reached the end of the corridor, and lifted the latch to my cell. It felt unusually dead and empty, no longer a nuptial chamber, my special meeting place with God. What had happened? I felt a rising sense of panic. Had I been wrong about everything all along? But all of this was irrelevant. I knew what I had to do. I had been trained. I sat down, looked out of the window for a moment, then, with a churning stomach, wrote that note.

That evening Suzi's play rehearsal was cancelled, as Mother Elizabeth had decided it was time for a mini concert, a festive gesture at recreation. Well, this was something! Although I sometimes played my viola for formal occasions in the choir, I hadn't had much chance to share the kind of music I most loved with my sisters. Now, on being asked to find something to perform, I decided to play one of my favourite movements from the Bach Cello Suites.

Soon the little concert was underway, and Mother was calling for a moment's silence. Then she asked me to do my bit. I stepped forward, introduced the Allemande, and took up a position near the garden window. I lifted my bow and let the hair sink, heavily, deliberately onto the two lower strings of my viola, then stretching, drawing the full length slowly from heel to point, moved it firmly across gut to take in the higher registers. The chord voiced itself clearly against the quiet, the full weight of arm and hand behind it, the angle of my wrist finely turned to draw some solid body from the thinner A string. I continued, losing myself in the alternate tensions and resolutions of the music, which meant so much to me. I birthed it as beautifully as I could, not because anyone was listening, but because I was helpless not to, compelled by the force of the unfolding harmonies. It was a relief, after the bruising emotions of the day, like coming home to something I had not realised how much I'd missed.

The arches of the structure rose and fell, and breathed

away into semi-silence at the longer notes. There were pauses, and repeats, lulls when the open octave sounded stark against the stillness of the evening. It was a luscious feeling, and somehow wonderful to be able to express who I was in the way that came most naturally. But just as I was raising my bow for the thematic developments of the second half, Mother's voice cut in, matter-of-fact, steely, like the closing of a book.

'Well, that's enough of that,' she said. A ripple of tentative applause spread through the room, more generous in some, more repressed in others, particularly so where Jennifer sat shut off in a pool of gloom. Why was she becoming resentful of me? Was she jealous? She'd started snapping at me recently, especially if ever I was shown any approval, but I supposed these sorts of emotions were natural enough. Who was I to judge? In the alcove the recorders were sounding the beginnings of a hornpipe, and feet were stamping, ready for the dance.

'Enough, enough!' Mother called again. She was looking anxiously towards Jennifer. 'Enough of all that seriousness – bring on the tambourines!' and at this Alison and Suzanne burst from behind a bookcase, thumping, banging, lifting high their instruments as they swirled into the centre of the room, to stand swaying alongside a flimsy music stand. Laughter was breaking out now, and then Ellen and Jane appeared, joining in, playing their recorders. Skipping, nodding, trilling, they moved towards me, until they stood next to me, the shrill notes discordant, Ellen desperately attempting to lead the tune. With a furious nod she brought the hornpipe to a close, while Mother began rising triumphantly to her feet, her arms spread wide like the sails of a ship. 'And so, to dance!' she cried in her best stage voice.

'*To dance!*' the sisters echoed. Their feet were tapping, stamping, itching to take off. The stronger ones were tucking up their habits already, hitching their underskirts into knots to free their legs. Sister Ellen called out '"Danny Boy"' and the tune changed to something we all knew. The relief among the older sisters was palpable. They loved the tune. It was easy enough to add some harmonies, and now I was merged, lost again in the melee, percussion thrashing, the oldies laughing, singing, swaying to the languorous beat. Jennifer remained on the sidelines, banging a knuckle repeatedly on the side of her stool, but no one seemed to notice her as the mood took over, and the intoxication of noise and play gathered the community into one loud, stamping wave of sound and movement.

By the time the bell went, everyone was dancing the hokey-cokey, even Jennifer now laughing with the rest. I played along as required, adding chords and decorations, my identity once more subsumed into the group. For a while I'd been like a small bird released, and had flown, oblivious of the cage. I had been able to breathe, to soar, to be expressive and true to the workings of my inmost mind. I'd plunged and poured myself into the Bach, sensed the authenticity of the moment, its force and weight, but now, the freeing flight aborted, I felt even more starkly alone than before. I could not relate to what had followed, which felt like an exercise in false jollity. Mother had steeled herself to show no response whatsoever while I'd played, just as that afternoon in the hall, she'd held herself aloof, had withheld the easy naturalness even of a smile. Trying to work out what was going on, to discern a rationale behind her sticks and carrots, was far harder than following a fugue.

If I'd been able to be honest with myself, I would have

admitted that my dream had turned into the beginnings of a nightmare. Later that evening, everything was swimming behind my eyes. Clarity had morphed into confusion, beauty into harshness, music into noise. My stomach was still churning. The prospect of a martyr's cross now seemed a reality, a grey shadow encroaching. But I knew the drill. What we thought and felt was not important. It was what God wanted that mattered, and God's will had been revealed by the deliberations of the chapter. Still, there was now the looming possibility, the anguished thought that it might all be a terrible mistake.

20. The Arrivals

'They can't just come here and bring their own customs,' Barbara had said when the possibility of one or two of the Holton sisters moving to Akenside was first floated. The subject had come up just as I was preparing to take my vows, and soon a range of long-buried Akenside undercurrents began to surface. Holton on the Humber had decided definitively on dispersal, not amalgamation ('thank God') and were only a small handful of the elderly, but Barbara emphasised that whatever happened it would be on our terms, and our terms alone. We would be the host Carmel, setting the tone, keeping things as they always had been. It was for them, the newcomers, to fit in. Of course, it would not be easy for them. We'd need to give them space and make allowances. Each house had its approach, and no doubt there would be a transition period while they let go of all that was familiar, and adapted to us.

Each community cherished its own customs, we knew that well enough. It did not escape me that the very customs or 'ways' (the purpose of which was to bring about detachment from such things as 'ways') were sometimes treated as absolutes, ends in themselves. There were those who were attached to 'how we'd always done things' for the simple reason that we'd always done them that way, and spoke as though we were the one house of the order that knew what was best. The circular nature of such thinking was only acknowledged by those who had enough hold on objective reality not to be in thrall to the centrifugal force that was Elizabeth. My new-found honesty with myself, my recovered ability to look and listen for what was actually the case rather than what everyone insisted it was, meant I was picking up on these dynamics.

Now the Holton sisters were at the door, and our first task was to prepare their cells and make them welcome. There was bustling to be done, windows to be wiped, and important details to be rearranged. Two new sets of initials were to be added to the Confessions board, and space made in the cloaks cupboard. There were ceilings to be swept (standing on tables, with long-handled brooms) and door lintels to be cleaned. Two places in the refectory had to be set up, and others shunted down to make room for them. Cubbyholes needed to be cleared and hooks allocated in the toolshed.

It seemed odd even to think of them as 'new' when they were older than Mother herself. Sister Marion and Mother Irene had been Carmelites for longer than I'd been alive. In her youth, Marion had been a lay sister, a 'servant' category of nun that had been abolished after Vatican II. Mother Irene, on the other hand, had been a grammar-school girl, and (it had slipped out somehow) a scholarship student. Although a 'late vocation' (she'd entered in middle age) she, unlike our own Mother, was steeped in rigorous theology, and in the more abstruse teachings of the order.

Marion and Irene. The names had been passed around in furtive undertones, and moved in ripples across the ranks at recreation. The Holton sisters. The newcomers from an unpropitious suburb of Hull. By day, the buzz of unheard conversation and the whirr of unseen wheels hung in the air. Elizabeth looked preoccupied, Jennifer disconsolate, and Sister Barbara told us to 'stick to our guns'. Not all communities had our traditional practices and our sound understanding of obedience, but we must be sure to set a good example, and the right tone from the start. Holton had failed for a reason.

I tried to read the faces of my own community. I'd stopped idealising them by this time, and had started looking, listening, searching for what was real. I thought I knew each sideways glance, each flicker of the eyelid – but nobody was giving much away. Were we all as good at pretending as each other? How impenetrable were these masks and veils? As for Holton, if they had had to close, wasn't that simply a result of their age and falling numbers? There was no shame in their realising it was time to sell up and start again. We all had the same Rule and Constitutions. The charism was the charism, after all. We were one bread, one body, and we shared in the one spirit. Sisters in Christ.

Holton was not one of the more glamorous monasteries. It was humble. It was modest. It was in the wrong part of the country, according to those sisters who prided themselves on their Geordie heritage. Nobody envied these poor sisters, and they had no special reputation to maintain. Of course, such considerations should never have raised their ugly heads at all among religious sisters, but – human nature being what it is – I'm afraid they did. People liked judging and comparing, even though they insisted on the gospel precept 'Do not judge, lest you be judged,' and made a big thing of holding others to those high standards. 'Do not judge' meant 'Be very careful to speak just as is expected of you, and never to betray your honest mind.' But there was always room for the odd snark.

In the unofficial hierarchy among the houses of our order, Mother Elizabeth and Sister Barbara thought that we were up there in the higher places. Our numbers were well into double figures, and had an impressive count of musical sisters. Music, to Mother's mind, was quite an indicator of status among the monasteries. Having a good quota of the able-bodied and of musicians equated to flourishing. Plus, we had guitars. What of the other houses? Mellerby Hall was amiably tolerated, since most of their number had begun at Akenside and there was a distant family resemblance (notwithstanding all their liberal nonsense). There were the Scottish and the Welsh Carmels (both more-or-less off our radar), and a smattering of others we barely knew. Any snippets of news, or other insights, came via a recently set up monastic support group called the Garth Alliance.

The only serious competition came from Norrington Grange, and we forgave them. They were everything we aspired to be, but unthreateningly so as they were a 'Mother House' in all but name. That is, we were directly descended from them, and from a common Parisian lineage involving their revered 'foundress', who had planted the seed that she'd brought over from France. Other than that, well, there was Danbury Hall, somewhat further afield, a large and rather grand community in Shropshire that was subtly envied and revered for all the wrong reasons (although it was genuinely flourishing). Holton, however, was not in either of their leagues. They were from a benighted land where God cast his shadow, a dubious sea port, cradle of the Civil War, and now they were dwindling so badly they were down to eight.

Mother Elizabeth was not keen on interaction. Autonomy was her watchword. None of us thought in terms of 'autocracy', but anything that required her to work together with, or to accommodate, other sources of legitimate authority was most unwelcome. If there were other monasteries who were living the Life as faithfully as we were, all well and good, but the fact was, while doing their best – God bless them – they were not Akenside and did not really 'understand our ways'. Yes, we shared a Rule and Constitution, and a common ancient heritage, but, at the end of the day, we were called to be hermits-in-community, solitaries living alone with God. We were called to be apart, self-governing, autonomous. No, the bishop and the monks did not have our insights, and their advice could safely be discounted. Although we'd somehow managed to vote to join the Garth Alliance, which meant getting annual newsletters and being asked for moral support every now and again, we were not encouraged to set any store by this connection with other monasteries. It was a token thing, a safety net perhaps, and if that meant we had a visit once every five years from a representative, so be it. We'd put on an informal concert or buffet supper for the visitor, tell them jokes, and send them packing, our smiling faces imprinted for ever on their retinas. We were a cheery crowd when we wanted to be, and a flurry of light entertainment could go a long way towards distracting visitors and inmates alike from potential or actual problems in our midst. Not that Mother would ever have admitted to there being problems. We had guitars! A promising novitiate! We were flourishing!

Nevertheless, it worried me that Mother Elizabeth took such obvious pride in our collective status quo, when what we'd been told was to humble ourselves, and accuse ourselves of unworthiness at every turn. If self-abasement was expected of individuals, did it not follow that the same attitude was expected of communities? Was not pride the sin we'd been most stringently warned against? What about Mother herself, was she exempt? Yes, she had the 'grace of the office', which gave her a guarantee of being right in all circumstances, but that did not absolve her from practising the efforts and attitudes she required of all. It was indeed very curious, especially as she must have known that her own lapses and deviations from the Rule would never have been tolerated in another sister. She led, not by example, but very much from the top.

Finally the day came, and the two newcomers arrived. They were red-faced and jolly, and little ripples were felt in the community. Some held back, while others were impressed at the stoicism of these welcome-and-yet-unwelcome arrivals. Some of us perhaps felt a little sorry for them. Sister Judith was the one charged with showing them the ropes, and she had already got some simple work lined up for them in the linen office. Mother Irene would be sewing veils and mending our frayed habit hems. Marion would be peeling potatoes. The important thing was to keep Marion away from any duties involving outsiders, Elizabeth had said, and certainly from anything to do with the extern.

People nodded knowingly when it turned out that Sister Marion was even more talkative than we'd expected. Some perhaps felt relieved to find her positively indiscreet; their preconceptions had been confirmed. Yet it was actually quite interesting to hear her unguarded chatter at recreation, very different from our stilted and formal interactions, and to soak up her frank descriptions of the pre-Conciliar era when she'd first entered. How tough it was, and how badly treated they had all been as lay sisters! Up skivvying for the others at 4 a.m., milking the cows! Eyebrows were raised among our ranks, but mostly people just looked down and smiled. She was from Holton. People made allowances.

No-nonsense Irene was a much more stolid, sober

character. She had none of Marion's chattiness. By comparison she seemed taciturn and made of a particularly unattractive, bumpy granite, with tiny, thick-lensed spectacles and a large, podgy face. Mother Irene was grounded, but she also had a brain. She knew the recent Vatican documents in some depth, and held clear, informed views on contemporary developments in the Church with more intellectual confidence than was generally approved of at Akenside. She'd read not only Karl Rahner (a progressive Catholic) but Karl Barth (a Calvinist). In other words, she had a breadth of outlook and knew what she was talking about.

Mother Irene's ponderous, earnest approach did not sit well with Mother Elizabeth's 'funny little ways', the authoritarianism that sat alongside her deviations from the Rule, none of them theologically founded or thought through. Mother Elizabeth was not an intellectual, and found people who were able to argue a case with any degree of philosophical confidence or coherence somewhat worrying. People like Irene were not the sort to be palmed off with skipping ropes and Plasticine and sweets. No one could convince her to ditch her gravitas and 'become like a little child'. Or could they? The two women looked at each other from afar, appraised, noted their differences, and took a few deep breaths.

Irene presented a smiling front at first, but after a few weeks was seen to baulk a little at what she saw going on around her. Her reactions came wrapped up as jokes at first, then as subtle looks, or the odd downcast expression, or a few comments, some of which were so honest and open they were quite a relief. You could almost hear the low hiss of air being let out of a big balloon in the room, the easing of pent-up tension in certain quarters. In others, dark looks were shared, and mutterings emitted. Having a new influx of

Carmelite life was the first sobering reality check we had had, the first hint that there might be another way of doing things, even in the One True Carmel.

These new sisters were inelegant and physically rough-hewn. Nothing about them was obviously impressive or likely to catch the eye. Next to them, Mother Elizabeth's beauty and mystique shone even brighter. Now that we had another prioress (albeit emeritus) in our midst, you realised that not all Mothers were equal, or the same, nor did all Superiors see themselves as exempt from aspects of the common life. It was clear from Irene's lowliness – her way of making herself unimportant – that she was living all that Mother Elizabeth had always taught us was required of 'simple sisters', everything in the spiritual exhortations of the order, but that Elizabeth herself had somehow managed to avoid. It was refreshing to see Mother Irene rolling up her sleeves and scrubbing floors! Tacitly, the community fell into those who saw Irene's example as edifying, and those who treated it as a threat. For them, any proposed changes to our Akenside ways would have been unwelcome.

The Holtonites quietly stuck to the horarium. They expected us to do so too. Implicitly their fidelity held up a mirror to what was odd or irregular about our own approach. Why were some people always missing from the Office? their looks seemed to ask. What were they doing? Why was it we hadn't had a Visitation (an official inspection from the hierarchy) in nearly twenty years? They also asked aloud, one recreation, why we didn't have the weekly community meetings enjoined on us by the Rule. These 'Sunday chapters' were supposed to be occasions of wise leadership and mutual support, where the growth and health of the community might be 'trustingly' addressed and 'openly' discussed. If any areas were getting out of balance, or in need of correction, this was to be done 'in charity'. The truth was that Elizabeth had stopped them partly because of Jen's aversion to serious discussion. It was as though she needed to be accommodated at all costs.

Irene and Marion stood tall and strong, but slowly we saw how much it cost them, this generosity, this displacement, this sense of upheaval, and being away from all they'd built up and been accustomed to over decades. How hard it must have been for them, on top of this, to be told their thoughts and views, their ways, their interpretation of the Life just did not matter, and that it was their job to adapt to us, with no hint of reciprocity. Our customs had to be respected and maintained, even if it meant discounting genuine insights, not listening, not embracing spurs to growth. In cases of an amalgamation – where two dwindling monasteries pooled their resources – there'd have been an attempt at give and take. But the Holtonites were outnumbered by a ratio of one to nine.

The months passed, and the new sisters got used to our pale faces and we to their ruddy ones. Irene's plodding footfall became a regular ambient backdrop to our world. Marion's excitable chatter was not quite what Akenside was used to, but she had many redeeming features – she was relentlessly cheerful, and undoubtedly very brave – and most of us cut her a bit of slack. Some sisters, subtly noting her verbal indiscretions, seemed to relegate her to the category of a harmless fool.

One thing that needed to be brought home to the new arrivals was the Akenside approach to recreation. With us it was not all silence and custody of the eyes. The sessions we had each evening were a counterbalance to the inwardness and toil of the working days, and Mother Elizabeth, as always, encouraged a hearty, even boisterous approach. Her whims and unspoken agendas were not always explicit, but one thing was sure – while we were bound to be silent the rest of the time, at recreation we were bound to talk.

It was at recreation that you really noticed things about each other. When still green, a newcomer might drop a reference to a special interest (one poor aspirant's talk of Sylvia Plath comes to mind) only to incur the cold edge of Mother's blade, her cruellest look. I recall how she cut me off once when I was waxing lyrical about polyphony. If she thought conversation not suitable, by which she meant not accessible to everyone, you'd find out quickly enough. The offender would be exposed and humiliated to show her where the boundaries lay. Nothing was meant to be said that did not, on some level, involve all present. Personal preferences were meant to be suppressed, and exclusive cliques avoided.

The other Akenside custom the new arrivals needed to be told about was the Rule of Three. It was an old tradition that Mother Julianna had brought back decades ago during a phase when there had been a problem with 'murmuring'. This was a dark word only ever uttered in tones of the strongest disapproval. To murmur was to share confidences privately with another sister in a way that criticised or undermined the prioress, and this could be anywhere – in the garden or outbuildings, or while waiting for others to arrive for recreation – that two sisters might be tempted to put their heads together. Three sisters were less likely to murmur than two (it was to be hoped at least one of them might have a loyal conscience) and so the rule of three became standard practice, although only the older sisters really knew why, and remembered the incidents and arguments that had sparked

off Mother's concerns. They remembered the year many of
the sisters left for Mellerby, and knew something about
the reason behind the steady trickle of Akensiders to that
younger, more liberal community, a trickle that, while now
sporadic, had been a liability ever since. Pippa had been the
latest defector, and Mother was determined to discourage us
younger ones from doing the same. Akenside was the One
True Carmel, the Barque of St Teresa, and Mother Elizabeth
was the only one fit to sit at its helm. Anyone who questioned this did so at their peril.

21. Stairway to Heaven

'*Kumbaya, m'Lord, kumbaya . . .*' The voices fluttered like uncomfortable birds. '*Kumbaya, m'Lord, kumbaya.*' Suzanne was a good guitarist. There she stood near the grille, leading the singing, with Ellen and Jennifer at her side: three guitars, one harmony, six hands, one ripple of crystal-clear arpeggios. Jen's head was down, intent on the crab-like action of her fingers across the strings. Ellen nodded in time to the beat, her round face flushed, her soft lips pursed while articulating the interesting, unfamiliar words.

Things had moved on since Sister Magdalena, an able organist, had left. Maggie had been a briefly dazzling presence when I'd first visited on my trial run, had shown herself a brilliant joker, but she was also shrewd, and too clever by far for Mother's liking. After she'd gone to Mellerby nothing much was heard of her. Any news was likely to be an 'unsettling' influence. She had got above herself. She was disobedient. The wise among us did not talk about her. Following her departure Mother had made me organist, after an awkward phase during which Jen and I took it in turns to play for Mass. Jen was not a natural player, which meant there was quite a lot of tension and worry about her, although she managed well enough until she hurt her hand in the garden. After that she stuck to guitar.

Mother was keen for me to contribute musically. Although she discouraged pride, she knew a community asset when she saw one, and my musical background was the kind of thing that could give Akenside the edge over other monasteries, at least where the liturgy was concerned. Although individually none of us was meant to shine, as a community it was quite a different matter. Mother wanted other houses to see that we were flourishing, to take note of us, and what better way than to have a very public display of talent from the young. Everyone under forty who had a musical instrument or a good voice was encouraged to do their bit, and musical recreations soon became a thing, showing the Holton sisters what we were made of.

Unlike Jen, I was able to accompany hymns without having to practise them first, and this time-saving factor meant that, finally, once life got busier for both of us, I was the one entrusted with the role. I threw myself into our musical life with gusto. By a quirk of providence, I'd slipped into my luggage not one but two shiny copies of *A Hundred Carols for Choirs* the day I'd headed for an unknown future. I'd produced them at one of the singalongs, and the next thing I knew I was teaching 'The Lute Book Lullaby' to my cohort and there was no looking back. Sister Ellen got out her flute, Jen had a go on tenor recorder, and Suzi – who had a wonderful voice – became the alto soloist. Fliss and Ellen had always been good soprano soloists, but nowadays it was mostly me. Ellen had put me forward as community cantor, happily claiming shyness, although I knew that she was really just giving me a chance. It was a relief.

Later some would joke that I was a Whoopi Goldberg among my companions, but – like many a community joke – there was a barb among the roses. In some people's view I was too dynamic by far. In the act of making music, I got animated and expressive in ways that were beyond the usual ways of doing things in our world. It was not that I stopped being demure, more that I became hyper-alert and intent on communicating. I actually looked around me, mouthed words and made eye contact, for example. The allocation of gifts and roles in a community is never without its controversies. Although it seemed to me that our musical efforts were modest compared to what I'd been involved with outside, it began to dawn on me that, in as closed a world as this, there were bound to be some so deprived of stimulation as to find it quite exciting. Some, after all, had been inside since the 1950s, and, like Mother Elizabeth herself, had never known the changes to wider culture ushered in by the 1960s. Their expectations were both old-fashioned and extremely low. The musical changes I was bringing in were – in spite of myself – causing ripples of approval.

But not for all. Soon I noticed Jennifer looking moody and holding aloof from the general positivity about the music sessions. I had not foreseen this. Little flickers of strong feeling and resentment were darting between us, flaring up. Looking back, I suppose rivalry was bound to have been built into our twin-ship, the word itself a verbal handcuff likely to have us bridling within our separate spheres. Natural antipathy would perhaps be the best word to describe the problem between us, although it pained me hugely nonetheless. Weren't we meant to love each other? To be generous and make sacrifices? Later, I'd have risen above it and carried on, my mood undented. But at the time I had no way of understanding my twin's mentality. I was still so naive and deluded, expecting everyone to be as kind and gentle as my aunt, or as courteous and self-deprecating as my father.

From finding instinctive joy in our music-making, I started to feel apprehension before our choral sessions. It had started in a small way, but by the time I was regularly directing choir practice from the organ I was aware of clouds of resentment from the other side of the choir, where Jen sat glaring, and – slowly – criticism of everything I was doing. According to her I played too expressively, or too softly, too fast, too slow, or simply with too much dynamic variation. My introversion and sensitivity were such that I could not prevent this sort of thing from getting me down. The questioning mind started circling around, my inability to get a handle on the situation or to understand my companion's mentality, something so incomprehensible to me, a constant torment.

I guessed that part of the resentment directed towards me had to do with the fact that Jen was in thrall to the suave and beautiful Mother Elizabeth, and Elizabeth was a big fan of the music. It was as though she made an exception where music was concerned, and was nice to me, contrary to her usual starchy approach. What a relief those moments were for a while! For an hour or two a week the tightness of her frosty clamp on me was released, the screws on the vice were loosened, and, for the length of a musical interlude, I was off the rack. It was one of the Life's ironies that, as soon as suffering was removed in one area, it was supplied in another. If Mother Elizabeth smiled on me, I could be sure that Jen would frown.

In the quiet of my cell, I'd turn in on myself, curl up, holding my pain close, then call on the unseen spouse to come to my aid – which, in the early years, he did. Something happened in those moments, something that allowed me to release the pent-up anguish I was feeling, and to slump into a pile of tears. At those times, I'd look up at the huge black cross on the wall, commit myself to it as to my allotted path, mouth words of acceptance while inwardly struggling to cope with what felt so wrong. There was a cognitive dissonance at work, something I was coming up against that seemed insuperable, a brick wall around which there was no logical or obvious path. I'd come to Carmel to seek the highest things. What I was discovering now was that being 'only human' didn't just mean needing to laugh and play and let off steam, it meant having a shadow side, it meant everything I thought was the opposite of Christianity. I was having difficulty reining in my indignation.

My mind began working overtime. Thoughts and words in which I sought to make sense of my community and of my own vocation were a torment. Nothing was ever explained to me or resolved. Instead, I was entering a long dark tunnel. Instead of focusing on Jesus, I found myself wrestling with the shadow of my twin, and facing my own shadow too – while doing everything I could to repress it. I so much wanted to be good, however hard it was. The image of St Thérèse hovered before me, showing me that to which I aspired, that of which I was surely capable if only I steeled myself and 'set my face like flint'. But there was a wheedling agony worming itself into my mind, a terrible pain at the lack of friendliness and acceptance from someone with whom I'd been thrown together and had tried so very hard to get along with. The reality of our differences gnawed at me, opening wounds that would not close. I smiled at her, reached out at recreation, and, while she sometimes did the same, it became impossible to ignore the dark clouds.

One day we heard the bishop would be visiting us. To Mother's mind a bishop was someone to whom one grovelled, just as everybody else grovelled to her. She would be very happy to kiss his ring! 'My Lord' was the usual mode of address, just as surely as an archbishop was Your Grace, and the Pope was Your Holiness (in the unlikely event you got to meet the Holy Father). Yes, the bishop was coming on a nice, friendly visit.

Although Mother addressed him as 'My Lord' he was very much a 'call me Tony' type of person. He'd been a couple of times before, always very 'informally' as he liked to say. In fact, even I could see he was the kind of person you could sit down and have a chat, and perhaps enjoy a glass of wine with. There was something about him that reminded me of relaxed times from long ago. This time it had been decided we'd put on a buffet supper in his honour, to round things off. As our canonical superior he was one of the very few people allowed to come inside the enclosure, and only on rare occasions such as this. Let's leave aside the fact that it was also a Visitation, and thus an undercover inspection. Apart from bishops, cardinals and popes, the only people allowed inside were doctors and workmen.

Anyway, we were all gathered round like sheep around their shepherd (even if it felt more like hens around a cock-erel) and things were going swimmingly. Tony loved the gingham tablecloths we'd improvised to hide our work-like trestle tables, and of course he loved the quiche. Second helpings? I don't mind if I do. It was a semi-festive occasion, like an irregular recreation. At times like this, or when not-able representatives of the hierarchy appeared (such as, once, Basil Hume), the usual restraints around speech were lifted, sisters circled round the room with plates and trays, and stood around in little pools chatting and laughing, while keeping a good eye on the top table.

Tony wore a dusky mauve V-necked jumper, an open-neck check shirt – no dog collar – and had Hush Puppies on his feet. He came not as a dignitary but as an informal and approachable man of the world among us. And how among us! There he sat, one ankle slung over a knee, his paper plate perched, a tumbler of orange squash dangerously close to his elbow. He was almost boyish. Next to him Mother Elizabeth purred, sticking to 'My Lord', however many times he softly corrected her. 'Please, do have another sandwich,' she said, leaning slightly towards him as though confiding. His eyes were now scanning the room. It was time to draw others in. Barbara was bustling about, having wheeled in one of the invalids. Ellen was smiling coyly while seeming to talk with Suzanne. Older sisters nodded sagely. Jennifer gesticulated while telling Ruth all about the time she'd been on pilgrimage to Walsingham – Oh, it was years ago, part of a college effort. She was starting to demonstrate an elaborate banner-waving sequence, getting quite loud now, bordering on the boisterous. This was not normally a problem for Elizabeth, but not in front of the bishop, perhaps?

Mother clapped for our attention. There was a wave of rattling as people put down their crockery and cutlery.

'Well, how wonderful to see you all, dear sisters,' Tony said.

'My Lord, the pleasure is all ours,' Elizabeth reciprocated. Her cheeks were just a little pinker than usual. 'Really, it's been some time, hasn't it.'

'Too long, too long. But how are we all these days?'

'We do our best, Father, I mean . . . My—'

'Tony.'

'Er, yes, we do our best. Sometimes it's a case of struggling on. But aren't we blessed with all our young ones? And so musical!'

'So I hear. News travels, you know, in the diocese.'

And with that, Mother called for the guitars. She did not quite say 'Bring on the dancing girls!' but she may as well have done. We young ones had a special number, a surprise up our sleeves. Sister Barbara had written the words, adapted from a well-known prayer, of course, and fitted them to the music. But first (a bit of build-up, we didn't want to peak too soon) we would play him some of our staples: 'I, the Lord of Sea and Sky', and 'Rejoice in the Lord Always', rousing ones to get us going.

Soon the whole room was swaying to the strums, Tony beating time with his foot, his trousers only slightly riding up his leg. Were those hairs adorning his exposed lower calf? I shuddered but did not look too long. The sight of his folded hands resting on his crotch could not but worry me. It seemed so crass. Why didn't he hide them, move them, put them away? But by now I was rising, gliding across the room, and everybody was drawing back their chairs, making a central space for us, the young ones, to dance in.

The folded hands still worried me. Surely he could feel them through the material? The thought of it made me feel squeamish. But it was time to apply myself to the task. It was time to dance for the bishop. And then the lovely notes and the sweet words Sister Barbara had written started up, and everyone went moist and dewy-eyed. It was everybody's favourite: 'Stairway to Heaven'! The bishop beamed – it was his favourite, too. Gosh, how it took him back! And what a good idea to write new words.

Plip, plop, plip, plop, the delicate plucking gathered strength. Suzi and Jane were humming harmonies. Barbara rocked the chair of her invalid back and forth. The latter's eyes lit up. The words rose into a dreamy crooning, words of deep emotion tugging at all our hearts. For a moment our dancing felt stately and ethereal.

Then the mood changed, and I was up and swirling, my

habit spinning round my ankles like the dress of a flamenco dancer, my hands high over my head. Ellen was dancing, too, her breasts bouncing under her habit. We were changing places with each other, turning our faces this way and that. Everyone was enjoying it. As glimpses of the bishop spun past, I could see his folded hands still resting in his lap. Please put them away, I thought. Please. Or was it just me who noticed? But now the tambourines were out, and people were clapping to the beat. Phew, at last his hands were up and working. That was good. He was clapping, joining in. And now we were on to a livelier number. Now it was 'Majesty', a modern chorus, a song fit for a king.

The Visitation had gone off well enough, although visits from any outsiders always left uneasy ripples in their wake. Elizabeth described such effects as 'unsettling' and told us to take the bishop's advice and example with a dose of scepticism. Even priests didn't really understand our ways, not being members of the order, and never having lived the Life as we did. This Visitation, our first for over eighteen years, was not remarkable for any drama. It would be some time before cats, and all they represented, became a serious problem, and life in the infirmary was left to rumble on as usual. Visitations every three years would henceforth be the norm.

What was remarkable though, looking back, was the way we were all instructed by Mother to watch our tongues during the one-to-one interviews requested by the bishop. He needed to hear from everyone, he said, and all needed to be free to speak to him in trust and confidence. The signal was clear, but the countersignal was stronger. In the novitiate, Barbara told us that we were only to say our Faults, praise the virtues of the community, and show him how contented we all were. It did the priests so much good to see smiling, contented nuns. Above all, we were to say nothing critical about Our Mother. It was up to us to make it a really happy, friendly visit.

Years later, Father Gregory was to sit me down to talk about the situation, by then grown out of hand. He and the bishop were there to help us, he reminded me. They needed to know what was going on. And it 'does rather defeat the purpose of a Visitation' if nobody is allowed, or is prepared, to speak the truth.

PART THREE
The Truth

On a dark night,
Kindled in love with yearnings – oh, happy chance! –
I went forth without being observed,
My house being now at rest.

St John of the Cross, *Dark Night of the Soul.*
Translated from Spanish by E. Allison Peers.

22. Father Raphael

'Raphael?' I asked Ellen, who was still my angel, but only just. She'd seen me through the early years, and through the difficulty of first, temporary vows, offering practical advice (never spiritual 'intrusion'), but once I'd made my vows for life, I would be left to my own devices. That, however, was not the most daunting aspect of what lay ahead. It was the momentousness of it all, the irrevocability . . .

'Yes, that's right, Father Raphael. He's a provincial, you know.' Ellen's words brought me back from my internal meanderings. Provincials were the priests elected as local superiors over a large geographical area, called a 'province', in this case that of England and Wales. They really should have been called 'provincial superiors', but linguistically things had slipped. Anyway.

'He has a cousin in the Carmelites, one of the friars at Faversham. He himself is a Franciscan, of course, so, er . . . well, he's not quite on our wavelength, but . . .'

'I think Mother said he was a counsellor?' I asked.

'Yes, we understand he runs some kind of therapy centre over in . . . er, Alnwick I believe. But that is neither here nor there. You'll be seeing him on your own, Catherine. So, do think carefully before you speak, and do pray for discernment before you go in.'

'Yes, I see. And . . . Jennifer?'

'Yes, her too. You'll see him one by one in the upstairs parlour tomorrow – afternoon and morning respectively. He knows what to expect. One hour each, and then he'll be having a meeting with Mother and the Council.'

'The Council?'

'Yes, well, it's directives from on high, I'm afraid. We've never had to do this before, and have managed perfectly well without so-called "professional" opinions. But it's the *mind of the Church*, or so it seems. Times are changing.' Sister Ellen sighed.

'I see,' I said. 'So, what did you do in the old days?'

'Well, it's not a case of the old days, particularly. Right up to, oh . . . only four or five years ago proper spiritual discernment was considered enough. It was all done in house, in the old way. You know, prayer, silence and detachment, and the candidate would be left to sink or swim. It's the best way, of course. If someone's not meant to be here, they usually go under in the early years. It becomes evident, as a rule. But then, there have been mistakes, and nowadays the bishops are calling for a thorough screening process.'

'Screening sounds very clinical. Do you know what it'll consist of?'

'Oh, I believe it's just a glorified chat, really, and then a medical opinion. Dr Gill will be seeing to that, all routine stuff. Blood pressure, digestion, sleep patterns.'

'Oh yes. I did see him last time he was here. Just a swollen knee cap, nothing too serious. It's . . . it's better now.'

'Overdoing the kneeling again, were you? Remember, even though we are ascetics, a measure of moderation is still required. "The best is the enemy of the good," as Mother Julianna used to say. Not that she stinted on her self-giving. The phrase was a counterbalance to her other maxim: "God will never be outdone in generosity."'

'That sounds like Mother. I remember her penitential

excesses. It was as though she had some extra source of energy. When I was new I somehow thought that, after a few years, we'd all be like that. Walking on air. But . . .'

'Yes, the Life is much harder than young, untried sisters tend to realise in the early days. I'm always warning people, and reminding them that, to the extent that you've felt the delights of prayer, and the sweetness of enthusiasm, so will you taste the bitterness of the low points later on. The great thing to master is the detachment of your will from the influence of your natural (even your supposedly "spiritual") feelings. Otherwise, the long fallow seasons of aridity come as a bit of a shock. We've all had to face them for ourselves, nevertheless . . .'

I nodded, recalling Barbara's words that 'The closest we humans come to consistency is undulation.' It sounded good at the time.

'Anyway, Jennifer will be seeing Father Raphael first. Then it will be your turn in the afternoon. Do remember, Catherine, this is just a formality, something we are obliged to do, but not quite in line with our spirit. The priests don't really understand our way of life, you see. Even the bishop has a very different way of looking at things. They don't have our charism.'

'Surely they know enough about us—'

'No, sister. Remember that outsiders don't understand us at all. Not even priests, and certainly none of the other orders grasp our values. Franciscans embrace nature quite differently from us, and see us, the desert orders, as negative and world-denying. It's a common misapprehension. The best thing is to keep as quiet as possible about anything that's worrying you. You know, it could give the wrong impression. Our hermit spirit is so misunderstood.'

'It's completely pointless, of course,' Elizabeth had said, as she did of anything that involved communication between individuals. 'And it can be quite unsettling for novices to be persuaded to unearth stuff about their so-called selves—' She shuddered here '—their battles, and their inner lives. I think they call it "sharing" nowadays. All this opening up is very disturbing, as you know. It encourages sisters to give in, and to reach for human supports rather than for God alone. The last thing you want is a shoulder to cry on. Your mind should be on God, not on yourself. Certainly not on your misleading emotions. What you need is not softness and understanding but some stern reminders that you need to leave yourself behind. After your profession you'll be much more on your own.'

The next day crawled by, slow and grey, with extra flutterings in my stomach and the awareness that Jen and Father Raphael were upstairs, quite possibly in momentous conversation behind the parlour door, exchanging words that could not be retracted. Words on which so much of such great import hung. Then it would be my turn. I had to be vigilant. I had to be careful to avoid disloyalty. But at the same time, this was a chance, perhaps my only chance, to have somebody disinterested as a sounding board at this vital stage.

And then I was there in front of him, his blue check shirt, no dog collar, everything about him proclaiming his normality through the bars of the grille. He was a stocky man with a round, pudgy face, warm brown eyes, and greying curls of dark hair on his high-browed head. He had the considered, slow reactions of a careful listener. I immediately sensed myself in the presence of kindness, a refreshing human goodness. It was a blast of energy from another world. It seemed obvious that this was someone I could trust. How could I not? The idea that someone might actually want to listen to me, might not begrudge the time spent with me, or treat me as an irrelevancy, was irresistible. Yet, habitual inhibition still hemmed me in.

Loyalty. The word slid around like oil, off which other words skidded or repositioned in my mind. Loyalty was not a theological virtue, it was not even a proper moral one – or was it? I'd need to check it in the Catechism. But one thing was certain, it had no direct relation to intrinsic truth. And in the great scheme of things there were more important imperatives than aligning yourself with another's particular interests if those interests were in fact flawed, or misguided, or somehow wrong. So much at Akenside had taken me by surprise.

'So, I understand you are preparing to go into your final vows?' he said.

The question brought me up short. Yes, I'd been in temporary vows for nearly three years, was due to make my life commitment, but all sorts of feelings were flooding me. Feelings of anxiety about it all that I very much didn't want to reveal.

'Yes,' I said. But now I was all out of kilter.

'And you are sure about this?' The pudgy face spoke again, the warm eyes searched.

'Yes.' The word came out automatically. After all, I'd been wanting to make my vows for years, hadn't I? I'd been preparing for this step so carefully. So surely . . .

'You understand the seriousness of what you are undertaking?' he asked again.

'Yes,' I said a third time. Of course I did. That's what I knew I had to insist, but then I wondered, would I have requested it if nothing had made me feel obliged, pushed me towards the decisive moment? My mind was suddenly one great fog, struggling for clarity. My stomach was churning. Why was I so passive? So willing to go with the flow? Should I tell him now of the true nature of my feelings? No, let's not confuse the issue. Feelings did not matter. I'd focus on being perfect and obedient.

'You are looking anxious, sister. Is everything all right?'

'Oh, well, it's naturally a big step, and . . .'

'How old are you?'

'I'm thirty-two.'

'Ah, so old enough to have had some experience of the outside world.' He smiled.

'Yes, I certainly have. I've lived in Paris, studied composition, worked in experimental music, studied for a diploma on the viola. My father died when I was twenty-four, and that's when things changed dramatically in my family. I found God when I was at rock bottom, experienced his love and presence for myself . . .'

As we talked on, his warmth felt like an invitation, and his encouragement to confide a relief, like going back to a place I'd once inhabited but had long forgotten.

'So you haven't had it easy, have you?' he said at last, gathering a few threads together.

'God has been merciful to me,' I said. 'But there have been times when I've felt very alone. Not in the sense of solitary – I've embraced the solitude. It has helped me in many ways, enabling me to look inside myself, search for truth. But in the sense of . . . I suppose . . . having felt abandoned. Been cast adrift. I don't know . . . Here at Akenside I believed I'd found something deeper than the transient. But it still hurts when Mother . . .'

I paused. There were a few moments of silence.

'What?' he asked.

'Well, when she brushes me aside. Or deliberately cuts me dead or harshly makes an example of me. It's as though there's something about the core, the reality of me, that is rejected. My outlook. My personality. That stringency would be easier if I saw it also applied to others. But it's very clear that there are different yardsticks being used. Double standards. In my case, it seems it's all about "letting go of props and embracing the cross".'

'It's tough, isn't it. It sounds like she's pushing you. Maybe she sees your potential? Thinks she is helping you to grow? Or it may be that she has no idea how you feel.'

'She doesn't ask.'

'I know, I know. The rigid mask, the stiff upper lip. That's the culture. It may be that that's what she grew up on. But yes, these closed-in communities can be crucifying.'

'I think that's the point.'

'Mother sounds as though she doesn't have a lot of time for you.'

But why, but why . . . ? He'd put his finger on it. That's right, I thought, no time for me, no interest, no connection. It was as though my whole vocation was to suffer.

'I've always felt she was discouraging me. It may be because I'm a convert. Or from an atypical background. You know, I went to boarding school. Down south. They don't like that around here. Anything that makes you look different or better off than others, or even more keen, more hopeful, more anything, she just tries to crush it down.'

'She sounds ruthless. Your humanity, your unique experience of life is as valid as anyone else's. It's a lazy approach to judge people on externals, especially when, as you say, she's asked you next to nothing about yourself. Never really tried to get to know you, the real Catherine, or understand the nuance of your past experience, or to go deeper. It's an old mistake we've made in the Church, this dismissing of people's humanity . . .'

The tears were rolling. My monastic hankie was getting wet. A quarter of someone's threadbare pillowcase was being transformed into a salty, soaking cloth.

'Does she know how much difficulty you went through before you entered?' Raphael asked. I'd spent little more than half an hour with him, and he was already getting to know me better than my sisters. He was already going to the heart of things.

'Very little. Just that my father was much older, and died before I entered, and that my mother's always been very remote. Eccentric really. She doesn't mean any harm, but . . .'

'It's not surprising that you are having trouble, Sister Catherine. Not one but two distant mothers, a forever precious but inaccessible father, a silent God. But what you do have is the gift of prayer. Somewhere in this dedicated cloister you are finding your own way. You are learning what it is to be true to yourself.'

I nodded. His words were kind. I was having to find my own way.

'It sounds to me as though your heart is very much in the right place, sister.' Father Raphael seemed to be winding things up. 'You are young, and brave, and you know how to think for yourself. You are not going to find it easy, though, whatever happens. If you were a plodder, with a less lively mind, you'd probably have an easier time of it. But if the cloister is still what you feel called to, if it is what you really want . . .'

I assured him that I still wanted to go ahead. God may

have gone quiet on me, and the way might be surrounded with thorns, but glorifying God was surely what I was born to do. Making the best of things. Engaging with redemption. Yes, I missed my music, but – could there be a higher vocation, a greater life's work and purpose than this?

The atmosphere in the parlour had lifted. Father was now smiling, sitting back comfortably and leaning his head to one side. He was a pleasant person.

'To sum up, Sister Catherine, what do you see as the hardest thing, for you, about the Life? What, overall, is the thing that presents you with the greatest challenge?'

The question struck the space between us, and its implications coursed through me like a laser beam. I needed a moment to think about it, and then, as though drawing out a line with great difficulty from some deep lagoon within myself, I said: 'The hardest thing is the feeling that I am not actually loved. Not supported, wanted or accepted here among the other sisters. There's hurtfulness, too, on the part of some of them. A harsh, impersonal approach. I just find it strange, and difficult to reconcile with . . .' I was crying freely now, and my words petered out.

'The love of God?' he finished my thought for me. I nodded, wiping my eyes. 'Has the obsession with the status of the order caused them to lose sight of the bigger picture?'

I nodded, and wept a bit more. 'Thank you, Father. Sometimes I just feel so crushed. So rejected and alone.'

No shock waves. Just accepting silence. No attempt to reconstruct or remould what I had said. And the long, velvety brown look. The relief was palpable, extraordinary. During our conversation some real, authentic part of me had escaped and had been entrusted to another sentient being. The white light of the truth was out there, suddenly filling the whole room. Instead of becoming anxious, though, I was relieved. There was a surge of inner strength even in the saying of the authentic words. A burden lifting. Through the intersections of the dark wooden grille, I saw only a plump man at peace. There was no judgement, no 'snap out of it', or 'don't be so silly'. Just a nodding and an understanding. A kindness that was in itself a kind of healing.

'Communities like this all have their problems,' he said. 'And as a newcomer – you've been here, what, five or six years? – you won't know the messy human history of what you are inheriting. How could you? The sisters will never talk about this. The factions, the past tensions with Mellerby, for example. They've had issues here for a long time, Sister Catherine. What you are taking on is already a difficult situation. Has been for years. There are all kinds of reasons for it. Just try to realise their hurtful attitudes and their prejudice towards you are not your fault. If they are rejecting of your individuality, of your unique background, and of who you really are, it says more about them than it does about you as a human being. Be comforted, Catherine. Be assured the Lord loves you, opens his arms for you, has a heart as tender and loving as any father's, any parent's. He is as accepting of you as a true friend.'

And now the tears were pressing up again. I let them flow, hung my head, and my whole body shook for a few moments. And then I waited, while Father Raphael waited kindly too. And when I'd finished, and he had waited again, I wiped my eyes and we laughed a little bit. We even smiled for a few moments.

'How long are you staying?' I asked him.

'Oh, just as long as Mother needs me,' he replied. There was a long pause, and then he said: 'And you?'

'Well, my intention was to stay for life.' I giggled, inexplicably.

'I thought you were going to say that. But remember, the choice is yours, Catherine. The choice is yours.'

So, you're not going to stop me, I felt like saying. I've told you everything – and this is how it's meant to be? But, instead, I smiled again. In a funny way it hurt. I knew he'd be gone the next day and would very probably never be back.

23. Solemn Profession

Mother Elizabeth could see that I was in a bit of a flurry. 'Jen's all in a muddle too,' she told me after Raphael had gone. Her point was proved. These outside advisors did far more harm than good, stirring us up, over-stimulating us, disrupting our quiet and recollection, and asking difficult questions that were better left unaddressed.

I realised that Jen had resented and resisted his questions as much as I'd been relieved by them, and that she had felt affronted by his prying. He'd tried to get her to talk about such things as feelings! Feelings! Can you believe it? And he'd asked her about sexuality, of all things! Mother was most disapproving. What did 'that sort of thing' have to do with us, with our chastity and consecration? But these days, of course, it was apparently all people talked about. Such a waste of time, and quite unsuitable.

How had I got on with his approach? Mother had taken me aside into a handy alcove and wanted to know. I told her that I'd liked him, and found the conversation natural, but still quite emotionally draining. Yes, it was helpful, but I'd felt churned up and tearful afterwards, and did not quite know why.

'Well, yes, we all noticed that – you big baby. Really. What would Father have thought? I hope you didn't give him the wrong impression. No one wants to see a weeping nun. As I always say, misery is a luxury none of us can afford. Making a cheerful impression on outsiders is very important. It's a form of virtue. And considering he's got a relative in the order . . . Talk gets around, you know. Now you just need to get back to work and settle down.'

As usual, my and Jen's reactions were diametrically opposed. Could Mother tell that my tears were not because I'd found the conversation intrusive, but because I'd found it a relief? Was she able to see beyond what she called 'misery' and recognise that cathartic emotions were at work, things that needed to be dealt with and acknowledged? Did it not occur to her that a conversation that stirred things up was not necessarily something to be avoided? Who knows how emotionally honest she was with herself, in the still hours of the night when she was alone in her cell. What stories did she tell herself while she was stroking the cats, feeding them tit-bits? But Mother was not one to sit around. She was needed and had work to do.

If only my twin could acknowledge the tensions and dif-ficulties between us, I thought, and just admit she'd been unkind to me at times. That alone would make so much dif-ference. I was always the one tying myself in knots to please. Apology and thoughtfulness apparently came more naturally to some people than to others. To my mind it was obvious – if you slammed a door in someone's face (something I was getting used to as Jen's moodiness grew darker by the day) you just said sorry. What was so difficult about that? Well, there was one thing against it, I supposed, and that was the rule of three, and the prohibition against sisters exchanging words that did not count as either 'practical' or 'recreational'. Confidences and soft-heartedness were seen as infidelities to the customs and spirit of the house. If a sister was upset, that was her problem, and for her to sort out with God's help. The problem with things like personal apologies was that it never stopped just there. No, emotions came to the surface, and you could end up with sisters crying in each other's arms. Most definitely to be avoided.

Now we were going into the seven-day retreat usual before the rite of solemn profession. With life vows now on the cards, and with our usual pairing in a single public ceremony there was an inevitability about the way things were going to be done. We'd go up to the front in our white novices' veils and kneel before Mother Elizabeth, Jen first, then me. We'd place our hands between Our Mother's in an attitude of prayer, and look into her eyes as she asked us certain questions. We would give the customary responses, already learned by rote, and she would then remove our white veils and replace them with black ones, signs to the world that we had now died to ourselves and were 'buried with Christ' for evermore. It was terrifying, of course, but we didn't talk about that side of it. Instead, we focused on the 'grace' of the occasion, and of the privilege of being brides of Christ.

When the retreat had almost run its course, Mother arranged for the two of us to meet her in the day room in the infirmary for a final chat. Was it to be a pep talk or a tea party? Was it a chance to recreate and 'let off steam' or was it a time for reminding ourselves of the seriousness of what we were taking on? One thing clear to me at this late hour was that this was the last chance for novitiate confusions to be cleared up. I was feeling tender and wobbly, and who knew, maybe Jennifer was feeling the same? Might it not help both of us to be able to clear the air of past misunderstandings and to make gestures of good will for the future?

I knew I would never feel resolved about the ups and downs of my relationship with Jennifer if I didn't at least try to address the issues. With the three of us present, with

Mother Elizabeth herself as witness, all would be legitimate, and I could lead the way in making a generic apology to Jen, that way making it easier for her to say sorry to me. Sorry was all I wanted to hear, some kindness and an acknowledgement of how difficult things had been and how much pain she'd caused me with her harsh and domineering manner over the years. Surely I could count on her to reciprocate? She was a Carmelite. And it was such an easy thing to say. Humility was our way of life.

Once we were settled in the day room and becoming accustomed to each other's voice and close proximity after the five days of retreat, Mother Elizabeth asked us how we were managing, and whether there was anything we wanted to ask. This was our last chance, after all. It was the big day the day after tomorrow. So now or never, going, going, gone! I appreciated the jolly tone was meant to put us at our ease, and hoped an informal chat where we opened up to each other might now be possible. As she had said, it really was now or never. Jen and I were on the verge of being united in twin-dom for life. And so I spoke.

'I just wanted to say . . .' I began, looking in turn at Mother and at Jennifer with sincerity, 'or rather, I wanted to reach out and offer a general apology of my shortcomings over the years, and to say sorry for any failures on my part. I thought now might be the time . . .'

But here I faltered. No sooner had I spoken than I watched, with horror, as a slow, cruel smile spread over Jen's face. She locked smiling eyes with Our Mother. It was clear she had no intention of reciprocating. Instead, she sat there, smug, smirking, exchanging looks of open satisfaction with Elizabeth. And Elizabeth, no less than Jennifer, held herself magisterially aloof from all I'd offered them, the expectation of generosity, the hopeful gesture, the desire to connect. I'd come forward in trust, only to find them sticking the sword in even deeper. Had they no sensitivity, or humble human feelings of their own? Had they no natural instinct of how to meet someone halfway, if only out of courtesy?

I left the day room in more pain than I had entered it. I had humbled myself willingly, only to be kicked while I was down, further humiliated. You want to say sorry? they seemed to say. Go on then, you stupid sinner. They, of course, had nothing for which to apologise, no faults of their own. That was their level of humanity. There was no reciprocal courtesy in this place. I should have known better, but still these realisations came as shocks.

During the final day of the retreat everything about the monastery seemed under a cloud. The spring weather was in danger of scuttling away, blown by high winds and interspersed with stormy squalls. Then the sun came out, just for a moment. The next day was the great event. I'd done everything I could to prepare myself. I hoped I had at least purified my heart by my pathetic confession. The morning would come and would see me kneeling. The bishop would don his mitre, and the guitars would begin to play.

And indeed they did. The strumming could be heard an hour beforehand, a silvery tickle of notes behind the antechoir door, and then a concerted chordal section, G-D-E-D, with someone adding a descant on the recorder. Then came an added seventh and a suspension, before the resolution. Neither Jennifer nor I were to be taking part in the playing – it was our day – which meant the instrumental side of things would feel (and sound) a little different from our usual style. But we'd had a say in the choice of readings and hymns, a potentially stressful area we both did our best to navigate without making it too obvious we had different preferences when it came to the liturgy. Secretly, I wished I could have had a day of my own, a solemn profession that really felt personally meaningful, something I had fully chosen. But as it was, we were going forward together and individuality had to be set aside, which – when you grasped what the vows were all about – was appropriate. 'Keep nothing back for yourself,' Old Mother used to say.

Soon a bell would be ringing and it would be time for me to gather myself together and tidy myself up, and appear, a beaming bride, on the threshold of the antechoir. Soon the visitors would be arriving – a cohort of priests from the diocese, an old, dear friend from London, now a Jesuit, and various members of our families. This, of all occasions, was one that would be opened unreservedly to the public. Out in the extern chapel they'd sit, an unseen collective, an army of supporters singing us on. And then, together with Sister Jennifer, I would process into choir and up towards the sanctuary where the clergy would be waiting for us in an imposing semicircle. But perhaps – and here I was clutching at a straw – perhaps things would work out differently, perhaps Jen might see things in a new light. Perhaps she would realise there was something amiss, perhaps back out at the last minute . . .

As the day rises up in my mind, I am back there again on that brave threshold, a moment never to be reversed or recaptured in its entirety, back at the very moment of fear and decision, with the bell going, and the footsteps of a whole community arriving with a great shuffling sound like water, and the rustling of many habits in the hall. I am back there being greeted by the Council, my cheeks flushed with indefinable emotion, a posy of spring flowers being thrust into my hands. My mind is still swarming with all the things I haven't said, still haven't done, the bridge-building I still so much desire to bring about with the truly distant and the half-remote, with those whose smiles hide a world of fulmination and frustration. I yearn for the honesty I seek to be not only permitted but reciprocated. But now it is too late, and we are being ushered along towards the sanctuary, led like garlanded oxen to the sacrifice. The guitars are tuning up.

Soon I am standing alongside Jen on our side of the grille, right on the edge, almost touching the wooden bars, and within sight of the outside chapel. There are far more people out there than I had expected. The sight of so many of them, of my family, and especially the large contingent of robed priests, makes me feel a little sick. My stomach is wildly lurching. The first hymn is already over, and there is a strong buzz in the air. Even the breathing of the many priests assembled so close by seems to add to the tense mood of expectation. Then I see a nervy man with a moustache going up to the lectern – it is Jennifer's father – and preparing to read the first lesson.

The rest of the ceremony passes in something of a haze. I've been waiting five and a half years to know for sure whether I would ever reach this point, and whether Jen would reach it too. So many questions. But now Jen is up there ahead of me, her hands pressed between Mother's palms, gazing into her eyes as she recites aloud the words of dedication. Mother is making the sign of the cross on Jen's newly black-veiled head, and Jen is rising, returning to her place next to me in her special seat. She has gone through with it.

And now it is my turn. There is no longer any ambiguity about what to expect, no longer any possibility of a different ending. I realise I could still make a dash for it. But no. I've come this far. I've stuck it out. And so I rise and walk over to where Mother sits near the altar. I kneel and place my hands between her palms. I lift up my face to look at her and try to smile. And soon I am saying those words aloud, words that have so terrified me in recent weeks, and yet that once held such a strong attraction. Poverty, chastity and obedience . . . and the deal is done.

24. Reversals

The climax of final vows and the emotional exhaustion that followed it had taken their toll, and I'd asked Mother for an exceptional permission to go away for a short break, either with my sister and her husband, or at another monastery. Such restorative retreats away were rare, and yet not unheard of. One or two other sisters had been to Mellerby for a rest when things had got too much for them, and had returned the better able to live the Life. Naturally, some of them got ideas about transferring, but, if they did, presumably that just meant that Mellerby was where they were meant to be. On the other hand, after Pippa's defection, Elizabeth had told us she would 'never countenance' anyone else looking to move to another Carmel. What misguided notions some people seemed to have.

The Holton sisters at least were settling in, although they sometimes made comments at recreation, indirectly reminding us they'd chosen Akenside from all the other Carmels, expecting to find us an accepting and compatible lot to live with. Perhaps it was the beauty of the grounds that had mesmerised them that first visit, or perhaps the broad beam of Mother Elizabeth's smile, the special smile she reserved for strangers. They continued to hint that things were not quite as they'd expected to find them, particularly our disregard of those customs that prevented the concentration of power in the hands of one personality, and the community's readiness to reinforce this time and again. It had happened with

Julianna, and they could see that things were going in the same direction with Elizabeth, already so established as a 'perennial prioress' on an unapologetic pedestal. They were less adept at covering up their natural feelings than us lot had been trained to be. At Holton they'd been allowed to challenge and discuss, to speak their minds.

I'd done my best to submerge my natural instincts, to resist the wide-ranging thoughts that sometimes came to me since my talk with Father Raphael. What would life be like at Mellerby? Might I be more able to open up and express my thoughts, be true to myself there, where I supposed the Akenside prejudices and constrictions did not apply? As though reading my mind, Elizabeth had produced a new dogma, one that said the grass was never greener on the other side. Looking for 'escape routes', as she called relief from suffering or any sort of consolation, was frowned upon, and those who'd transferred to other Carmels were seen as bad examples. All suffering was penance, and penance had a purpose. Understood correctly, it was redemptive. 'Giving in' was a form of failure, and – until now – I'd avoided overt failure like the plague. Failure, I'd supposed, was an enemy of holiness. How little I'd really grasped of human complexity, and of what it took to grow profoundly as a sincere person in search of the truth. Sometimes the image of oneself as good needs to be shattered, to make way for deeper realities. The days when I'd assumed I'd found what I was looking for, simply by becoming a Catholic and a Carmelite, were running out. Any sort of truth worth knowing was not an automatic result of rule-keeping, of never stepping out of line, but rather of myriad experiences and a readiness to face reality. And now I was ready to push a little at the boundaries.

'No, you can't just go and see your sister,' Mother was saying to me. 'What do you mean, she needs you – of course she doesn't need you. She can manage perfectly well without you. She's a grown woman. Why on earth would she want you around? What stuff and nonsense. What use are you anyway to anyone? You big baby, you silly child.'

'But I feel—'

'No one cares what you feel. You're here now. This is what you signed up for. You just need to get on with it. Goodness me, Sister Catherine.'

The worry worming itself into my mind was about Frankie and had been growing steadily ever since the day of my final vows. The big shock that day, apart from the sight of all those priests spreading out onto the sanctuary, was the fact that so many of my family had been in tears. They'd all been so casual about my vocation until now. No worries, they'd always seemed to say. It's your life, Cathy. Do whatever you want. That was the easy-going mantra that went with our humane family vibe. So it never occurred to me that I was in any way upsetting (or even abandoning) them by becoming a Carmelite. Frankie, although an agnostic, had even said my entering Akenside had felt a natural step for me to take at the time. It was a step that she had seen as growing out of who I was, the deep-thinking older sister who was always losing herself in books, who liked long walks and quiet and independence. How little we still knew about enclosure!

I knew it was futile to press my point with Mother. But all I could think about was the growing anxiety about my sister. Her tears, her distress, her emotional outpouring. So uncharacteristic. Perhaps my responsibility. Everything was suddenly nerve-wracking, and nothing felt right any more. On top of this, I'd had some strange waves of extreme weakness in my legs. My feet and ankles were becoming feeble and tingly. If this was due to panic, I'd managed, and suppressed it as far as possible until now, but finally it was coming up through my limbs, surging through my very body. Sometimes I had to hold on to the wall just to steady myself, stop myself from falling. One day Mother had found me slumped in a pile outside the antechoir, my legs as soft as jelly, a heap of help-lessness. My head was aching. How she'd scorned this failure. How I needed to grow up, get back on my feet! It was 'normal' to encounter challenges, to start to feel spiritually disorien-tated after a while, she told me. Just deal with it, pull yourself together, and no, you don't need to see a doctor.

Yes, we'd been told about it, the dark night of the soul, told to expect everything to feel barren and miserable after a while. Feelings passed, while faith, hope and love alone remained. But those three virtues themselves had been rede-fined as something stony and unyielding. Faith was a decision, one which in its purest form was unsupported by the imagin-ation or emotions. Hope was the override button you pressed when in danger of desperation. Love was an objective duty, dispensed evenly and equally to all people at all times, no matter how you actually felt about them. Love of God was a more exclusive form of the same. Love of God was surren-der to the consuming fire.

I'd read all about these desert sojourns of the spirit, these wilderness experiences, in John of the Cross, had given my assent to his theory of the soul's purification. We all needed to be stripped of comforts and supports until we could love God for himself alone, not for how he made us feel, or any other of his benefits. John had described the process of 'stripping' in poetic terms, and, as a young nun, that was good enough for me. Bring it on, I'd said. 'Where has thou hidden, my beloved?' John had asked, comparing himself to a wounded stag left panting for further glimpses of transcendence. 'Was it a vision, or a waking dream? Fled is that music: do I wake or sleep?' It was Keatsian. Yes, fled indeed was all that beauty and transcendence, and what the hell was going on inside me, and why did I feel a sort of indefinable dread deep down in my gut?

Meanwhile, Jen was striding about triumphantly, on top of the world. Her family had been there in force at the profession ceremony, all so proud to have a fully-fledged nun to their credit. They were a Proper Catholic Family. They had brought piles of gifts and flowers. Their laughter floated across the sanctuary after the service, when people had been allowed to come up to the grille and congratulate us. My family and my London friends, up from the Kilburn Soup Kitchen where I used to volunteer, by contrast, had been inconsolable. This was hugely upsetting and confusing for me, especially given how relaxed they'd all been about my entering. Unlike Jennifer's entourage, who had tried to stop her once upon a time, none of my relatives had seemed to mind my locking myself away. Now everything was reversed. Jennifer's family could not have been more delighted, while mine, and my sister Frankie in particular, were in floods of tears. The way some of them had been sobbing was alarming. We were not used to seeing unbridled emotion like this in our cloistered world. It all seemed so extreme. What was going on? Against the backdrop of Jen's whoops, and Mother Elizabeth purring into the ears of her family, I felt this dissonance all the more deeply. What had I done?

Deep down the niggle worked its way into my entrails. I was the cause of my beloved sister's tears, her upset. I was the one who had made these friendly people cry. Something was amiss, and I was to blame. I wondered whether there was something of which these onlookers had all been aware, something ominous they'd all picked up on. What was it they all saw or understood, the day of my profession? What alien influence was there in the sanctuary working on their minds and emotions? However much I thought about it, I could not feel resolved or right about the situation.

On the plus side, there was light on the horizon as far as the languishing novitiate was concerned. Not one nibbler but two! Elizabeth was delighted. Another pair of twins! But what, I was wondering, do we actually know about dear Stephanie, the sweet girl with curly fair hair, from the sixth-form college? Or about Lucy, the dark-haired beanpole with a playful personality? How deep had conversations gone with them, how much did they know about what to expect, and how much would they be welcomed for who they really were, rather than what they represented for Akenside as a boost to our already 'healthy' numbers? How much did Mother really care?

Steph had first been brought out by Father Brendan on one of his pastoral visits, while Lucy had come out with a friend who had been considering entering herself, but had changed her mind. Lucy had been captivated by the beauty of the liturgy and by the silence. Both were fervent in their own ways.

I knew enough to realise that new entrants' purely natural personalities and histories would be largely skimmed over, because what mattered in an applicant was good will, malleability and the right disposition. As long as she was a Good Catholic, and free of impediments, a new enquirer was always seen as an answer to Mother's prayers. More than that, it would be taken as read that the best possible outcome would be her smooth entry into the Life, assuming there were no obvious contraindications. Poor health, debt or family dependents were things that surfaced early on, and made for a clear-cut case against a potential entrant. But, in the absence of those, the thumbs-up would be given, and everyone would wave her through until she found herself feted on her trial stay – elated at the beauty of it all, showered with positive attention for a few weeks, happy in the delicious sense of freedom from all worldly cares. And in that state of wonder all the seeds of future plants, both wheat and darnel, would be sown.

Back she'd come a few months later, having burned at least some of her bridges, and from that day onwards she'd hear over and again the mantras: It's for life, you know. In for a penny, in for a pound. Once the hand's turned to the plough, only lost souls would think of turning back. Uncertainties? Stare them down, push past them! Just act as though you were sure about it. Don't give in. Fake it until you make it. You are here because you have been chosen to be one of the special ones, God's bride.

At the same time, the standard phrases crafted for the benefit of outsiders would be rolled out and given their due from time to time. The words had a bland formality. Up until her Clothing a postulant is free to leave at any time. For vows to be valid they must be taken voluntarily and not under duress. At the expiry of temporary vows, a sister is free to return to secular life if she so wishes. A discernment period of five years is allowed before any final commitment . . . Words to that effect. Between these two opposing messages was a gulf of qualitative difference. It was clear which carried weight in practice, and which amounted to words alone – powerful things when people wanted them to be, but as flimsy as air when they didn't fit the agenda. On the one hand, we came as enquirers, free to stay or go, encouraged to 'give it a try'. Just come and have a look. No sooner were we over the threshold, however, than it seemed a crime to reconsider, to be uncertain, or to contemplate a return to life outside. Our free wills were to be handed over to God, as mediated and represented by the prioress. When the giving up of our wills was the primary requirement, what could it possibly mean to say we chose anything else, or 'didn't want' to stay at Akenside? What did it mean to want anything other than to obey?

Seeing these two new entrants, so keen and fresh, the question resurfaced for me again. My heart felt for them. For now, they wanted to be among the chosen, to have a place in the choir, a cell of their own, and a new, higher purpose in life. They longed to feel the urgency of vocation. But did they really know what they were asking? No, of course not. None of us really knew what lurked in the chalice.

The next year was the centenary of St Thérèse and there were grand festivities planned. The monastery would be hosting all sorts of special events, a tea party with a bishop, even a play. That kind of thing. Unsurprisingly, both Lucy and Stephanie had requested the date itself for their entrance as postulants. Another jackpot, Mother was already whispering. But I saw in the arrival of another pair of twins cause for apprehension. Was history to repeat itself? Were these two to be played off against each other? When Lucy wrote to say she thought she'd give it a few more weeks, I was relieved. Perhaps someone had recommended they space the new arrivals out this time, treat them as separate individuals, each on their separate merits. And so the weeks would pass, and gradually the novitiate would be repopulated, the empty nest refilled.

Even before Lucy and Steph applied to us, it had been

conveyed to me that the formation sessions in the novitiate would continue, but on a reduced basis, for Jen's benefit alone. This was immediately after our double profession. Jen still felt she needed some support, apparently, and was not quite ready for the far greater solitude and discipline the life of a chapter sister required. This was a surprise. Everything in the novitiate had been geared to profession, and now more novitiate sessions even though we were solemnly professed? Perhaps it was a good idea. But when I asked whether I could join in and be supported too, Barbara, Ellen and Elizabeth all said, with finality: No. The ongoing sessions were not for me. It was Jen who needed the extra help.

No longer being included or having access to the facilities in the novitiate, under these circumstances, felt like a rejection. It was hurtful being left out in the cold. And of course there was still more to learn. I'd been longing for the time we'd finally get to study the writings of the order more deeply. Longing for some real interchange of thoughts and ideas. Longing to feel there was scope for further attempts at understanding, and communication. Was Mother always going to distance and discourage me? On the other hand, I could well imagine the style of the reduced sessions, with only Jen, catering to her needs, and realised I was perhaps well out of it. Mother would have her boxes of chocolates at the ready and her party poppers. No one really wanted to do any work today, did they? The skipping ropes would come out.

There is a unique pain, neuroscientists say, that comes from being deliberately excluded, a part of the brain that responds as it does to bullying. I felt it keenly. There had been a double standard in our training all along, one whereby I was expected to live a certain way, alone, thrown back on myself and my own inner resources, while my companion was given a completely different blueprint, including far more support. I'd got used to a kind of spiritual loneliness long ago, but this – this deliberate, final, frosty distancing – was too much.

That summer, at least three big things happened. First Stephanie and then Lucy entered as postulants, filling our recreations with their cheer and buzz, and adding warmth and vigour to the life of the community. They were both lovely, and naturally we welcomed two extra sets of feet pattering up and down the central staircase, two voices adding to the swell of our liturgical singing. The centenary of St Thérèse was also a milestone, a time of special reflection and festivity. Later in the year, she would be declared a Doctor of the Church by Pope John Paul II, adding another Carmelite to the canon, alongside John and Teresa.

The third extraordinary (and in this case, tragic) event was the death of Diana, Princess of Wales. It was a Sunday morning, and I still recall wondering whether I'd heard correctly when it was announced from the pulpit. Poor old Father Stanley had a way of mumbling. But no, the news was true, and the fact that we were so unused to hearing updates from the wider world made it all the more dramatic. There was a kind of incredulity among us, and then, for days, the appearance of the first sheets of real-world newsprint we'd seen in years that a friend of Mother's sent in, and that she arranged on the community-room table. Page after page showing the weeping crowds, the flowers outside Buckingham Palace.

In Carmel we lived without television, radio and the secular press and other media. News from outside was strictly filtered, mediated via Mother or the priests, just as the books in the library were vetted for suitability. On this occasion, the sight of newspaper headlines, images and cuttings was a blast from the past, eliciting a range of reactions. We prayed for Diana that year (although, as Catholics, our prayers focused more on the big picture, asking for God's mercy, and for the graces of 'conversion' and 'salvation' for all members of the Royal Family), feeling sad that such a woman had been taken in her prime. The cuttings stayed on the hall table for days, triggering memories, causing us to wonder at the state of the world. Even the pictures of the crowds and their unfamiliar 'worldly' clothing were part fascinating, part repelling. We were only meant to read the relevant sections, of course, and made sure not to turn the cuttings over. Who knew what was on the other side?

That Indian summer, with a novitiate catering not so much for the newcomers as for the clique of which they were inescapably a part, there was a run of three consecutive birthdays, Steph's, Mother Irene's and Suzanne's. A triple run of celebrations! This was just the kind of thing Elizabeth famously enjoyed holding court over. A birthday was always a chance to single out some and ignore others, the differing treatments people received marking differing grades of approval in Mother's book. There were treats which were easy enough to devise and were a great way to get people firmly on side, loyal not so much to God or Carmel as to the inner coterie that made a point of excluding and disparaging those who did not serve their interests. Chocolates and guitars usually did the trick. Steph's and Suzanne's birthdays, which fell on days one and three respectively, were made much of, with loud garden tea-parties, festivities and balloons. From our cell windows the rest of us saw them weaving their way across the lawn at reading time, balancing trays of cakes with tambourines and guitars, as they strolled to the further meadow.

Luckily for them the weather was fine. But on the most radiant day of all, the middle day, Irene's birthday, a conspicuous
stillness fell over the monastery. Nothing happened. It was
almost like old times. But the snub to Irene could not have
been greater. Everyone noticed, but as usual no one spoke.

Lovely though she was, it was Lucy who inadvertently put
her finger on things one day at an open-air activity. It was
while we were having one of our optional midday summer
recreations, when talk was combined with gardening work,
the able-bodied generously raking dry grass into piles near
the bonfire patch. 'Good to see the gang out in force,' she
said. The wind was in danger of whisking the strands of
grass away, but we all leaned forward and managed to man-
oeuvre the unwieldy clumps of drying hay into one pile. At
that moment, seeing the separate strands stick together and
coagulate, something else solidified and came into focus.
Mother's coterie was not just an extended novitiate team or a
study group. From now on, by their own admission, they
were 'the gang'.

25. The Elections

The bell had been rung, and the chequerboard hall was dotted with black-veiled sisters putting on their great cream cloaks. It was spring and the elections had come round again. How quickly three years passed once you had got used to the rhythm of the Life. Like a well-oiled machine the monastery functioned as though it belonged to a higher order than the human norm, and we all continued to inhabit our allotted grooves. Each cog was there to serve the whole. But we all knew this status quo, painful for some, pleasant for others, was not necessarily inviolable. Now the arc of the broad stairway was filled with misty light, tiny flecks dancing in the beams, the smell and smoke of wax tapers coiling upwards and around in random directions. Sisters avoided each other's eyes.

Soon we were in place in our stalls. We rose to sing the invocation of the Holy Spirit. A confluence of voices arranged itself, pale and shaky. The flames of the tall candles on the altar flickered. And then the great moment arrived: Father Gregory rose up in his own sea of vestments, which followed him like a wave, turning as he circumnavigated the sanctuary. He arrived at the threshold of our side of the raised wooden platform, where the grille had been half opened to let him look in. We saw him before us, a figure of humanity, a figure of the authority we were bound to honour by virtue of our membership of the Church. Mother coughed. We all stood, intent upon him and on the sacred duty to cast a vote for our prioress according to our spirit-enlightened conscience. The 'scrutators' would triple check the slips of paper, then Father Gregory would announce the result, which was a clear expression of the will of God. We'd been prepped and drilled in the procedure. Now he was preparing to speak – a prophet acting as the mouthpiece of God. He was spreading his enclosing arms. And then he was asking us to sit for a moment. 'Dear sisters . . .' he appealed. It was customary for there to be a mini-sermon on the import of the proceedings.

'My dear sisters in the Church, we are come together, as we do every three years, to beseech God to reveal his choice of prioress. He will surely do so if we trust in him, and allow his grace to be supreme. It seems only last week that Mother Elizabeth was voted in for her second term in office. And what a term of office it has been! A double profession, a double entry – the blessing of two new chapter sisters, two new novices! Much to celebrate. And how helpful for all of us, consecrated religious, that we have the Holy Father's latest pronouncements on the religious life to support and shed light on the path. I trust you have all been studying the latest encyclical which, while new, is already not so new now. What is it, three years already? And how timely and how very much needed an encyclical it was.'

What new pronouncement was that? I wondered. Surely he couldn't mean *Perfectae Caritatis*? That was issued over thirty years ago, and yes, certainly we knew it well.

'So, building on *Perfectae Caritatis* – which in the days of the Second Vatican Council set a new standard of authenticity for enclosed communities – the Pope has now offered us new spiritual directives and encouragement in *Fraternal Life in Community*. This document has clarified monastic values, pointing us back to our source charisms, if ever there was any doubt.'

Father Gregory was the soul of diplomacy. He looked up and out at the two long rows of chapter sisters in their stalls, surveyed us with a gentle smile. Yet I could discern a subtle undercurrent of concern. He went on: 'The old model of leadership, with its pitfalls of authoritarianism on the one hand, and infantilism on the other, is no longer acceptable in our communities. The days of putting our leaders on pedestals, the days of permanently enshrined prioresses, are behind us, dear sisters. The time has come for sharing and collaboration, for the generous delegation of duties, like the Pope's own more collegial model. As you all know, your own Constitutions discourage perennially repeated terms of office, and only allow them in communities who really have no alternatives but to re-elect. That is, where there are no other sisters young and fit enough, or capable of leadership. And even then it is a rare exception, requiring a special permission from the Pope. It is not something to be undertaken lightly.'

The air around me was tightening. How does one sense these things? Somehow I knew that Sister Barbara was fidgeting in her seat. I knew Mother was all tight and tense, up there at the top, and that Jen was indignant, I knew it by the working of my antennae, although I didn't know quite how red Jen's face would be, or how stormy her expression. And what was this new document he kept on referring to? The title, *Fraternal Life in Community*, was unfamiliar. In fact, we'd never heard of it. Never so much as seen a copy. Yet it was addressed to us enclosed nuns from the Pope himself, a new articulation of the Mind of the Church.

Then he was going on: 'You will all of course have read it, and perhaps studied it as a group. Perhaps in your weekly community meetings? I trust all sisters have been given copies. As you know, a range of enclosed monasteries and abbeys were consulted around the world, since, after all, it was for you, the cloistered contemplatives in the Church, that it was written. And how helpful you have probably been finding it. A real beacon for the practical implementation of the Mind of the Church. A very insightful document . . .'

There was a certain amount of coughing and computing going on. Yes, it was inescapable, there had been some sort of important Church pronouncement withheld from us. Not any old one, but one addressed to us specifically, one drawn up with us in mind. Hadn't Judith once alluded to it? Or was it Irene? But the topic had been brushed aside. Perfection, Mother Elizabeth told us, lay not in reading much, or speaking much, but in 'loving much'. The definition of love God was to obey. To know God was to submit, as simple as that. Everything else was a distraction. We all needed to let off steam from time to time, fair enough, but what we didn't want was too much intellectual stimulation.

The proceedings continued. I knew very well what I'd decided on, this my first time voting as a chapter sister. My choice for prioress was Sister Suzanne, someone clearly endowed with leadership qualities and intelligence, but I still needed to concentrate, and there were protocols to be observed. I watched as the processions to the top began in order of religion. We, the youngest, had time to compose ourselves. The novices, meanwhile, were in the day room, praying for God's grace and guidance at this crucial hour.

'So,' Father Gregory raised his voice for one last rally, 'dear sisters, let us take a minute to compose ourselves, and let us pray. Then we shall begin.'

One by one we moved forward, processing to the front to cast our votes by means of a slip of paper with a name on it,

placed into a box. Then we returned to our places. We waited
for what, to some, might have seemed a foregone conclu-
sion, a long-expected result. But then Father moved forward
and raised his voice to say something. And, as the air focused,
he announced that Mother Elizabeth was out. She sat down,
looking quietly at her hands, while the rest of us remained
standing. There was no outward reaction, no stirring.

Out at the first ballot. It did feel like a shock, and I took it
in quietly. It was not unthinkable, given all Father Gregory
had said, but – let's just say, unlikely. Elizabeth was the
embodiment of authority among us, to an extent that had
always felt unassailable, even though many of us could see it
was so flawed. She was the figurehead. In the silence of the
great choir, a similar reverberation was resounding in people's minds. Who now would take her place? A stretch of the
imagination was needed. People needed to dig deep, look
into their souls and think of who else among us might make
a good prioress: a humble leader of the group, someone who
was a good listener, as well as an administrator. Someone
who cared not only about the institution, but about individuals and their spiritual growth. A second and a third ballot
followed, and Gregory announced their results. A tie each
time, which meant we'd have to try again. But still the stubborn tied result remained.

Finally, recourse was made to the Rule and Constitutions.
The latter outlined that if after a series of ballots the result
stubbornly remained a tie, the older in religion of the two
candidates would be elected. The chosen one would then rise
from the obscurity of the ranks to be the new Reverend
Mother, a major religious superior in the Roman Catholic
Church, just under the bishop himself in authority, a force to
be reckoned with. And then the grace of the office would

follow, just as surely as Jesus rose from the dead, as day follows night. This was no more nor less than what we had been taught to believe. And so Father Gregory rose, stepped forward and said: 'Dear sisters, we have a result. The Lord has spoken. The Holy Spirit has indicated your chosen successor. Will you please stand, and get ready to welcome Mother Irene, your new prioress.'

For a moment a chasm of even deeper silence opened before us. The very air was startled. The chasm yawned. Tall candles were being passed round. Elizabeth wore her unchanging mask of expressionless composure. Sister Ellen, next to me, caught my attention and tilted her lit candle towards mine, offering its tiny flame. Her large eyes flashed me a meaningful look. What was she saying? Opposite us, Sister Jennifer was looking round wildly, trying to grab the attention of each sister in turn, as though expecting someone to act, do something, intervene, or at least to join her in reaction. She was flailing, her body swinging this way and that. Her flushed face suggested a crisis, and yet – here we were, a community of nuns quietly doing what we were supposed to, a routine procedure, selecting our new Superior. This was standard stuff.

From her position two-thirds of the way up the choir, Irene, once prioress of Holton, now our own Reverend Mother, swung out with muted panache. Her face was fixed ahead of her, beaming towards the priest standing on the sanctuary. Her hulking frame, broad, heavy and ungainly, moved decisively up to the front, the drag of a weak ankle only slightly apparent under the movement of her thick cloak and habit. Her bottle-glass spectacles were impenetrable, misted over, although the emotions were strictly controlled. She reached out and brusquely shook the hand that was offered her, a manly gesture, then crossed herself, wobbled and knelt.

Outside in the hall, people were putting away their cloaks. The next step was to move on to the community room, where a buffet lunch had been set out on a big festive table at the top with an arrangement of flowers and a large swinging coloured cut-out sign that read OUR MOTHER draped elegantly across the front. There were little bowls of fruit and jugs of water. There were even paper plates and – something we only had once or twice a year – a tablecloth. Under other circumstances someone would have appeared with a guitar by now, or perhaps even had their finger on the cassette recorder. The gang would be talking amongst themselves, making sure to avoid mixing too much with the rest of the community. That's how far things had already gone with them. But as it was, the community room was half abandoned and subdued, as Mother Irene sat there not quite alone, but flanked only by Judith and Marion at an almost empty table. Ambrose, Alison, Jane and a few others were dotted around the room, eating their sandwiches and soup demurely at the smaller tables. But voices were lowered. The mood was not quite right. Elizabeth and the gang, like the ferals, were nowhere to be seen.

26. The Murmuring

It started as a whispering behind closed doors. Voices just out of earshot. Habits sweeping faster than usual, doors clicking with determination. Somewhere out of sight people were gathering, people in twos and threes, people with opinions, and things were being said. You didn't need to have particularly acute antennae – although most of us did – to sense a storm was brewing behind the infirmary doors. And whatever sort of storm it was, it was something purposeful and very determined indeed. There was resistance in the air. A Holton sister at the helm! To certain minds – those who'd lost touch with the principle of faith that was supposed to govern the elections – this seemed unthinkable.

'They have no idea how we do things here,' someone was whispering.

'Our Akenside ways are under threat,' another said.

'The point is, sister, Holton was never like us. Never will be in a million years! As for so-called Mother Irene, heavens! What are we coming to?'

'She's even got the new style of veil, you know, a clip-on one like Mellerby.'

'You don't need to tell me that. She's gone along with all the fads and reforms!'

'Oh, it's all Vatican II stuff – that's what comes of too much talking. Stirring things up. Questioning our customs.'

'And she entered very late, you know.'

'Yes, a late vocation. Only been a Carmelite twenty-five

years. She might be over sixty-five now, but if you haven't been properly formed when you are young . . .'

'That's why we've always done so well here. We've nearly always got some good young ones in the novitiate, thanks to Father Brendan and the chaplaincy.'

'Quite right, too. People lose their malleability after a certain age. You need to break and set the bones while you can. Make the best of youthful good will.'

'But look at Irene, she's only just arrived! How long is it?'

'It's getting on for five years now since Holton closed, but what is that in Carmel? Mother Elizabeth has been within these walls for over thirty years.'

'Five years at Akenside, five years . . . Even if she's had her silver jubilee and been a prioress before, that was elsewhere. In another house.'

And so it went on. A muttering. A murmuring. A mutiny was brewing. Elizabeth, as was customary for an outgoing prioress, retained her honorific title of 'Mother'. It was a vestige she clung to, while those particularly attached to her person began to give the word a new kind of emphasis when referring to her. She was not to lose her aura or her crown. Unsurprisingly, the atmosphere changed dramatically over the next few weeks. Disorientation set in. Tempers were rising. Elizabeth gathered her chosen coterie around her and kept apart in the infirmary. For days, which turned into weeks, we did not see her. There was something stewing, something wrong. Meanwhile, Irene held her head high.

After a couple of weeks I went to see her. The door to her office was open. It was not the large wood-panelled chamber that all the other prioresses had had before her. This was a hurriedly converted cell, thrown together to save Mother Elizabeth from moving her things out. There was far too much stuff in there to have to relocate, and no point taking everything away if you were just going to have to put it all back again in three years' time. Irene's office, by contrast, was a simple, empty room in an out-of-the-way corner of the building, its door permanently ajar. She welcomed visitors, and was pleased to help and listen.

'Ah, Sister Catherine! Hello! How are you doing?' she asked.

'I'm OK, I think,' I said, smiling. I was keen to make a start, to take her up on her invitation. So glad that she was encouraging. So glad to feel some openness and availability on her part towards me. But first, I made to offer the customary gesture . . .

'Oh gosh, sister, no need to bow! No need to put me on a pedestal.'

'Oh, yes . . .' I said, correcting myself and noting the fresh approach.

'And while we are talking about these routines, may I just remind you what I've been telling everybody? I'd like you all to call me Sister Irene, please, not Mother. I'd really prefer sister, like everybody else. A lot of the Carmels switched years ago, and we at Holton certainly felt that using the title "Mother" fostered the wrong kind of attitude.'

'"Wrong" as in?'

'As in . . . infantile, you know. We've come a long way in the Church since the sixties. It's important for everyone to feel aware of their own share of responsibility.'

'Yes, Mo—I mean sister,' I said.

'I know it's a change, and a change of mindset, Catherine, and I can see not everyone is going to make the switch that easily. Some here are very stuck in their ways. But the Mind of the Church really is very clear about this. There is a new model of authority these days. You really all should have been told about it, and have read *Fraternal Life in Community*. It was written precisely for us cloistered nuns, as Father Gregory explained. It's to help us implement a healthy model of authority and obedience. Change has been slow percolating into the enclosed orders, but Vatican II happened over thirty years ago, Catherine, and we really do need to start engaging with the wider Church on this.'

'I understand,' I said. 'The outward way we do things, and even some of the peripheral teachings, are means not ends, and ... if they are means to something more important, it makes sense for us to know when to let things go.'

Irene's moss-green eyes, like small wet buttons through her thick, round spectacles, lingered a few moments on my face. I noticed the heaviness around her jowls. She was appraising me, getting the measure of my dispositions.

'I had to make big leaps of faith, and other changes to my life when I became a Roman Catholic,' I said. 'Had to let a lot of things go. That's why I'm not too bothered by external changes to the way we do things. Isn't it the interior spirit that counts?'

Irene nodded. Her head was leaning to one side. She was looking closely at my face, intent on listening, actually listening and allowing me to speak my mind. She was open and entering into a mutually respectful exchange. I went on: 'All along we've been trained, as novices, to keep our eyes on the transcendent. Haven't we? That's all as I expected it would be. What does bother me, though, is the tension I sometimes see between the two sets of teachings, the old and the new. Surely there are implicit contradictions between the pre- and the post Vatican II outlooks. They can't both simultaneously be true or right. They contradict each other. Yet no one has admitted this or brought it out into the open. That's what worries me. Shouldn't we be cooperating and helping each other to understand these things? There's been no thorough discussion . . .'

'You want to get things straight in your mind, I can see, Sister Catherine. You chose the Church with all its history, and theology, and you expect it to add up.'

I nodded – of course I did.

'You converts always expect miracles of the Church. But this is Christianity, Catherine. We can only go so far as human beings. The rest is mystery. But you do well to ponder and to want to tease things out. Still, you need to set your expectations realistically. In a mixed bag of a community – and God knows Akenside is a mixed bag – there will always be those incapable of considered discourse and philosophical discussion.'

'I know, I know. Mother Elizabeth was insistent that talk could get us nowhere. But . . .' The air hung heavy for a moment. 'But I'd like to read the new encyclical, Sister Irene, and to look in more depth at theologians like, oh – like Karl Rahner and von Balthasar. We've never been taken down that route in any detail. It's always been the Catechism and the Constitutions. I know those formulae by heart. They are essential, but I'd still like to enrich and supplement my knowledge with wider reading, and with trying to see things from every side, to dwell on the different outlooks, at least theoretically understand them with all their implications. It's so frustrating having no intellectual or cultural nourishment at all. I've never said this before, but – Irene, is it really like this in other monasteries?'

The new prioress's expression left me in no doubt that she knew the import of my question, but she chose to let it hang some time in the air. She'd as good as told me that Akenside was in a peculiar state, not for want of 'vocations' or a stock of vigorous young sisters to do the chores, but for a lack of coherent vision and integrity. I left Irene's office that day feeling a window had opened in my mind. It was a relief. She'd reassured me my perceptions were justified, and had had such a natural, easy manner with me! None of that crushing, cruel distancing, none of that punishing me for my supposed 'advantages' or for being a southerner, that dismissal of me just because I spoke, not like the majority, but like me. And I loved the north! Hadn't I fallen in love with it and chosen beautiful Northumberland over London? Hadn't I made all the adjustments and renunciations I possibly could? I always took care not to draw attention to cultural differences. But nothing, absolutely nothing I did could make me accepted by Elizabeth.

Now things were changing, finally. The new prioress took me as she found me, with all my complexity and my actual lived reality, not as her prejudice and preconceptions suggested. And she was so ready to communicate. It was a good thing, I told myself, that Irene had taken over just now. The lovely Benedictine monks who had been coming to us for Sunday Mass, and fortnightly for Confession for years, were moving away, their pastoral centre being taken over by my old friend Sister Agnes's order of nuns, and I had been wondering who in the world there would be to talk to once they were gone. It was not that they were especially chatty – they stuck to their remit strictly and did their job – but they represented a nuanced approach, and kept us in contact with some sort of informed and thoughtful way of doing things. Father Brendan was set to take over and I knew that that would feel like a loss to me. One or two of the Benedictines had almost come to seem like friends.

*

That year there were high winds and summer squalls, and the mood at Akenside was queasy. One day, Irene was late to the refectory. There must have been a good reason, as this was most uncharacteristic. Perhaps Father Gregory had dropped by again. I'd noticed he'd been coming more often than usual. Sisters were asking for him, and some were being called out of meals to see him. Even with your eyes on your food you picked up on these ripples of energy and fluctuations.

The door to the refectory swung open, and Irene appeared, more strolling than processing. Her head shook slightly from side to side. There was none of Elizabeth's dignity or grandeur. Elizabeth had regularly come in late for meals, as she did for the Office, and we had been accustomed to her regal entries. It was always a moment when she commanded a special sort of attention. All would stop what they were doing, whether eating or reading, serving or carrying trays, and stand up with a clatter of cutlery, and bow low while she walked to her seat. The reader at the spotlit pulpit would be poised mid-word, and there would be a suppressed shuffle as habits and muslin napkins were rearranged. But with Irene today it was different. She started laughing quietly as she walked in. 'No, sisters. Really, please, please—' She was raising a hand, still laughing quietly '—you don't need to stop what you are doing for me. Please – please sit down and get on with your lunch.'

The odd thing was that, even as I made to sit, I could see that no one else in the refectory was stirring, let alone doing what they had been asked. For half a minute, not a single person moved a muscle. I was wavering now, wanting to sit, but sensing a collective force somehow keeping me on my feet. What was going on?

'Sisters, please sit down,' the prioress said again, a little more forcefully this time. The room remained in suspended animation. People were blanching, distancing themselves with disapproval. Still no one spoke. Inside, I was flustered. I wanted to obey, knew that was the correct things to do. Presumably it was perfectly clear – the prioress had issued her command. But still I froze, and looked around me. Still no reaction. The atmosphere was so hard, so brittle you could have cut it with a knife. Eyes were staring ahead, heedless of Irene and her words. She repeated her request yet again. This time there was no laughter in her voice. Finally she reached the prioress's seat at the top and sat down without saying anything else, but in what sounded like a rush of annoyance.

Slowly and sheepishly everybody followed suit, sitting back down at their benches, and the meal continued. When it came to an end, twenty minutes later, Irene held up a hand and asked us all to wait a moment.

'Sisters, just to let you know that—'

'Mother!' It was Sister Suzanne. Irene swung her head and looked at the younger sister.

'Mother . . .' Suzi repeated, her usual quick-to-laugh character now tough and assertive, her full mouth and bright brown eyes taking on a hard, decided look.

'Yes, Suzi. And please, it's *Sister* Irene.'

'*Mother* Irene,' Suzi resumed, openly correcting her.

People were flushing, frowning, looking across with heightened concentration.

'Look, I have already made this clear, Suzanne. I am not here to lord it over you; I am here among you, like Jesus, as one who serves. If you need to say something to me it really isn't necessary to contort yourself into formal knots. I've said many times already, I would like you all to call me Sister. Just Sister Irene. That is what I have requested as your prioress. We are all human, Suzanne, all women, all sisters here together.'

There was an uncomfortable rush of energy in the air. It seemed quite incredible to me at that moment the extent to which Suzi was sticking to her guns (imagine if anyone had treated Elizabeth with such contempt!) and the sense of harshness and anger that was now heightening on both sides.

'*Mother* Irene,' Suzi went on. 'I am sticking to Mother, please note, because it is the correct form of address. It's traditional. We *always say Mother at Akenside*. It's what we've always done.'

Irene must have known there was no point replying. She hung her head and seemed to be studying the cracks on the floor.

Suzi continued, now raising her voice: 'I don't think you understand, Mother Irene. Please allow me to put you right. It's always Mother in Carmel for the prioress. It's the Akenside way. It's what we have always done, and what we, as a community, prefer. If some Carmels have updated, we have no intention of doing that here. You are not fully integrated as one of us, coming from Holton, and you will now need to take the lead from us, not the other way around.'

'Sister Suzanne, may I remind you that I am your elected Superior, your new prioress,' Irene said. 'I am the one you all voted for as a body, and you are now all called to respect as your leader, and to obey. I have the grace of the office . . .'

How the exchange ended I do not now recall, but I do remember Suzi ignoring Irene's words, turning on her, telling her off for dispensing with some minor permission or other. Permissions had been everyday events in the past, the trad-itional practice by which we had to ask the prioress for a whole range of mundane things, from the borrowing of a book, to the writing of a letter, to the skipping of one's daily 'sweep' in order to help another sister with some heavy lifting. But according to Irene it didn't help sisters grow if they had to ask for every single little thing, even paper to write upon. (Stamps were very much the prioress's province, and even after permission was given to write a letter, only she could seal and stamp the envelope, at her discretion.) It was counterproductive, she thought. Suzanne's point was that even our canonically elected prioress should not be allowed to absolve us from permissions. The community were divided between those who agreed with her and thought the prioress was called to obey the community, and those who believed, as we'd been taught by Elizabeth herself and Julianna before her, that the vow of obedience entailed that we respected and did what the prioress asked of us, regardless of whether we personally agreed with it or not.

One night later that summer, Elizabeth and the gang were again missing from recreation. I expected them to appear at halftime, as they so often did these days, late but with some credible excuse involving the infirmary. But no. They obviously had other fish to fry. Had Irene given them a one-off exemption? Were they having one of their infirmary parties, separate from the rest of us? Soon people were looking round expectant, puzzled. Irene was saying something in a hoarse stage-whisper to her neighbour. There was the feeling of something edgy, like danger, yet the muted conversation went on. Even with our depleted numbers people seemed to be speaking even more quietly and cautiously than usual.

Then, quick as a flash, Irene got up with a rush of her habit, and strode decisively towards the door. Her footsteps could be heard loud as cymbals banging along the corridor.

The atmosphere in the room grew very quiet. On the knitting needles clacked, on flowed the murmured voices. It was difficult to stick to inconsequential exchanges when everyone in the community room was thinking the same thing. Where were they? The gang was really taking things too far – were we as a community now finally so divided we were taking recreation in two separate groups? What of all we'd been taught about unity and self-effacement? What about kindness and humility? What about all pulling together?

Then there was a clatter and a rush of noise, a rabble approaching down the corridor. The door swung open, and first Irene burst in and strode fiercely through the room to take her seat, in a condition I'd never seen her in before. No longer meek, she was boiling over, agitated, her face moist with emotion, bright red. I felt sorry for her. Then in they straggled, the rest of them, in twos and threes, first sisters Jen and Suzi, then the novices, then Barbara and Ellen, and finally Elizabeth herself, all smirking, giggling, darting looks among themselves. You even sensed they were enjoying this. But why? I tried to adjust my vision and interpret it. One thing was clear: they had pushed humble Irene too far, tried her tolerance, and finally begun to break her down. Their faces said it all, and I was disgusted to realise they were gloating at her downfall. Glad to see her losing her temper. Now didn't she look bad next to Elizabeth?

The community was by now openly divided. I say 'openly' because it can take a lot to push things to a point of open admission in as closed and secretive an atmosphere as this. In some ways 'openness' was the antithesis of everything we had been taught and trained to value. You hid your emotions, you did not show partiality or antipathy, you swallowed your reactions, held back independent judgement, and turned critical thinking into its opposite, a blanket of accepting praise. If a sister particularly annoyed you, you made sure to make a point of praising some aspect of her work or character. If someone's conversation bored you at recreation you made sure to draw her out and to exclaim 'Fancy that!' There was so much you were not allowed to talk about, so many truths you were not allowed to say, and I think many nuns had literally forgotten what it was to be intellectually honest and direct.

Now the mood was altering. Although there were still blankets of denial everywhere – no one openly admitted Mother Elizabeth's role in dividing the community, for example, even though the situation was obvious – there was now a mood of combat and resistance in the air. The gang reinforced its position by taking more recreations separately in the infirmary and on the days they did turn up in the recreation room, they invariably sat apart in a clique, with Elizabeth on a fixed chair at the exact opposite end of the room to Our Mother.

The novices, inevitably and through no fault of their own, were bound to get caught up in this. The novitiate was the mirror image of the infirmary. Things were done differently there, and lives were lived decidedly apart. Flanking Elizabeth, or sitting in settled, separate pairings with Barbara and Jennifer, Stephanie and Lucy seemed ignorant of and oblivious to all we'd been taught as novices about recreating with impartiality, and about integrating, making Suzi's words about Irene's supposed failure to integrate all the more ironic. Irene was in her sixth year among us, about seventy years old by now, and knew the Rule and Constitutions by heart. She was trying to live by their teachings.

One day, I had reason to talk to Stephanie in an alcove

about something or other. It was probably just to do with work, or dishes, or some arrangement that needed to be made about the liturgy. When I suggested she ask Our Mother about the arrangement, Steph flushed hot and said 'Barbara would kill me if I ever went to see Mother Irene. We are not meant to talk to her.' Not talk to our Reverend Mother? What was this about, and if things had changed in how we practised obedience or related to our superiors, why had we not all been told about it? Still, I kept my counsel. What could I do?

Another day an even more startling thing happened after an Office. I think it must have been None, and, when Mother Irene made some minor announcement after the doxology, Jen leapt to her feet and began literally shouting at the old woman. After all the boiling undercurrents and half-restraints, this was an eruption, an outburst like nothing we'd ever witnessed in the monastery before. Jen was unmoored, losing her temper in a completely unfettered way. What was going on, what ill wind from the underworld was affecting us? Finally, she hurled her breviary across the choir, aiming directly at Our Mother and shouting insults before it landed with a big bang at Irene's feet and Jen stormed out.

Shock waves in Carmel were always muted, but they were felt. This was the last we saw or heard of Jennifer for a while. Like all those whose religious aura had been seriously dented or become unstuck, she was segregated in the infirmary. Nothing much was said about the incident. After some weeks we were told she would be going home for a break. In her case – allowances inexplicably being made as usual – this was a permitted relief. So attached was she to the charismatic Elizabeth that she had openly rejected the new prioress, just as Suzi had rejected her that day in the refectory, and as

Barbara had rejected her in ways too numerous to recount. Some of these were more subtle than others, but what it all amounted to was a schism. The community was split right down the middle, both intellectually and physically, along the wall dividing the novitiate and the infirmary from the rest of the house. The novices, Lucy and Steph, were unwittingly caught up in the fall-out of months and years of murmuring, and had no choice but to be part of the gang, dependent on its older members, while Ellen, who guarded herself so closely and had always been inscrutable, managed to remain both passively involved and mysteriously on the fence.

27. The Infirmary

The bodies were piling up in the infirmary. No, I'm not refer-ring to the cats, whose procreative faculties were soon to be curtailed. They'd been fruitful and multiplied for many a long year, until the corridors slunk with them, and their fleas fed fat on our anaemic veins. But they'd had their fun. Just as the flea-infested mattresses had been taken out and burned, so the hazards of potential slippages in the corridors and the smell were soon to be things of the past. One day a bishop's visit occurred unlike any normal Visitation. Tony listened to the long string of issues surrounding the lack of control and potty-training, deemed 'untamed nature' out of place in the cloister, and instructed that all the ferals be rounded up and taken to the vet for neutering. It was the only time I remem-ber Elizabeth apologising for anything, something she did at Compline, in measured tones that sounded less contrite than 'obliged'. It was obvious that the situation needed to be cor-rected, and it was done so, clinically and quietly, and life in the corridors became a little more predictable.

At the heart of the infirmary, meanwhile, Elizabeth, the ousted queen, had (whispers said) fallen into depression since the elections. It was true we did not often see her. It was true there seemed to be some major problem no one named. A couple of months after the elections she, like Jen-nifer, went away 'for a rest' for a couple of weeks. When she reappeared you sensed a certain loss of energy and confi-dence. If I'd thought of being voted out of office and the consequent loss of power as something undesirable, I would have felt sorry for her. But since we'd been taught such things as power and status did not matter, I took it as read that there was nothing for her to be upset about. If everything both Julianna and she herself had taught us was true, and God's will was revealed at the elections, I could not see any reason for there to be a problem.

If Gregory was coming and going these days, summoned by senior members of the gang, I was only vaguely aware of it. Only certain people were getting to see him, cross at how he'd supposedly steered the elections by pointing out the Vatican's latest teachings about humility, dialogue and *Fraternal Life in Community*. His interventions had been, to their minds, unwelcome, and they felt incensed that the outcome had not gone their way. No one else got told about our official overseer's presence in the parlour or his newfound availability. Any letters I had written to him, I was later to discover, went unsent.

Eventually, more serious interventions were required. When did it become beyond clear to all of us that we could not help ourselves? Did it start with the spate of breakdowns, always treated as health issues rather than manifestations of spiritual, emotional or mental conflict and repression? Or did it only begin in earnest once the veil of silence was lifted, and people started to speak their troubled minds? So unused were most of us to expressing ourselves verbally beyond standard formulaic phrases, euphemisms and old party lines, that it all got very clumsy and overcharged. It's difficult to pinpoint the beginning of the avalanche. Some of the early boulders that presaged the tumbling and toppling of our world, though, stick in the mind. After her outburst in choir, Jen fell into the grips of mental illness, and was now invalided out and on medication. Perhaps the silence and restraints demanded by the Life, never mind the detachment, were too much for her outgoing temperament. Certainly she was unable to live by the Rule without a supporting trellis of concessions. However difficult she'd been towards me in the past, however rough and harsh, at least this medical diagnosis made her behaviour easier to accept. But if only they'd picked up on it before now, if only somebody had noticed or cared what was going on.

Sadly, another breakdown occurred in the run up to the new millennium. Lucy had been with us well over a year, and she and I had bonded brilliantly, partly because she was a skilled musician, a fine violinist, meaning there was now someone on my musical wavelength I could play duets with, and partly because she, like me, was interested in art and poetry. We'd laughed and joked and got on like a house on fire. She was also quick-witted, in the verbally clever sort of way I liked, and few recreations passed without the pleasure of her puns. None of these qualities had endeared her to Elizabeth. She'd coined the term 'the gang', herself involuntarily a member of it, but she could also stand apart and make up her own mind about things, something that was bound to push her to the edge, and to cost her support from the religious Mothers of our world.

One day the bishop came to talk to us, sniffing around our problem areas, and Lucy decided to stand up in front of all of us, quite dramatically, and challenge him. She certainly knew how to choose her moment. She also knew how to raise her voice to make her point. What was the bishop doing about things in the Church and in the world? Had he no sense of responsibility? Where was his spiritual backbone, and his prophetic spirit? Did he really think we, as a Church, were embodying the revolutionary spirit of Christ? Shouldn't all of us be rousing ourselves more, living less comfortably and complacently?

For days after, Lucy was treated with a very cautious kind of 'concern'. Poor thing, some said, she was clearly finding the Life stressful. She was not herself. She had changed. She was not well. And then came the terrible day that she slid from her stall at Lauds, and landed in a great thrashing, beating pile on the echoing floor. Her limbs were in spasms, flailing everywhere, her head lolling, the whites of her eyes showing scarily, rolling, twitching, everything about her unrecognisable. For a few minutes I thought she was dying, her face blue-grey. True to custom, nobody stopped what they were doing or tried to help. Our duty was to keep our eyes averted and carrying on praying, and apart from a moment when shocked eyes were raised, we continued singing. Finally, Irene stumbled over to where Lucy lay writhing on the floor, waited for her to regain consciousness, then raised her to her feet and guided her out of the door.

Like Jennifer, Lucy vanished to the infirmary. However, in her case the outcome was very different. She was not yet in vows, even though she was in the habit. She had given Carmel a good go, but clearly was not well enough or what Mother called 'able for it'. Two weeks later she was gone, another case of mental breakdown. The word that slipped out this time was 'psychosis'. Not that I understood it, nor did we have the kind of dictionaries that would have given much information on the subject, nor the internet. But psychosis sounded serious, and people bought it. Lucy had once described the community as being split between the forces of good and evil, the good side headed by Sister Ruth and the dark side by Elizabeth, as the Antichrist. That had sealed her fate for ever. Her own mother came and escorted her off the premises. The Life had got to her, had worn down her defences. I realised that, like Felicity and Jen, and others before them, she was just another casualty.

Once people started leaving, I could not fail to ask myself how long it would be before all of us succumbed. Was it something to do with the Life, an inherent danger? Surely all these cases could not be a coincidence, as Ellen tried to insist when I once mentioned the phenomenon to her in private. I'd noticed that psychiatric problems, now admitted in our midst, were on the rise in other Carmels too – news filtered through to us – invariably affecting those in my own age group the most. The elderly stalwarts, with their wartime upbring-ings, were less overtly affected, although there were at least two older nuns who had had eating disorders in the past, as well as one 'manic depressive', as we used to call it. In the enclosing silence of my cell these realisations started rising up against me in startled moments, like taunts. What was this sacred Life that I had come to? It was a pressure cooker. I felt the danger hanging over me, swirling round the corridors like a miasma, filling the whole monastery, a foreboding. Vowed religious life was described as the 'state of perfec-tion', but what was perfect about this?

We were what I'd always known we were on one level, a group of twenty imperfect women thrown together to learn to live charitably with each other and in harmony with God. But was it working? If the strictures and customs we observed – the absolute nature of enclosure, the rejection of outside with its diverse, questioning, searching influences, and the demand that we live without friendship and intellec-tual or emotional support – had once supported people's best intentions and helped them to grow, all well and good.

But today, on the cusp of a new millennium, could such rigid ways still be justified? For my generation, those born after 1960, let alone anyone younger, could the hermetically sealed interpretation of the Life not be counterproductive?

I looked around me, and my eyes saw the bald facts of the situation. There was something wrong, something rotten in the state of Akenside. In the early days, the demands of monasticism had all felt easy. My spirit had been full of joy. Now I had to set my face like flint just to get through a standard day, to constantly use a form of prayer that was nothing but an act of will, pure determination. Such naked faith was what we had always been told to expect and even aspire to. Faith, hope and love, unassisted by fine feelings and consolations, were a purer offering to God than the state of romance that often characterised the early stages. The will was the core, the volitional centre of the human person, and to act in its power and under its energy alone was seen as the highest virtue. I willingly accepted all these teachings. But still, unwanted thoughts came to me around this time, about ropes, or pills, or one-way journeys to the Mere. If there was no kindness here, no natural kinship, no relief and no escape, could I survive in my right mind, let alone flourish in my vocation as a Carmelite much longer?

28. The Chapters

Then one day a bright bell was ringing. It was Sunday afternoon, and the community was drifting down to the largest of the three parlours, prayer stools in hand. We'd been told by the bishop that we needed to start having weekly chapter meetings again as the Rule entailed, and now the Garth Alliance had asked that we respond to a series of questions.

It had been so long since we had met as a group to discuss serious matters, that some were looking anxious, others sheepish, others relentlessly upbeat. What would it be like facing each other in considered conversation again? Wasn't there a nervousness now in the air between the obedient majority and the members of the gang? Wasn't so much unsaid, and unsayable, that any attempt at interaction would be a charade? Still, in people trickled, and slowly took up their places in the standard circle round the room. Nods were exchanged and reverent silence kept. Then Mother Irene began with a gathering prayer. She was in the prioress's big wooden seat, while Mother Elizabeth, directly opposite her, was flanked by Barbara and Suzanne. All of us had a copy of the Rule and Constitutions, as well as notebooks, biros and handkerchiefs. We had come prepared. Finally, once the shuffling and coughing had subsided, Irene began to talk.

'We've come together, sisters, as you know, to respond to the questions asked of us by the Garth Alliance. It is part of the order's effort at honest self-evaluation and reflection as we approach the milestone of the new millennium. It is also in preparation for the visit of our superior in the order, Father Camillo, who has requested that we take time as a community to reflect on the meaning and value of our charism in the modern world. It is important that we all have a chance to think about these things, and to feed back.'

The atmosphere was turgid, a heavy sense of reserve almost a presence in the room.

'So, Ellen?' Irene cast a glance in Ellen's direction. 'I think you will be taking down the minutes, and typing up our conclusions afterwards, is that right?'

Ellen smiled and nodded.

'I think you have all had time now to consider the list of points that were sent round, and I hope you will each have your own insights to share. What we need is to put together our answers in writing, point by point, but only once we've heard everyone's thoughts on the matter. So, who would like to begin?' Irene looked around the room with a warm, inviting smile. 'It's up to you, sisters. This is your chance to express your thoughts on the matter. There's no right or wrong answer to any of this, remember. What you are being asked for is your own opinion. It's all grist to the mill, and meant to be constructive. So, any thoughts on the first question? Feel free to use this time as a chance to share what you really think.'

We all looked down at the sheets of paper given to us in advance. It was important we tried to keep the game up, at least go through the motions of turning up for a chapter meeting.

'I think it would be best if we went round the room,' Sister Barbara put forward. People nodded. Several other sisters murmured agreement.

'Good. So, the first question on the list is little more than a matter of common sense that we are called to consider,'

Irene went on. 'I expect some of you have thought about this yourselves from time to time.' She looked up, then down again, enunciating the point slowly. '"What changes might we consider making to adapt to the needs of young women coming in today?" Any thoughts? Let's take a moment to sit quietly and get it into focus.'

It was a straightforward enough question, offered in a straightforward way. At least you would have thought so – the Garth Alliance was a realistic group. The room was still for a while, some sisters holding their biros, others recollected in an attitude of prayer. Mother Elizabeth held herself particularly steely and erect, totally composed, eyes cast down. Then the tour of the room began and each sister was asked what points she would like to put forward.

Some pointed out that many new entrants these days had college qualifications, or university degrees, and may have held positions of adult responsibility in life outside. We'd had a young policewoman enquire not long ago. Although still in her twenties, she'd been in charge of a small team. These were the kinds of realities some people mentioned. And the fact that people were tending to enter later nowadays. Perhaps we should consider them women and no longer 'girls'? It was the braver ones who made these points. Finally, the talk had circled most of the room, and came round to me.

'Sister Catherine?' Irene raised her eyebrows.

'I'd like to pick up what was said earlier about regarding newcomers not so much as girls but as women,' I began. 'Even if people coming in are school-leavers, I think it's important that we don't treat them as children. My own view is that people coming in today may bring with them not only openness, and readiness to change, but also a spirit of genuine enquiry. They may come to us with a desire to study and learn. Questioning and discussion are part of life nowadays, and most educations will have encouraged both. So I think we should acknowledge that fact, and build on it. Our approach to spiritual training and formation could be stifling otherwise. I think it's time to encourage people to use their minds, and to be nourished intellectually, not just told what to do without any sort of genuine human interchange.'

I'd not spoken long, but there was an atmosphere of sharply felt resistance. Barbara and even Suzanne were looking concerned. Others, however, nodded and seemed to accord with what I was saying. But the clock was ticking, and I was the bottom of the pile. If I said much more there was a danger we'd be going over time.

'Thank you, Catherine,' Irene said. 'That's a very helpful observation, and I think we can all say that sounds very much in line with common sense and with what the Church is asking of us. Sister Ellen, are you getting this all down?'

Ellen nodded. She never gave anything away.

After the session, while bodies were bustling back and forth, people keen to resume their routine duties, Mother Irene shot me a very deliberate smile in the corridor, and confirmed an arrangement we'd recently made, that we'd be meeting for a chat the next day.

'See you at three o'clock tomorrow,' she said.

It was refreshing not to have to wait for hours outside her office as I'd done in the old days, when I'd so rarely got more than five brisk minutes with my prioress. But here was Mother Irene, all expansiveness and encouragement when I turned up at her open door. It was impossible not to be grateful for her support.

'Ah, Catherine,' she said, indicating a seat, 'I'm glad to see you. I wanted to say how pleased I was with your contribution to the chapter yesterday. You spoke very well, and I think it is important for people to get used to airing and sharing different points of view. There seems to be a lot of anxiety in the community, a fear of sharing. But it's important that younger voices be heard. After all, what do we older ones know about young women today? As one of the more recent entrants you have insights to bring to the table.'

It was such a relief to be asked to contribute and listened to, to feel included for once, not only as an individual, but as one of the younger sisters with a valid perspective on the topic in hand. Recently, the title 'the young ones' had been treated as synonymous with the gang, even though I was younger, both in natural age and in religion, than several of its members. Barbara, Suzi and Ellen were all well into their thirties now. The Alliance's questions could not have been more timely or relevant. It was so good to make progress in the interpretation and adaptation of our charism after a long period of stagnation.

Then, midweek, Mother Irene called me up to her office to see her again. This time the mood was different. She seemed torn, slightly saddened, her face contorted. She leaned over her big, folded hands on the tabletop and sighed. She told me that she had something delicate to say to me. It pained her, and she was genuinely sorry, but someone – she could not say who – *someone* had come to her and insisted I be 'disciplined'.

'Disciplined? How . . . ?'

'I am so sorry, Catherine. I know you've done nothing wrong. You've tried to take things seriously, to answer the questions. But I am afraid it seems inevitable now that you will need to be made an example of. You see, according to the person who came to see me, what you said at the chapter last weekend was damaging, and wrong in her view, and therefore will need to be taken back. That's how she sees it. She believes you gave the wrong impression of our formation process, and she needs you to apologise and make satisfaction. I am terribly sorry, again, sister, but I am going to have to ask you to make a full public apology.'

My stomach did a kind of lurch. 'Oh,' I said. 'Oh . . . I see.'

'Yes, I know it's difficult. It's a very hard thing for me to ask of you.'

'Hang on, if it's hard for you, Irene, and if you have no problem with anything I said, why are we even in this position? I really don't quite understand it. I thought you agreed with me, and that what I'd said had been helpful, opening things up . . .'

'I know, I know. I said I agreed with you, and I still do. But I am sorry to say there are certain people among us who cannot be negotiated with. People of influence who feel they need to have the last word. It's very difficult for me. My hands are tied.'

The injustice of the situation flared before me. Mother Irene was bending this way and that to avoid offending a Certain Person. She was going back even on her own convictions. Against her better judgement, she was allowing herself to be stripped of her authority, of the grace of her role, to become a puppet, and one controlled not by any old other, but someone she did not even agree with. That someone was herself too cowardly to come out and discuss things openly with others on a level playing field. Was it that she'd played this game so long she had forgotten how to communicate? Had she forgotten that we were supposed to be open to truth?

'I am so sorry,' she said again, shaking her head. 'Things

are all wrong here for now, but this is your moment, Catherine. This is your chance to rise to the holy challenge, like Jesus, who bore our sins and suffered the stripes. It is your chance for a crown. There is no greater virtue than the sacrifice of obedience, do remember.'

'Yes, Mother, I agree that it is a virtue, as we've been taught all along. But in that case, why are others also not practising it? If the supernatural spirit of obedience and the grace of the office are real, what does it mean when those who themselves taught us, and insisted on those things, cast them aside?'

Irene looked down at her thick-fingered, bluish-purple hands. Her lips were moving wordlessly, and her head rocking from side to side. Her heavy jowl wobbled.

'These are all valid questions, Sister Catherine, and fair enough. I have had the same thoughts myself. The situation is very difficult for me. I am the prioress elect, and yet there are those who would control me. I am having to keep the peace with them, to tread very carefully. Perhaps there will be a chance for genuine dialogue eventually, once the community gets used to talking, and some of your hopes to interact more truthfully and meaningfully with others will be satisfied. But for now . . .'

The conversation ranged widely that afternoon. Irene was clearly tormented at her predicament, but simultaneously glad that she had a few followers to back her up. She was a woman of conviction. After being treated like a newcomer for over five years, like someone who barely knew the ropes, now she was at last in a position to make a difference to how things were done, and to bring a ready, listening ear to all who might want or need to see her.

The next Sunday another meeting was convoked. This

time Jennifer was present, on day-release from the infirmary. Knowing how much she'd baulked at chapter meetings in the past, this was surprising. She'd always taken Elizabeth's view that talking things over was pointless and distracting; we were hermits-in-community, and all we needed was to do as we were told. But now she was here, ready to see the spectacle. Stephanie was also allowed to come, which was most unusual for a novice. Articulate and bright, the only one left now in 'formation', she was in danger of being cut off from the wider group on the one hand, and of cabin fever on the other. Finally, Elizabeth was in a corner, holding herself straight-backed and aloof, her face giving nothing away, her demeanour an outward demonstration of what she regarded as perfection. It was not like her to get involved in the talking; she let others do that for her. At least Barbara and Suzanne, who flanked her like bodyguards, could be relied upon to react and verbalise on her part.

Mother Irene sat solid yet visibly squirming near the door, her bulging green eyes restless as she surveyed the group. Inaugurating the proceedings with a prayer, she gathered us into one mighty focus, and the community meeting began. But before anything else was dealt with, she had an announcement to make. Sister Catherine had 'something to say to the community'. It was a moment of burning focus. My stomach swam. So this was really happening. The gang, of course, knew what was coming and prepared for their amusement. The entire circle had their eyes upon me. Among the wider, innocent community, faces swivelled, breaths were held. I took up my position in the middle of the room, kneeling upright, then beat my hand across my chest in a customary gesture of contrition. 'I have an apology to make,' I said. 'I want to say how sorry I am if what I said last week caused any upset to anyone. That was not my intention. I am sorry if I was tactless or hurt anybody's feelings. Please accept my sincere apology.'

'And? Anything else, sister?' Mother Irene asked.

'Well, I know how headstrong I can be with my idealism, and that this approach is not necessarily shared by others. We all have our different points of view. I stated mine, as I believed the Alliance questionnaire required of us, but if I did so too forcefully, or if my views caused upset, for whatever reason, I do apologise.'

There was a bit of a pause. Was I supposed to say something else? Why did everything feel unresolved, and did I even know what I was meant to be apologising for?

The next step in a public apology was for the sister apologising to prostrate herself in front of everyone, and kiss the floor. It was an easy enough attitude to assume if you were spiritually compliant and physically fit and supple. As required, I doubled myself up on the floor, forehead to the ground, and waited for the word that would tell me to rise. In the old days when this happened (which was all too frequently), Mother Elizabeth had always said 'Get up' quite promptly. That was the signal to sit up and go back to one's position. She was well practised at this ancient art of staged humiliation, one Irene had wanted to set aside (she considered it medieval and unnecessary), but she had been persuaded to retain the custom, as an integral part of the Akenside 'ways'. This time, however, as I lay there, forehead to the floor, time stretched out indefinitely. Mother said nothing. On the minutes ticked, and still no word was given.

At last, after what felt an age, I heard the words of release in Irene's now quavering voice. She sounded affected, as though something had happened non-verbally while I was down there on the floor. Had somebody been signalling to or prompting her? My face was hot and damp as I resumed my position in the circle, my heart banging wildly. My face was probably very red. For a minute or two I avoided looking at anybody. I'd had no idea this gesture would make me feel so bad. Then I felt my heart slowing and opened my eyes on the assembled circle of long brown habits. What I saw next was worse than the correction itself, and confirmed my worst imaginings. It was not a recollected gathering of gentle nuns, eyes cast down in prayerful consideration. It was a ragged crew of spiritually weather-beaten characters that included a row of gloaters, the faces of the gang locked on to each other in smug satisfaction. They sensed my discomfort. That alone was enough to make them pleased. Gone was all charity. All they wanted was my invalidation.

Later, when the chapter was over, I passed Elizabeth in the hall wearing her blue overall, a saucer of chopped liver in one hand, and heading for the infirmary. She was moving briskly, but I mouthed 'Mother Elizabeth' to her, gesturing to an alcove. She stopped, all flushed and pink, and seemed half amenable for a moment. We stepped into the alcove by the back garden door. I wanted to talk to her, she understood that. But when I asked her how she felt the meeting had gone, she stiffened and pulled herself up.

'You did not say what you were meant to say,' she answered, in words like shafts of steel. And again, she repeated: 'You did not say what you were meant to say!'

I looked at her in bewilderment. What on earth was this? Surely what I was 'meant to say' was what I meant truthfully, no more nor less. I'd made my gesture. I'd apologised if I'd upset her. But taking my words back was a form of lying, something I would never do. It seemed incredible to me that

Mother would tell me what to say in a community discussion that was meant to be about honest sharing. The whole point of the questions sent us by the Garth was to elicit from us what we really thought, something each sister was asked carefully to consider.

But why did it seem so strange to me, when I'd known Elizabeth and her ways for all these years? The summer was nearly upon us, and in October Jennifer and I would celebrate our tenth anniversary in the Life. In three years' time I would be turning forty. Why was I still so stubborn in expecting the best of everyone, and clinging to the belief that everything was perfect in reality? Was this how I'd learned to navigate the dysfunction of my mother and my family as a child? Was the relentless cheerfulness I showed to the world (I still managed this most of the time, at least when I wasn't overcome with 'weak' emotions) and my acceptance of the trials that came my way just a continuation of my peace-keeping role? I'd always been a mediator. But who was I to mediate between now, when it was clear that the one Mother was puppet and the other puppeteer?

It dawned on me that for nearly a decade I'd had nobody to share my deepest thoughts with, and – apart from occasional formal stutterings in the confessional and the long, unsent letters to Father Gregory – nobody in whom to confide. If Jesus visited me from time to time as a consoling presence, more usually he was elusive. Where had he hidden I sometimes wondered, together with John of the Cross (who taught us to endure the dark nights and the apparent barrenness of a 'maturing' prayer life), what was going on? I waited for him at the foot of the big black cross in my cell. I murmured his name during my prayer time. I called on the Spirit, and on the Father, I intoned scriptural mantras, and dwelled on favourite phrases from the psalms. I closed my eyes and visualised my Spouse, my Redeemer, but often felt there was just a blank. No ripples or responses from the other side.

It must have been just before Irene's own descent into complete confusion that I went to her and asked for permission to meet with Sister Judith one afternoon for spiritual conversation. You'd never have known such meetings were provided for in the Constitutions, so vehemently had Elizabeth forbidden and blocked all such possibilities. Perhaps she (of all people!) was afraid there would be 'murmuring'. But now I remembered that Teresa herself had allowed sisters to meet from time to time to 'edify' each other, and to help each other on the way, and all of a sudden it made sense. If ever a spiritual confidante was needed it was now. And Judith had always seemed to me a beacon of good sense. Free from Elizabeth's constricting control, and knowing that Irene and Judith had always had a strong relationship of trust, the way ahead was open.

And so it was that one Sunday afternoon I made my way along the dormitory corridor and, instead of stopping at the vestibule near my cell, I carried on and opened the low door at the end of the passage, and took myself up a spiral staircase, and felt a sense of wonder as I emerged at the top and the light streamed in from every side. The tower was a beautiful strong turret with tall, mullioned windows on all four of its sturdy facets, a room from where the view seemed almost aerial. The gravel drive stretched and petered into the distance, a vanishing trickle. The trees of the woods looked like bushes, and the lake stretched far, its meandering shape like the body of a swan. In the corner sat Sister Judith, who rose to greet me, and gestured to a sturdy stool.

Our words wove a skein of silk that day, and as we shared and wept together the skein became a cloth to cover us, a blanket of hope to keep us warm. Finally, there was someone who understood me and who saw what was going on. Finally, there was the shelter of a tentative meeting of minds.

As summer opened out before us, and our weekly meetings in the tower brought light and strength, Judith spoke to me of Mellerby, of the days of its foundation, long ago, when she had been a novice herself, and of the conflict that had arisen between the pioneers of the new ways there, and the old guard – Elizabeth, back home at Akenside, in particular. The banning of discussion and debate, and the clamping down on dialogue and chapter meetings could be traced right back to those times as could the Rule of Three. Elizabeth had then taken on the important roles herself, trying to combine the positions of novice mistress, bursar and infirmarian, until finally she became prioress too. She then had complete and utter sway over every aspect of her sisters' lives, and had become so used to this situation that, by the time Irene entered, it seemed unthinkable to Elizabeth that she should ever give up her power and her privileges. She was a woman who, while challenging and correcting others, had hardly been challenged or corrected herself. Her sway was absolute.

Although I did not have the ear of Father Gregory, who despite visiting more frequently was only ever seeing Irene and the gang, I did at last have somebody to talk to. Sadly, things were not progressing as well for Irene, whose tendency to stammer and tremble was becoming accentuated. It was obvious she was being worked upon, told what to think, how to act, what to say to the community, frequently marched off by Barbara or Suzi to the infirmary, where the powers that ruled that separated space would persuade her she was wrong. Not just wrong about being prioress, or about details of the Life such as permissions, but wrong full stop. She was a Holton sister. Was this gaslighting or open bullying? Even from a distance you could see she was beginning to fall apart. Finally, she became so unsure of herself, so torn, that she walked about with her shoulders slumped, her chin shaking, her head hanging low. At other times she would flush a violent shade of red and boil up with indignation.

Ultimately, Irene did not have the force of character to withstand the pressures and abuses of the gang, nor the buoyancy of temperament to keep cheerful and positive in her outlook indefinitely. Something in her was changing, caving in to the expectations that were being laid upon her. The segregated zone that was the infirmary had staged a mutiny against her, had reinforced its separation from the monastery proper by walls that were invisible but no less significant for that. Would she ever be able to fight back, push against the power of the infirmary, or make her mark?

And now Elizabeth was calling for a general meeting, a convocation at which the boundary lines could be redrawn, and proper discipline meted out, including corrections of those who were in error.

It's difficult to forget those July chapters. I am back there often in my thoughts, face downward on the floor in an attitude of prostration. This time it is in the antechoir, and everyone is present. I am flattened, the sweat trickling down my forehead. It has settled in deep salty pools around my nostrils, seeped into a stinging crack where the underside of my nose meets my upper lip. My eyes are closed. I am praying hard. Praying for clarity. My heart is thumping. How much longer can this silence stretch? And how many pairs of

eyes are feasting, boring into me? How pleased with this outcome are my many loud accusers? Are they satisfied yet with
what they have done to me, to Our Mother, to the community? Have they finally had their fill? Has Elizabeth got her
way at last?

This time it is not just me. It is not even just me and Sister
Judith, as it was a week ago when further corrections had
taken place, Judith having bravely spoken out about the divi-
sions in the community and called for the need for dialogue
and honesty. This time there are seven of us down there,
prostrated, arms outstretched, bodies in the shape of a star,
a patchwork of brown and white and black, our veils askew
on the wood, a mass of not-quite-monochrome medieval
clothing covering the polished parquet. We have apparently
spoken 'damagingly' of the 'way we do things'. We have
questioned the status quo. Over us sit the members of the
gang, with Mother Irene a mute figurehead on the prioress's
chair by the door. Her expression is confused, neither a smile
nor a frown. Has she lost her bearings now completely? Or
has she finally yielded all influence and authority to another?

The windows are open onto the orchard. The fervid July
heat presses in on us like a heavy palm. One of the Mothers –
it doesn't matter which, the puppet or the puppeteer – gives
the knock, and then there is a shuffling as seven bodies
rearrange themselves back into a kneeling position. Some
make of their right hands a fist to beat their own breasts. *Mea
culpa*, they are muttering. We apologise, we should not have
spoken, should not even have thought. Others reach for their
handkerchiefs, wipe their brows, catch furtive glimpses of
the spinning room. I hold myself in, but in a single sweep get
the measure of it. It is them against us, us against them, sister
against sister, mother against child, truth against lies. It is an

open schism, yet one the gang are intent on denying even exists. How dare anyone suggest we have a problem? How dare anyone speak of there being a lack of unity among us?

The farce of it is that even the fence-sitters like Ellen have been asked to retract something or other. As for me and Sister Judith, our forced apologies have been a pageantry, a sacrifice to the Akenside idols, a warning to others not to suggest Mother Elizabeth is in the wrong. We have said things that have been intolerable, truths 'too hard' for the community to hear. As a result, we have been verbally flagellated, disgraced, made to lie prone, saying sorry yet again for everything we have said, and done, and are, sorry even for our truthfulness. *Especially* for our truthfulness. It was ever thus where vested power was at stake. Today, though, it is Ambrose, Ruth, Jane, Alison, and yes, even Ellen (who has too sensible a head on her shoulders not to know what is going on). It is all of us who took up the lead given by Judith when she said the inflammatory words: 'two camps'. It was like an electric shock sending paroxysms of defensiveness through Elizabeth's supporters. And now sisters Barbara and Suzanne are talking both at once.

'Two camps? Two camps? What a thing to suggest!' It is Barbara's voice that cuts through the clamour, her cheeks red as she leans forward firing her words towards the offenders. Then Suzi rounds on us, her arm pointing, as she echoes: 'What on earth do you mean, two camps? Of course we're not in two camps! That's ridiculous. We're a traditional Carmelite community here at Akenside, a Carmel doing what we have always done. Who says we have a problem or are disunited? Who says we need to re-examine how we interpret the principles of authority and obedience? How dare anyone suggest we have a problem!'

Words and voices held back over years are now firing randomly and aloud, abrupt as gunshot. The antechoir is in uproar. Previously regulated voices are giving way beneath emotion, threatened, defensive, in denial of our all-too-evident situation. Some are shouting now, several sisters talking at once, interrupting each other. The call for truth has unleashed a panic among the clique surrounding Elizabeth, held in by the strictures of silence for so long that they have forgotten how to talk reasonably to each other, or to anyone. Once the formulaic expressions have been put aside, there is nothing for some of these women to fall back on except repressed emotion, fear turning to anger, anger turning to rage and desperation. And underneath all of this is the unspoken assertion that personal loyalty to Elizabeth is more important than loyalty to God, to truth, to kindness and humanity. That it is loyalty to all that she embodies that makes of Akenside the perfect place it is, the One True Carmel, better than the rest. Anything other than this must be eradicated. The influence of Holton. The querulous and questioning inbetweeners. The converts. Those who dare to put their finger on the problems in the community. Problems – as if we have problems!

I don't risk catching Judith's eye, but we both know that what we are witnessing is something incredible in Carmel. In our usually silent world, where individual points of view are not normally heard, violent voices are rising, and there is a torrent of noise and aggression swirling all around us. Barbara has fully exploded and, now uncontrolled, is letting forth a barrage of protestations as a jarring counterpoint to Suzanne's harsh defensiveness. Both are pointing fingers, Suzi's now thrusting at arm's length and jabbing towards me – 'You started this' – while Barbara aims for Sister Judith.

'How dare you?' she says. 'How dare you?' Between the two of them, Elizabeth is pulled up as stiff and straight as ever, saying nothing, her gaze casting beams of silent reproach across the room. The last thing she will do is relinquish composure. She will not let slip the mask. She will not be seen to falter or fail.

No one has openly defended Judith, who is now fully ostracised, a battered scapegoat made to retract and prostrate herself so many times it is becoming predictable. The things she has said have been intolerable to some. Too challenging. Too true. As for Mother Irene, whom Judith has stood by all along out of respect for her election, she has not risen to the challenge, has not dared defend her. She vacillates, a broken staff amid the battering rams feeble, ready to topple. While I have been quick to add my voice to Judith's plea for honest dialogue, I realise that asking for it is tantamount to saying that truth and dialogue are lacking, which makes of such asking a crime in itself. Asking that we address problems implies we have things that need addressing. But no one openly addresses things at Akenside, where everything is already perfect, and where all we have to do is obey. The question is, whom do we obey and why, and how do we understand the elections, the grace of the office, and supernatural spirit of obedience? Have all these fundamentals changed?

None of these monastic essentials is something we are allowed to talk about, even though they were presented to us during our training as the bedrocks of our lives. The fact that obedience, for example, has either been put aside or acquired a new definition, is taboo. The fact that it is no longer the prioress's word that counts, but that of a self-appointed overseer and her coterie, is something all can see but no one can allude to without incurring punishment. And so here we are, gathered in the antechoir, the fan whirring loudly in a corner during the pre-millennium heatwave, the blue touch paper well and truly lit. There is no stopping the torrent of wild and flailing talk now that Barbara and Suzi are engaged and taking a lead in defending Mother Elizabeth's indefensible position. As for Elizabeth, she continues to say nothing. Not one word. The ice-blue eyes are not engaging.

The shock waves were felt again at Vespers, and again at supper, and no one was surprised (was everybody in fact relieved?) when it was announced that the discussion would be resumed at the same time next day. And so it went on, the talking, not for two days but for three. After years of the silencing of views and opinions, years during which the practice of weekly chapter meetings has been suppressed, years during which people have forgotten how to speak civilly to one another, and forgotten the non-formulaic use of language, it seemed we really were unable to stop talking. The results of that week were unforgettable. Multiple forced apologies all round, from everyone except the resolute fence-sitters and the gang. Irene being marched off between sessions to the day room, where we could see them working on her, three or four black veils behind the cloudy glass door, Mother emerging each time red in the face and shaking from head to foot. Her visible disintegration.

That summer no appeal was made to the bishop or to Father Gregory, nor were they given any scope to intervene, or exercise their pastoral leadership. We'd got to that point. People in the gang spoke ill of Gregory, said they had lost trust in him, even if he was our canonical superior. He had forfeited their allegiance ever since he had presided so tactfully and skilfully over the elections. As for the bishop, he was irrelevant. As was Father Camillo. What do these outside people know about how we live at Akenside? What do any of the Church's representatives, outsiders to the proper Akenside way of doing things, understand? We don't need the bishop, the priests, the father general of the order, or – heaven forbid – Mother Mellerby – to sort us out. Of course they won't be of any use to us at all. Mother knows best – that is, Mother Elizabeth.

Judith and I took one last stand, made a final request – could we not invite a trained, outside facilitator, someone with skills in dialogue and mediation, to enable us to communicate with each other more effectively? Could we not admit that we as a community needed such help? Could we not actually try to 'speak the truth to each other in a spirit of love' – because what was truthfulness other than a form of love? Sister Barbara's face turned pale again. A week later we heard that a facilitator would indeed be coming to us. She was none other than Mother Patricia, the Prioress of Norrington, an old friend of Sister Barbara's. Years ago, they'd been young sisters in the same novitiate; memories and camaraderie bound them together. Mother Patricia had been fully informed of the situation. Mother Patricia could be relied upon to sort us out.

The months passed, and, as we waited for Mother Patricia, the need for an interim facilitator arose. While Judith and I and a few others suggested Father Raphael, the loudest voices in the room decided on everyone's behalf that Suzi could do the job as well as anyone. From that point on, Sister Suzanne became the sole judge at meetings, choosing which raised hand to note and which to ignore, whom to allow to speak, and whom (no surprises here) to silence. The chapter discussions that had erupted, almost out of thin air, as a free-for-all, now settled into a new standard form, one which above all served the old status quo. It was as though a spell had been cast on Elizabeth's gang, making of these otherwise good earnest women acolytes of an orthodoxy that was as unorthodox as it comes. Religious obedience was forgotten in favour of partiality. With the influence of the bishop and Father Gregory now successfully sidelined and Mother Patricia poised for action, there really was no recourse to objectivity. And, when the visitor from Norrington appeared, everyone put on their best faces (we even held a tea party for her) and got on with the charade.

29. The Beating

By the time I called for help I was on the floor. My tunic and night veil had been stripped from me, and I was foetal, knees under my chin, arms wrapped round me, shielding my torso from further blows. I felt for my nose. My hand came away hot and wet. But it was still there, the bone intact. Mother Irene stood over me, still shouting. She'd shaken and dragged me, nose to the floor, and, without releasing her grip, had thrashed my body from side to side on the cold lino. My nose took the weight as I rose and fell, left, right, left, right, the bone and cartilage twisting and pounding with each pull and thrust.

For a while, the sheets had held me, straining against her current, but finally came off like slow-stretched pastry, and I lay there, my feet and calves entangled, my breasts and shoulders open to her gaze. The curves of my hips were scooped-out hollows, my kneecaps red and swollen, the inner white of my thighs stained with watery pink. I'd spent the last ten years oblivious to the reality of my body. Now it pulsed and shivered like meat on a butcher's slab.

When she took away her hand, and air rushed through my nostrils once again, the blows proper began. Cheeks, arms, stomach, cheeks, midriff, arms, cheeks, my backbone nobbly against the hard floor. She had that morning smell about her, fresh soap.

'Toughen up!' she kept saying. 'I thought Scots were tough. With a name like yours you should be tougher than this. You should be tough, tough, tough!' Her brown-sandalled foot kicked and prodded at me, as though testing for reflexes. 'What's all this nonsense? You're not ill. You need to toughen up, tough, tough, tough . . .' Her voice rose like a hoover. 'There's nothing wrong with you – you – you malingerer! What are you doing here? There's nothing wrong. Get up!'

I lay and looked at her, numb within my battered body, at a woman twice my weight and almost twice my age, her loose red cheeks quivering with the blows, her lips moist with spittle. I had no energy with which to fight or weep. I watched and listened with strange detachment, with pity, and – I can admit it now – fascination. Such extreme ventings of emotion were new and still out of character within these walls.

'You've duties . . . should know better . . .' She was shaking, coughing now through her words, breathless, struggling to get them out. 'Get up, I'm telling you for the last time. No, you don't need to see the doctor. Get up, you – you southerner, you southern wimp!'

Maybe this was when I called out: 'Get her out of here. Get her away from me!'

It went against the grain to call, against the years of silencing, but finally the words flew through me like an escaped bird. Then, swift as a feather, the latch clicked and Sister Barbara appeared, as if she'd been standing there all along. No footsteps.

Mother sprang back, smiled like it was normal – me on the floor, bedclothes everywhere. Barbara enquired with a single look, then: 'I'll deal with this.'

They swapped places. Barbara's gaunt figure swayed into the cold space with satisfied efficiency. Yes, she was pallid, as drained as any of us, but did I detect the hint of a smile beneath the surface? Was it satisfaction? Witness-status?

After all, this was evidence. Irene was a failure. This was enough to bring her down with the rest of them.

'She shouldn't be in the infirmary,' Mother Irene was saying. 'A tetanus injection is nothing to make a fuss about. If she'd needed a half-hour lie down, all well and good – at a stretch – but she should have pulled herself together by now.' She spoke in a voice like gravel, leaning in to where the white of wimple cloth rumpled into Barbara's black veil. The two women stood like medieval washerwomen conferring in a marketplace, floor-length brown serge and arms hidden under sleeves like tents, the half-turned backs, the sideways glances. Then Irene moved towards the door. 'There's no need for her to lie in. No need for rest. People don't get ill just like that. Not without any warning.'

Mother strode the five paces of the cell's cold length. I staggered to my feet and found the bed. The high, white washbasin, the smell of pine, the low winter light, all clean and pure as ever. The apple trees stood bare beyond the window, angular, unmoved. Sister Barbara pulled out a thermometer from underneath her scapular. She rolled up her wide sleeves and began to shake it. Mother Irene's hand rested on the wooden latch before she tugged the pulley. One push, and she was out. The felt-lined door sighed and breathed back into its enclosing frame. I was finally alone with Barbara. The room folded round me.

For two days I barely spoke, just slept. Being in the infirmary was odd and new. Barbara brought me biscuits and Ovaltine. Mother Elizabeth appeared with orange squash. I had had a funny turn. Perhaps fainted. No one was seriously worried about me, and the fainting feebleness had passed. I didn't have a temperature. Was I faking it, malingering? I hadn't been in need of 'bed rest' in the infirmary before. I was fit and healthy, apart from my occasional asthma. I shouldn't be taking up an infirmary cell, or other people's time.

The last thing I remembered was going dizzy after my injection, then falling to the ground in the infirmary corridor. The jab had been a standard procedure, nothing to worry about, and no one else had had a reaction. It was more likely, the infirmarians thought, that I was just stressed and exhausted. I nodded. Yes, that sounded like an explanation. I was stressed and exhausted. Utterly exhausted.

One day I was told Dr Gill would pop in to see me. Barbara didn't like sparing him from the proper invalids – after all, there were no further symptoms. Just a temporary collapse. Otherwise, I was physically fine, my pulse normal. Dr Gill's time was precious. I didn't really need his attention.

Elizabeth floated in and looked at me. I seemed to be myself again, she said with a pale smile. I felt a rush of sadness for her.

The room felt very peaceful, and much warmer than I expected. I was pleased of that, now it was winter. Having a rug under my feet when I got out of bed was a nice sensation. And I quite liked the sense of activity going on nearby. The rattle of a trolley in the corridor. A flurry of feet. The sound of Barbara on the telephone. Mother Elizabeth's steely laugh. The tinkle of her spoon on a saucer and her calling to the cats. It was both more lively than the main house, and yet oddly calm. Almost ominously so. Yet something about the place was making me feel better. One of the best things about it was the sight of the lovely apple trees right outside my ground-floor window, an arc of trunks and branches, interlocking. Although it was winter, there was beauty in their ghostly company. Their brave branches reached out and touched each other in places, an overlapping asymmetry that would one day course with new life. The sap would rise in the spring, the buds would blossom.

I'd eased out of bed gently, testing my legs for wobbliness. Having my own loo was amazing, and the little washbasin with Lifebuoy soap. The room even had hot running water! And, instead of a ragged rectangle of cut-off roller towel with big hospital lettering on it, I had a velvety yellow one with a neat *St Michael* label folded along its seam. The comfortable room was almost like a return to the outside world. Seeing myself in the mirror was a big surprise. I looked weary and yet half startled, my face surrounded by a great, white, crumpled night veil. Didn't I used to have freckles?

At last there was a knock on the door, and there was Dr Gill. In he came, all pleasantries and bonhomie, just a touch of condescension. So, what's going on in here then? Like a policeman with a stethoscope. Soon he was casting a shadow on my bed, leaning over, asking me to sit up and open wide. He was nice enough, and even indulged in a bit of banter. So, you're the community musician, I take it? They're going to need you for the carol service! You should be ready to go back to work tomorrow.

Out he strode, carrying his case, and in Mother Elizabeth glided. She brought me a tangerine on a plate and a cup of tea. For a while she stood there with her head on one side, looking at me for the first time as though I were a proper human being. Almost off-guard, she had a go at chatting. How was I feeling? Were those bruises she noticed on my arms? Had the doctor seen them? Any difficulties to report? I knew better than to spill the beans about Irene's attack. It was likely they knew anyway. Barbara's entry had been swift and smooth, and there were keyholes everywhere. Who knows – maybe Irene herself had told them what had happened. Or had they seen evidence of her bruising fists? Was there blood on my nose?

As the days passed, my mind cleared and I felt ready to return to my cell. The subject of the beating never came up, unless you count a passing reference between Irene and me in the community room some days later. I was sitting in one corner when she had hobbled in and was arranging books from the mobile library during a quiet moment, while everybody else was at work. She'd sunk into a state of semi-somnolence of late. Was she too having a breakdown? Had she already had one? What was a breakdown anyway? I wondered whether her violence against me had simply been a blind release of misery, a taking-out on the most unresistant person she could find of all her pain, her pent-up anger and frustration. Or perhaps they'd turned her against me, finally. Naturally I had to forgive her. She had become a victim too.

She pretended not to see me for a bit, continuing to arrange the books. On her way out, however, she looked sideways at me, made a detour and brushed close past me, too close, while croaking something fuzzy and deep-throated in my ear. There was no one else around to hear it, but I suppose she wanted to be sure.

'I'm sorry I beat you,' she said, almost offhand.

'It's all right,' I answered, quick as a breath, equally softly, barely looking at her. And that was that. You knew when a subject was closed, or best left well alone. Then she moved away, and heaved herself out, all swaying hips, the door clicking into place behind her.

Back in the cell that evening, I heard the rustling of the wind. The corridors were still. Ten years had passed since my first Advent. I'd moved from fervent postulant to eager novice,

and then on to the trials and turbulence of the dark night of
the soul. At that point, on the very verge of making my vows,
I'd lost my bearings, as, like everybody else, I was bound to
lose them. All of us beginners on the contemplative path were
bound to drift in fog and then walk into the dark of unknow-
ing at some point, as John had taught. The explanation had
not convinced me at the time. It had seemed too neat, too
easy. The reality I was undergoing had felt much worse, like
some dereliction, some drastic loss caused surely by some fault
on my own part. But that crisis too had passed. In time I grew
strong and God's spirit spoke to me not in ecstasies and consolations but in moments of quiet contentment.

So what was the cause of my collapse in the infirmary? If
Dr Gill was right that there was nothing wrong with me ('You
are young and strong!') and that the tetanus injection was
innocuous, what had really sent me over the edge that afternoon, when I'd not resisted the urge to slide down helplessly
onto the floor and allow all the fight and energy to seep out
of me? However strained things had become among us, my
instinct to keep quiet about my struggles, my learned, trained,
deeply ingrained and practised faculty for silence and for
keeping my troubles to myself meant that I had said nothing
to anybody about Jennifer's outburst at a recent music practice. I was beginning to see that such things were not out of
the ordinary at Akenside any more. I told myself it was her
illness, and perhaps it really was, the surliness and tendency
to storm, the dark looks and attempts to undermine what I
was doing. I told myself to keep my eyes on God, and not to
take it personally.

It was that time of year again, and we were busy with the
preparations for the carol service. As always, Father Gregory
would be coming. As always, I was writing an instrumental

medley for the occasion, one that would show off the talents of the community to their best advantage, and would involve as many contributors as possible, from the most modest recorder player to the best of the singers. In the past, Jen had always brought along her French horn, and we'd found a way to incorporate her efforts into some of the more lively carols. Ellen would have been there with her flute, and Suzi with a selection of instruments, and her beautiful singing voice. This year, though, the buzz of protest in the air had put a strain on things and, although Barbara wandered into the choir from time to time to check up on proceedings and add her own modest voice to the singing, we were definitely a depleted group. When Jen sauntered in, looking both cowed and swaggering, I was surprised she'd decided to join us, but then sad to find all she wanted to do was sit on the floor and comment, while banging a couple of percussion instruments. She'd found some maracas and a drum, and was intent on making her presence felt, but not constructively.

Poor Jen, now heavily medicated, was treated as an exception in everything and often exposed by her increasingly frequent and very public rages. I did not know how to handle her, or how to cope myself with the combative energy she threw in my direction. Our twin-ship had never been an easy one, but we'd tried hard in the early years, acting cheerfully around each other, and succeeding in convincing the older sisters that we were friendly – although officially 'friendship' in Carmel was for God alone. Towards and among each other we were encouraged to be 'supportive sisters', and as far as I knew Jen and I had pulled off the act quite successfully. We were, as she'd intimated in the beginning, partners in this extraordinary exercise, this rash dare. However, so much of what passed for virtue in the monastery was a form of covering up, of masking, of avoiding our true thoughts and feelings about almost anything. The more perfect you were (look at Elizabeth!) the less you gave away of yourself, the less you outwardly betrayed the least glimmer of your own reality. One rule of thumb, for example, was always 'to say the opposite' of what you were thinking, if your thoughts did not fall into the expected pattern. Similarly, we were called to 'do the opposite' of what we instinctively or wanted to do – all part of the purification of our natures in conformity with the Mind of Christ. The intention was honourable, but the method was deeply flawed. It relied on suppression of facts, of honesty, and of that simple, universally recognized virtue of speaking the truth.

On the cusp of the new millennium, and at that almost midnight hour, it was still too early for me to feel sorry for Jen, the sister who had so long antagonised me. The pain I felt (and that I dutifully buried deep inside) was too acute. If it was Irene who had rolled up her sleeves and beaten me, it was Jennifer who had hurt me more with her covert opposition, her barbed comments and black looks. It had been going on for years. Part of me knew why, could sense the differences between us, and how they affected and tormented us. In close proximity to each other, unable to get away from the hothouse of the enclosure, these things were magnified. And all too easily in the cloister, no outside help or reality checks from the wider world permitted, small differences and resentments could get totally out of hand. The fact that so many of our generation of younger sisters had already fallen prey to illness, and mental or emotional breakdowns of one sort or another, was evidence enough that something was not working as it should. That there were underlying problems with the 'way we did things' that urgently needed to be reviewed, possibly changed.

Sometimes I wonder, had I been less intent on the mirage of 'perfection' I'd once so ardently espoused, had I spoken up earlier, told someone of the bullying behaviour that was torturing me, driving me deep down into myself with the years, might Jen's condition have been noticed and seen for what it was – and treated – earlier? Was it that Mother Elizabeth really did not know what was going on, that she imagined Jen was a perfectly well-adjusted candidate for the Life, and that there were no problems requiring outside attention? Or would my voice have added nothing to the situation, been dismissed as nonsense or as feeble complaining (because commenting negatively on others' behaviour was always wrong) and made no difference to anyone or anything in the end? How had a cheerful young woman been allowed to get so low, so broken? Of course, you were not supposed to ask or even think about these things. You minded your own business. You kept your eyes on the Lord, on the crucifix, and on that redeeming, tortured, bloodied body of his, making of your own life a replica of his wholehearted sacrifice.

The black cross still loomed over me in my cell. Sometimes I felt I was half nailed to its sturdy, uncompromising beams. The sacrifice I'd taken on at vows was coming to fruition. At others, I feared the driving in of further nails and that, somehow, I too would crumble, break into a thousand pieces. I feared the losing of my mind. I feared the half-comforting lure of self-destruction. Others had done it before me, at other monasteries. Even Jesus had faltered and begged for the cup of suffering to be taken away.

'Dear Father . . .' I sat, a crumpled heap of tearfulness in my cell. 'Dear Lord,' I said again, and for the millionth time. 'Dear Dad . . .' My shoulders were shaking. The skin on my winter, work-worn hands was chapped, the knuckles raw and cracked, the garden, the laundry, the 'simplicity' of our lives having taken its toll. Dear Mother Mary. I called on all of them, the saints and angels. I held out my hands to Teresa, and to John of the Cross, those mentors I thought of as my friends. I went into my innermost Carmelite heart, whisper-ing as I did so, knowing there was someone there, a loving presence that would not budge, or change, or ever let me down. I am glad I did so, and that I'd learned, long, long ago, to find the place of strength and stability within, the very core of me where the still, small voice of calm abided. Yes, that presence was still there, and had been all along. The fount of life, the way of peace, and the source of truth had not deserted me. He wanted me to continue to love him not because of, but in spite of the community. He wanted me to rely on him alone, in spite of problems, in spite of the cog-nitive dissonance that had tested and driven me towards doubt and disillusionment. He wanted me to come out into the light. And now that light was shining. The moon was high above the monastery.

'Our Father . . .' The words came naturally. 'Who art in heaven . . .' The sky showed an infinite horizon. 'Thy will be done . . .' That will was clear. The One True God was bigger than the monastery. He was bigger than the Church. He was a God of life not death, a God who had originally made us for his own delight. He had even told us he would rejoice in us, his people, dance over us 'as on a wedding day'. This was the God I would believe in and hold fast to, a God of love not punishment, a God of kindness not cruelty, the one who would never desert me, wherever and however far I went.

'"If I take the wings of the morning and dwell at the sea's furthest end, even there, thy hand shall lead me, thy right hand shall hold me fast."' Indeed. The words sent the tears rolling hot and salty down my cheeks. The beauty of them. Their deep resonance of truth. Yes. My mind was settled. I would 'choose life' not death. I would trust, I would not fear.

30. One Dark Night

In my mind I am still running. Running towards the road. Running. Running. Running. The night is a dark wash, a slap of wet around my head, my veil twisting and turning in the wind. My feet in their sandals pound onwards, first over gravel, then over grass, until, losing the road, I find a field and throw myself down, my heart thumping, amazed at what I see around me. The skirts of my great habit are spread wide, the leather of my heavy belt anchoring my elaborate medieval clothing at the hip. Too big for my frame now, its loose tip hangs low and digs into my legs. Above me is nothing but the vastness of the moonlit sky and an infinity of staring stars. The bone-white moon glows reassuringly through a drifting mauve-grey penumbra, and then reappears, stark with splendour. It sees me and I stare back.

It is impossible not to laugh, to spread wide my arms, to enjoy the singing and wild percussion of my heart, the feeling of expansiveness, and then to speak, at first in whispers, as though shy of the million and one stars, then in a great rush of declaration. I know you are there, great God, I breathe out loud. I know you are with me. I trust in you. Rolling over and pressing my palms into the wet grass, my mind and senses are unbound. Earth is newly my mother, dank and generous. I love the vital wet and midnight greenness of her, wanting more. The flattened winter grasses all around me are my friends. Then, thank you, thank you, thank you – the words, like the gratitude they express, come so very easily.

Two bright cars later – they sped too fast for me to see, blurs in the night – and I am up again, no longer running but walking steadily. Although trustful, I am now anxious and apprehensive, getting tired. My viola strap is digging into my shoulder. As the first domestic glow of orange light, then the tops of houses and a steeple come into sight, my mind slows. What next? What on earth am I to do now? I know nothing of how this world works. Here, people have other rhythms, and live by other stories. I stop, taking in the cluster of what my mind processes as an alien settlement.

Fear had not come into it, during the two-mile walk from Akenside. Instead, my heart and senses had been singing, my mind phenomenally clear. But now I am here, in a village I have hardly ever seen, what am I to do? Knock on the vicarage door? No, the lights are off. And, seeing me standing there in my long black veil, my coif and tocque, how would they react? No, safer to lie low a little longer, then look for a phone box. Surely phone boxes and things like taxis are all over the place out here? A reverse-charge call to my sister would do the trick. Get me to her warm house for the night.

Now I am scouting the streets, horrified at the lack of phones. Horrified, too, at the lack of taxis. Where are the buses? Where is everybody? Isn't this the Outside World? Where is all the activity? Disappointed, my heart sinks. Now I am walking hesitantly down the main road where small, period cottages, with roses outside, seem more promising than the uniform, modern enclaves. I am walking in such a way as to avoid being noticed, not quite on tiptoes. I have no money. I have only whatever providence sends, that and the promptings of my guardian angel. 'Guide me,' I whisper. The night is cold around my face. 'Help me,' I say in a determined undertone. The streets are preternaturally still and empty. There is a deadness in the air. Unlike the freedom of the fields, this all feels clinical and disappointing. Everything is tidily shut down for the night. Traces of shadowy net curtains, soulless front doors . . .

Then I see a further row of cottages, raised on a higher bit of pavement behind a railing. I see an ebullience of shrubs and trees. There is a light on in a ground-floor window. 'Guide me,' I whisper again. 'Show me the way.' The answer to my prayer seems to have appeared already. A light in the darkness. A sign of hope. This surely must be the house. As I approach, my heart beats loud enough for me to hear it, like an orchestral instrument. Bang, it goes, thud, thud, as though building to a big reveal. I grip my viola case more tightly. I adjust my now inconveniently rustling plastic bag over my left shoulder. I'd left with only the essentials. I'd left with sandals on my feet and a staff in my hand.

The well-lit window is a beacon and I move towards it. From being a generalised village house, it becomes a proposition, its detail coming into focus. There is a poster in the window. It is something black and white and half familiar, hand-drawn and based on, perhaps, a Dürer engraving? Here, of all places, the face of my spouse looks querulously out at me, the expression inscrutable between coils of long-hanging hair. Is it a pleading or an invitation? Might it after all be a reproach? Are those thorns around his head? The image is indistinct in the moonlight. Above it, in calligraphic lettering, is the title of a choral concert, the date only a week away.

Finding the house is one thing, but having the courage to

knock is another. And how can I be sure this is the one? How safe is the certain otherness I'll find inside? How welcoming? Walls are powerful protectors. They are also guardians of mystery. I am stalling on the threshold. I look up at the moon; it seems a friend. I take in the wide expanse of space and stars. The sense of freedom is beyond glorious. It is a feast. Perhaps I should just keep on walking. Perhaps I should find some more fields to lie down and laugh and sing in. Perhaps dance my way to dawn and a friendly taxi rank. But then again – a door. A lamp. A concert poster. Titles of friendly Renaissance polyphony.

With my heart thudding I lift my hand. I turn my knuckle. I take a great gulp of night-pure oxygen. I knock.

Can I hear noises within? The door begins to move, and a column of light appears. In the centre of the column there is a face. It is the face of a plump middle-aged woman. She is mousey and short. Behind her the face of a heavily bearded man appears. Can I help you? they both say not quite together. Who are you? What has happened? Then I hear the bearded man whispering while moving away.

Alone on the doorstep with this stranger, I suddenly feel conspicuous. She, after all, is wearing a beige, mid-length skirt and fluffy slippers. It is difficult to tell the colour in the mix of lights, but I think there is a purple cardigan.

'Helen,' the man calls from somewhere off the hall.

She does a half-turn. 'Yes, David?'

There is some sort of interchange going on. It all seems a bit muffled. Then she's looking back at me, her face doing gentle interrogatives. Something behind her eyes is computing.

'You must be from the Priory,' she says, and my heart sinks. 'What are you doing out here at this time? Do they know, and do you need us to run you back there? I mean, we've got the car. But look at you, my dear, you're all soaking wet, goodness . . .'

My apologies must be sounding like the bleatings of a very lost sheep. I keep on hearing myself say the word sorry. Sorry to trouble you, sorry to disturb. But she is smiling now, seeing my viola. She is beginning to get purposeful. Soon I am being led into an Aladdin's cave, a room crowded with decorative lamps and furniture, rugs, tasselled curtains, printed tea towels on an Aga, mugs hanging from a shelf. There are dark-orange casserole dishes. Herbs and spices. Quite a lot of earthenware. And, on a table in a corner, a pile of music. Some vocal scores. 'O Magnum Mysterium' is written on the top cover. Then others in piles, 'Verbum Caro Factum Est', 'Omnes de Saba' . . .

'Oh, that's David's work. He's up late doing the programme notes. But we can clear a space . . .'

The sight of the music startles me, as astonishing as an apparition of angels overhead. The colour everywhere is like a symphony. The lamplight warm. Then David is back, filling a pipe with Old Holborn tobacco. Helen is settling me at the table.

'So, you're musical too, I see?' he says, half a question.

'Yes, I'm Catherine, and I really needed to get away,' I say.

'So we see,' they both say, almost laugh, and look at each other. But before I can begin to tell them anything more about myself and my predicament, Helen takes a firm seat next to me and pats me on the wrist. David leans back, a puff of aromatic smoke rising around his head.

'Yes, you need to tell us all about yourself and what has happened,' Helen says.

I nod. The tears are now rolling down my cheeks. David sucks carefully on his pipe. He seems to be extracting something elusive from it very slowly. He strokes his beard. I notice he has shallow, square-cut nails. Helen's hands are soft and plump.

'But first, David will put the kettle on,' she says. 'Won't you, darling?' She looks at him. Points to a tin marked 'Biscuits'. He rises and moves away.

'Tea or Ovaltine?'

'Or something stronger?' David calls over his shoulder.

'There's coffee if you need it,' Helen explains. 'After all, you've probably got lots to tell us.'

Soon he is back, and they are both lifting receptacles, filling cups. Some chocolate-chip shortbread has appeared.

In my mind I am still sitting there. In my mind I am talking to them, hardly knowing what I am saying. In my mind I am drinking tea, and eating biscuits, no longer running through the night.

'Thank you,' I say to them. 'Thank you for your kindness.'

Light will soon be peeping round the curtains. Cars will soon be driving past. I will soon be standing on their doormat, a little warmer, a little drier, ready for the lift they have offered me into Newcastle. Frankie will soon be running down the stairs, opening the door to her and Johnny's Victorian townhouse. But before I leave the protective cave and head out into cool fresh air again, I owe them another apology.

'I'm sorry I kept you up so late,' I say. 'I'm sorry . . .'

But now their arms are around me, and both their voices are saying something together. Never mind, it seems to be – never mind. And take care of yourself, Catherine. Remember to call us tomorrow. And David is waving me off with a smile. As I get into the car and Helen starts the engine, and the village recedes and turns to fields, I look back for a moment. I hold on to my viola. I have missed *matraque* and Lauds and Little Jug. But now a new world is dawning. Soon it will be time for breakfast.

Epilogue

Biscuit tins have never been the same since. Nor have orange casserole dishes. I'd never have given such domesticities a second thought, but now they speak to me of freedom, of a light in a window, of a table kindly shared. Twenty years have passed since the night I ran away and trusted myself to strangers, and found my trust repaid with generosity. After Helen drove me into Newcastle, and Frankie floated along the street in a nightie, weaving between the streetlamps, and Johnny stood incredulous on the doorstep in his pyjamas, and I was ushered into a house that smelled of toast, a new phase began, one that forced me to confront what I had done in leaving.

Getting away was one thing, and a relief, but negotiating the onslaught of the unfamiliar, the sensory overload, was another. Although I was finally outside Carmel, I was still a Carmelite inside. My inner ear waited for the bell, for hushed footsteps in the corridor, for plainchant floating up the lofty staircase. I instinctively sought silence and was perplexed by the great rush of noise. I looked for privacy, a bare room with a quiet door, and felt out of place among the coloured rugs and cushion covers. Pattern and decoration were alien to my cloistered, austere sensibility. I missed the stony corridors, the plain white of my cell wall, the big black cross that watched in solemn silence over everything. Carmel was all I'd known for over a decade. Carmel was my identity and my home.

The clatter of footsteps on the pavement outside the

window when I awoke, later that morning, was a new kind of morning alarm, and a new shock. Where was the thin blanket, the cold air of my cell? This was what freedom sounded like, but – what had I done? I had torn myself from the one world where I had a home, a niche, a purpose. A world that, in essence, I still loved. After over a decade of straining for the highest monastic ideals (and being shocked when others didn't) I'd broken one of the most fundamental of our rules, that of enclosure. I'd broken it, not out of laziness, or because I didn't care, but because I cared too much. I cared about what I saw going on around me – the breakdowns, the bullying, the hurtful cliques, the double standards, the sheer hypocrisy, the 'only human-ness' of it all. Carrying the conflict of this, the pain of reality together with the fear that I, too, might one day be pushed too far and break down, was slowly terrifying me. I'd heard of too many others in my age group being written off as unfit or crazy. If suicide or madness were the alternatives, then leaving was surely the lesser evil?

I may not have climbed out of a window, as John of the Cross had done, famously, after nine months of imprisonment by his own brethren, but I'd dared to cross a sacred threshold and to turn a forbidden key. I'd run through sensor lights and across gravel, had sped through fields, had even crouched amid gravestones under the moon. I'd presented myself at a stranger's house. And now I was here, lying under fluffy duvets on a sofa bed in my sister's front room, the light slanting in through wrought-iron city railings. I was here, a mug of tea cooling beside me, the sound of Frankie's two-year-old daughter running over creaky floorboards, and of my newborn niece crying on an upper floor.

I felt churned up by what I'd done – I'd gone from

goody-goody to rebel overnight. But I also felt amazed at all the possibilities surrounding me. The mix of guilt and euphoria was something I hadn't tasted in a long time, if ever at all. The wide, wide canvas of potential, together with the actuality of creativity and experiences I'd barely dreamed of, all of that and more was there. Those vistas, that excitement, that happy reality. But, underpinning it like a dragging weight, was the awareness of my fault, my rashness, that irregular burst of self-determination by which I'd removed myself from things that seemed no longer bearable. I'd been told Mellerby was out of the question and warned 'not even to think about' asking to see Father Gregory. And so I'd acted – fully, consciously under the eyes of a protector God.

I'd felt him close beside me under the vast dome of a black, brilliant, starry sky. I'd felt him accompanying me like a friend through fields and lanes, and I'd found him again, Emmaus-like, over tea and biscuits in a wayside cottage, a cottage that had drawn me with its light. If I'd had moments of doubt during my decade behind bars (and what nun doesn't?) I had none now. The power behind the universe was the same power that made my ears to hear, my eyes to see, my heart to beat. It was there in the crunch of gravel underfoot, it was there in the grass that sprang, lush and midnight-coloured, under my sandals as I ran, it was there in the inner confidence that said to me, run on, run on!

I'd trusted, but had I trusted too much? Was I being presumptuous in counting on him still to uphold me?

Frankie wandered in with scrambled eggs.

'How are you feeling, Cathy?'

'I'm OK,' I said. It was too early to start digging, and more important to focus on the immediate, this lovely breakfast. I smiled. 'Thank you for the tea.'

Later she returned and gave me a cloudy-silver key on an old piece of string. I turned it over in my hands. I knew what it meant. But when she produced two five-pound notes I had no idea of their value. It had been years. And I'd got used to thinking that money was alien, dangerous, unnecessary, a potential source of contamination. Instead of counting it, or counting on it, we were told to count on God alone as a provider. Everything came from him, and, since he loved us and wanted to look after us, we needed only to pray and to give thanks to enjoy his benefits. Any form of calculation, or desire for personal gain, was inimical to our way of life. Such social or survival skills were things I had completely forgotten. I had been reformed into the shape of someone who trusted so much that she no longer knew what it was to defend herself or feel suspicion.

'Can you remember your way around the city?' Frankie asked, handing me a map. The truth was that I had no way of orientating myself in this unfamiliar environment. My thoughts defaulted to prayer and praise, overflowed naturally into excesses of thanksgiving, and the idea that I might have to take care of my own interests had not yet impinged. Yes, I could walk along the river, could ad lib it, stroll here and there and look at things. I could take my pick of shops to walk into, or avoid, and could probably find my way back afterwards. But a map was definitely needed. As was advice.

For a few days Frankie and I just talked, sometimes long into the nights, while Johnny crept around the house, allowing us the space to chatter and – importantly – to laugh. Which we did a great deal. Lots of stuff was coming out in a big rush, and we often fell about, helpless with hilarity. One day she told me I had a couple of hairs growing out of my chin, something of which I'd been entirely oblivious, and the session with the tweezers was one of high drama and high comedy, me flinching, she insisting I sit still, and pulling hard. The whole business of having mirrors everywhere was extraordinary. I looked at the tired reflection in the bathroom cabinet. Was this faded person me? But baths were wonderful; long, hot, proper baths, with bubbles, and no one to ring a bell to tell me to get out. I soaked and sang, and let the time roll past in one long, lazy continuum.

One day I succumbed to my sister's suggestion that I try on some of her clothes. I did so reluctantly as, whatever I felt about Akenside and the problems there, the habit was still part of my identity. The jeans she thrust into my hands slipped on easily enough, and felt quite fun, but hung off me, making me look shockingly skinny. I'd lost weight and was now more like a fragile scarecrow than the rosy, freckled girl who'd entered on a spiritual high. My hair, too, was a shock. Johnny's teenage daughter visited and told me that people 'paid a lot to get that look' in Toni & Guy. Cool. It was an effortlessly spiky crop. Asymmetric, too. Did I want some gel? No, I didn't. If I was going to do without a veil, I certainly wasn't going to do without a hat or headscarf. I was used to being swathed and swamped in cloth.

Experimenting and relaxing were hugely therapeutic. I'd needed a holiday, that much was for sure. There's only so far you can stretch a piece of elastic. And all that unbridled laughter was a wonderful release. Something exhausted in me was responding to this natural human connection. Mum came up for a few days, something exceptional in itself. Johnny made a bumper evening meal. We lit candles, we played Scrabble, we ate chicken, we drank wine. I vaguely realised I was Cause for Concern. The runaway nun. The one who'd nearly cracked. But then again, I sensed a kind of

mirth, of suppressed comedy even, an atmosphere of celebration. It was muted but it was there, a collective relief.

One day I said I would be out for lunch and wandered off
in the only direction my feet knew well in that great northern
city. I went to a turquoise-painted door I remembered from
the days before my entry, the days of my conversion, when I
used to go for daily Mass at the Jesmond Pastoral Centre.
There were one or two people there who would remember
me, and I wasn't sure whether I wanted to dodge them or be
recognised. Part of me wondered whether I didn't just want
to turn myself in. It would be much easier. At the same time,
there was a feeling of shame at having walked (or rather run)
away from my vocation. I still felt I was a Carmelite, no
matter what I looked like or what I did, and I can't remember
to this day whether I was wearing my habit or my sister's ill-
fitting clothing the day I wandered into the centre and
encountered Sister Josephine.

Josephine was by now the Mother Superior of her convent, having replaced Aggie, but was only ever known to me
as Jo. The teaching order she belonged to didn't wear habits,
and Jo was known for her collection of flowery scarves. She
was a bright, bustling woman with a bold manner and a big,
pealing laugh, someone I'd met in my early days exploring
the north. I was a new convert then, interested in finding
somewhere to go for an Easter retreat. Jo had sensed potential and was soon inviting me for lunch. One thing had led to
another. She'd encouraged me, and things had taken their
course. Who knows what might have happened if I had I not
sought her out in this time of crisis?

I'd promised Helen, my night rescuer, that I would let the
monastery know that I was safe. The next day Frankie had
called them, had heard the disbelief, the stunned silence as

she told Sister Barbara that I was asleep in her front room. There'd been some crackling and Elizabeth had come on the line. After the initial questions they'd reached an agreement – give it a few days – and Fra had hung up, half giggling, half walking on eggshells. I'd drunk my tea and gone back to sleep. Days had passed and everything continued to shuffle around, like foggy slides on an overhead projector. Waking or sleeping, I was adjusting, assessing, praying, discerning, getting used to seeing things in a new light. But none of that stopped me from succumbing to the pull of the Pastoral Centre, and of the liturgy. None of my recent encounters with the secular could stop the feeling that I was made for the sacred.

As it happened, after Mass that day, Sister Josephine put on her best, most commanding manner, and walked me upstairs to a special room, an inner chamber with such un-monastic features as sofas and painted vases, and plonked me down in front of a telephone. Now, Sister Catherine, she seemed to say. Or perhaps she just said, Come on, Cathy. She smiled a steely, most decided smile. She folded her hands.

'I think we ought to phone the bishop.'

The truth is that, by the time I arrived at what I thought was safety, away from the mental and emotional pressures of the cloister – or rather away from Akenside – I had undergone such a deep reframing of my mind and heart that I felt I only belonged in a habit and inside a cell. If my mind had been 'remade', and my nature at least half transformed, if I'd responded to the formation process, I was now good for nothing but smiling, praising, chanting psalms and sweeping floors. Of course, that's to simplify it, but you get the drift. I might have been enjoying bubble baths, and the cool touch of a key in my pocket, I might even have been enjoying jeans, but everything inside me was programmed to prayer.

On one level it's been impossible to leave. It's been impossible to forget the sound of silence. It's been impossible not to wake each morning loving God. Impossible not to rejoice. Unresistant, my psyche had taken the imprint of something much greater and grander than itself, something indelible, when I'd entered a closed world all those years ago. My hands were strong and ready for hard work. I'd given all I had to God, to faith, to Akenside, had given all I had to become a New Creation. No, I was not going to walk away.

After the phone call with the bishop, and an agreed two-week stint in a Scottish abbey guesthouse, a place where I could 'recuperate' and have some 'spiritual direction', and after someone had driven me to the nearest station and I'd got on a train and crossed the Firth of Forth, and seen the seagulls flying, had heard their cry – after all of that, I returned with a mix of joy and reluctance to Northumberland and to Akenside. When I say reluctance, I mean I felt a bit shamefaced and apprehensive about how everything would work out, and how the old routines would seem after my brush with freedom. There was no doubt I'd enjoyed aspects of the Outside World. But the joy I felt crossing the threshold was the happiness of homecoming, and an extraordinary homecoming it was. I was ushered in under cover of something or other – no one had been told about my escapade, I was simply 'out of action in the infirmary' – and a breezy pretence that nothing serious had happened.

I must say, Elizabeth was magnificent, and – however flawed and blinkered she'd been at times, however messed up – I came to realise that she, too, had been formed by others, Julianna in part, and programmed to what she thought was perfection. It is remarkable how programmable we all are as human beings. In that lies our ability to learn, but also our propensity to be controlled. None of us are fully our own masters and mistresses. None of us is capable of acting truly independently. We called the power that hovered over our lives, filling and directing them, 'God', a simple word, a sort of name, a concept that is as abstract as it is personal. You may have your own word for that unseen guest at every table in your life, that miraculous feeling that you are not quite alone, that some purpose and potentiality are at work making of your existence something so much greater than the sum of its parts.

I have no doubt that God was over everything that happened to me, and that he is still over everything that fills me and motivates me and matters in my life. But how I would define that little word, that tiny, huge, potent enigma, is another matter. I won't even begin to try. The philosopher Paul Tillich got close when he said that God was the 'Ground of Being', the object of our Ultimate Concern, a reduction that nevertheless makes complete sense intuitively. Kierkegaard and Tillich are just two among the cloud of witnesses to the divine who have spoken to, and for, human beings of every creed and condition and colour everywhere throughout history. It's official, we can't get away from it – we have been 'fearfully and wonderfully made' (Psalm 139). Or, if you don't like 'fearfully', there is always 'awesomely' – an alternative translation from the Hebrew.

Awe has a lot to do with it, actually, and with everything that grabbed me by the throat as a young woman on hearing her beloved dad had died. Awe is powerful. It changes us. It can shock us with a sense of being tiny, insignificant and alone. Conversely, it can come with an overwhelming sense of presence. There really was something there in the silence of my cell, and in the choir, and there really is something everywhere worth bearing witness to, even if the only word you have for it is love. Especially if the only word you have for it is love. It is what keeps us alive.

Back to Elizabeth. Seeing me laid low, and disgraced, she became warm, and kind, and even quite funny. Irene was more or less invisible by now, sidelined, disregarded, and things were trundling on peacefully in the infirmary. I'd stopped commenting on the status quo, and was just glad of the space and the time to adjust, and of orange squash. As far as I know, nobody was ever told about my midnight flit apart from Barbara (who'd answered the phone) and Elizabeth (who knew everything) and Irene (because she was, after all, the prioress). It was our big secret, and for a week or two I was treated as an invalid recovering.

You can take the nun out of the monastery, but you can't take the monastery out of the nun. The saying is true. And neither can you put the genie back in the bottle once it's escaped. Nothing was to be the same again, once I'd pushed at the boundaries, run away, and felt the revivification of my raw and innate humanity through family, through food, and fun, and meat, and music, and above all through the freedom I'd given myself to act, to think outside the box.

I lived another two years at Akenside. Long enough to know that I could not turn back the clock. I was evolving, becoming a stronger, more aware and morally accountable human being. I was taking responsibility. Was my departure one dark night a rebellion or an act of faith? Was my inability to stop thinking about things – or to stop thinking, full stop – a failure of faith or a gift? God knows. What I offer is a story. A personal testament. A glimpse over the wall. It is an act of thanks for my survival.

My second departure was done officially and efficiently,

under the auspices of Father Gregory, and with a decree releasing me from my vows straight from the Pope. It sits in the least favourite compartment of my least favourite drawer, in a tall, grey filing cabinet in a corner of my study in Oxford, where I live. I cannot bear to look at it. It bears a blob of dark red wax. And a signature. But that is all history. It was a means to an end.

And what was that end? Well, the beginning of it was that I should learn and grow, and so I applied to go back to university. I became an undergraduate again (not having finished my degree in London the first time round), this time at the University of Oxford, thinking, This will keep me going. It was something to do. It was somewhere to live. There was an ivory-tower element to it, too, which felt familiar and reassuring. I was at home in stony corridors. Above all, it was a chance to read and think and question, and to delve at last into all those books I'd not had access to. And – of course – to write.

I've lived and thought and written long and hard. I've also prayed. I've stayed up through many a long dark night. John of the Cross was right about the not knowing. When we 'go out' from ourselves and our familiar routines and assumptions, into the dark night of agnosticism, when we stand with Elijah on the mountain and hear 'the sound of absolutely nothing', as one translation puts it, or, more familiarly, the 'sound of a gentle breeze', we are transposed to a place where awe can teach us, where we can be remodelled. There is a presence there that makes us new. It's not about staid religion. It's not about mindless conformity. It's about a very personal level of experience that hovers perpetually somewhere on the fringes of our consciousness, one that visits us uninvited from time to time. It's about letting it touch us. It's about hearing that silent music. It's about seizing the moment.

*

In time I heard that Elizabeth had been re-elected after Irene's three years were up. It was Judith who told me, in one of her beautifully written letters, also telling me (wryly) that 'things had gone back to normal'. Of course they had had to in the end. Irene remained chastened and downtrodden, finally becoming meek as a lamb. Marion remained the court jester, humoured but tacitly despised. Judith soon departed for Mellerby, and was allowed to transfer there permanently once it became clear that it was the obvious choice. She'd been cruelly hounded during the days of the Akenside Inquisition, bullied, made to tie herself in knots, and even to apologise for speaking the obvious truth. She would be better off at Mellerby, many of whose sisters were members of her own original cohort, contemporaries who shared her perspective. I was glad to hear she had found a beautiful and supportive Carmelite home elsewhere. Glad to hear she'd found acceptance. She was an honest soul.

We kept in touch. One day she wrote to tell me that the power of the gang had dissolved. The bonds that had once held its members ceased to be relevant. With so many sisters having departed or moved on, no common enemy left to fight, they'd slipped into their own new channels, new minor rivalries, new loves, partialities and antipathies, as was only human. On one level, the level Elizabeth liked to promote, that's what the Life was mainly about, just shared customs, shared surrenders, a club for the like-minded. They were just a group of people living a certain way by (perfect or imperfect) common consent. I'd gone there seeking and expecting a lot more. I'd gone there blinded by my love affair with the divine. Dazzled by a sense of discovery. I was giving it my all and expected, not necessarily rapture, but at least transfiguration, if not heaven in return. I still had a lot to learn, especially about the diversity and fallibility of human nature.

As the years passed, more news trickled through. Stephanie chose to leave after the expiry of her temporary vows. Like me, she opted to study theology at university. To the raising of one or two eyebrows, Suzi followed her to college life, where the two of them were apparently 'as thick as thieves', now living well beyond the dictates of the cloister. People had ways of reading things in, but I guessed the two of them were just good friends, although eventually they went their very different ways. As did so many of us. Felicity, Pippa, Lucy, Emily, all of us morphed into new creations of whatever sort best suited our eternal souls. Some of us kept in touch. One or two of our number came out as gay, when it felt safe for them to do so, while others, like me, moved from determined celibacy into relationships with those confusing, unfamiliar beings, human men. I thought it was worth giving it a try. I have always been open to new beginnings.

Life has changed for me beyond all recognition. I never thought I would find happiness in a domesticated relationship. But I was wrong. After years as a tutor and teacher, I made new vows, and am now something I never dreamed I would, or would ever want to be: a married woman, living in an east Oxford terraced house, not unlike my sister's old house in Jesmond. I make marmalade and cook dahl. I am active locally as a musician. I sing in choirs. I play in string quartets. I quite often go to church. But not too often. What I do do, and still need to do, is to seek out times of extended solitude and silence, and I still go on retreat to other monasteries. The power of the cloister has never faded.

I have never been back to Akenside, although I have often dreamed of doing so. I have often woken at midnight thinking

I have heard a bell, or the rustle of a habit hem outside my door, or the padding of a dozen feet along a top-floor corridor. I have dreamed of space, and extraordinary cleanliness, and unending psalmody. I have dreamed of wheelbarrows, and have longed to see those fields again from my high window, to run all the way to the hornbeam and back, to walk to the Mere, to dance in the Deep. I have yearned – most improbably – for the toolshed. And of course, I still miss the resonance of the choir and the silent beauty of my cell. These things are both indelible and irretrievable.

My last link now with the community is Father Gregory, who, although well on in years, still keeps in touch. He knows the truth, which is that I loved my sisters, and still love them and the remnant of the community – Elizabeth, Barbara, Ruth, Alison, Ellen and the rest – and especially that I loved the dream, the hopes we once shared of a perfect world. A perfect way of life. But, like all dreams, those illusions died at the breaking of the day. The dawning of flawed human reality was too painful. The rejecting politics, the mess, the dysfunction of the group; I was too deeply hurt by all of this.

Eventually I learned that Barbara followed Elizabeth as prioress. That everyone was very happy with the arrangement. In time, I learned that Irene had died. That Paula and others, similarly, went the way of all flesh. I learned that the community dwindled, and moved out of the great house into more manageable premises elsewhere, and that the beautiful building that we all loved was sold. Sadly, I learned that Jennifer never fully recovered from her illness. She has remained, a semi-invalid, looked after by Barbara and Elizabeth, to this day. As for those two infirmarians, the Loyal of Akenside, they have continued to take it in turns as prioress ever since.

One day I will return to Akenside. Or it will return to me. But it may be an Akenside transfigured, or overseas, or an Akenside of the imagination, or of the afterlife. Or it may simply be the pages of this book. The monastery held me, enamoured, too long for the core of the experience to be fundamentally renounced. Like all transcendent experiences, all true loves, its essence lives on long after its accidental signs and symbols have been lost or destroyed. The house as we all knew it is no more. The people, too, have surely changed, as have I. The essence of what it all meant to us, though, the spiritual heartland of the Life, was deeper than all of that, more permanent. Who knows where I will find it, or where, turning a corner, it will find me? Who knows how soon? And as for you, the reader, on closing this book, you never know. If you shut your eyes, you too may feel the cold of the corridors, may hear the cry of the low-flying geese, or the padding of sandals on stone. You may hear the distant tolling of the bell for Vespers. You may even hear the sound of perfect silence.

Acknowledgements

This book emerged, slowly and cautiously, from a world of silence, and owes as much to silence as it does to speech. Listening was a prerequisite for learning in the monastery, and I must thank my mother for the gift of attentive listening and a love of words, things she fostered in me from an early age. She was a poet and reciter of poetry and taught me to love Yeats from as far back as I can remember. Her voice had an emotive power and musicality that may well have shaped my sensibilities from the womb.

My father instilled a love of Mozart, Milton, and attention to minutiae (I hope adequately reflected in these pages – any sloppiness is entirely my own fault, like the impulsiveness he so deplored) and taught me to look at every side of situations, and to take stock. Aunt Winnie's gift was kindness and the King James Bible. Enid Canning and Michèle Crawford were inspirational teachers, sadly no longer with us, but co-responsible with my parents for the many opportunities my childhood afforded me to indulge my love of language.

Veronica Cecil, who saw my first attempts at memoir and encouraged me, did me a great favour, as did Jan Fortune, who decided I was worth publishing when I sent her some early short stories. Both offered constructive criticism and other insights that set me on the road to *Cloistered*. Both have remained supportive to this day. Adam Lively, Kathryn Hughes, Helen Smith and William Fiennes all gave me valuable feedback and taught me how to sift the wheat from the chaff, a skill I hope to perfect before I die.

ACKNOWLEDGEMENTS

A very special debt of gratitude goes to those bookish friends who shared their literary journeys and stood by me on my own road to publication. Sally Bayley has been a marvellous example of writerly courage, honesty, and integrity. Generous to a fault, she has always been ready to offer insights on my work. Anna Zaranko, literary translator and wordsmith extraordinaire, has been incomparable as a friend, an ally, and a confidante. The past three years would have been far bleaker without her on the end of the phone to laugh and cry and grumble with. Her sense of balance, eye for detail, and ear for the *mot juste* have been amusing and instructive by turns. Hers is moral support taken to a fine art.

Julia Hollander and Rachel Crowther, my fantastic East Oxford almost neighbours, were the catalysts for so much that went towards the making of this book, turning the dwindling months of the pandemic into a furnace of creativity. Our writerly support system and literary lunches at the Magdalen Arms have been unforgettable, and always enormous fun. Both women are proof that singing is good for the soul. Family and other friends have all been quietly supportive, and showed understanding of my lapses in communication when I was absorbed by work. Thanks are due, in particular, to my splendid sister Frankie, my amazing brother Rob, and to Nick Stogdon and Paul Lodge, who read various drafts.

MONK arts magazine has been an important part of my creative life over the past five years, and I thank Sophie Lévy Burton for the opportunities she has given me to develop my craft through the personal essay form. She taught me to take creative risks, at a time when my work tended towards the academic, and gave me the confidence to be myself and spread my wings. Blake Morrison, my tireless PhD supervisor, whose ability to grasp the essentials in a piece of writing and offer decisive advice has always astounded me, has been a spur to keep on moving even when the going felt tough. His sense of humour has been a much-needed tonic at times and I thank him for never quite giving up on me.

Had it not been for Patrick Walsh, who saw the book's potential while still in rough draft, this monastic memoir would never have made it to its present published form. He has been a wonderful agent, and his zest and dynamism have made all the difference. I can never thank him and all at PEW Literary enough for their generous encouragement. Finally, and most importantly, Clara Farmer at Chatto & Windus has been the most kind and insightful of editors, endlessly patient and forgiving, quietly dazzling me with her brilliant suggestions. Huge thanks are also due to Rosanna Hildyard, Rhiannon Roy and Jessie Spivey, also at Chatto and Vintage, and to copyeditor Eugenie Todd who steadied my nerve at the last minute.

No memoir can claim to be an objective representation of the truth. All I have is my own memory and the aftereffects of how my monastic journey affected me. As I hope this volume has shown, those effects have been both rich and profound. I thank from the bottom of my heart the other courageous women who shared that journey with me, in all its light and shade, through all its agonies and ecstasies. If anyone feels her experience has been poorly represented in these pages, may she take comfort from my admission that this work is imperfect, simply the expression of my own experience and point of view.

And so, to the present. My companion for the past twelve years, Neil, has been kind, caring and endlessly tolerant of the hermit writer in his loft. His understanding and readiness to make room for silence and space within our shared lives have been remarkable. It is unlikely I would have been able to keep body and soul together while writing this book without his help. For all of this, and for the inestimable gift of Carmel: Deo gratias.